THE DECADE OF UPHEAVAL

By the same author
THE DISTASTEFUL CHALLENGE

THE DECADE OF UPHEAVAL
Irish Trade Unions in the Nineteen Sixties

Charles McCarthy

INSTITUTE OF PUBLIC ADMINISTRATION
Dublin

© Institute of Public Administration 1973
57–61 Lansdowne Road
Dublin, Ireland

ISBN 0 902173 56 1

This book has been set in ten on twelve point Monotype Times New Roman and printed in the Republic of Ireland by Mount Salus Press Ltd., Sandymount, Dublin.

FOR MURIEL

Contents

	Acknowledgements	ix
CHAPTER ONE	Introduction	1
CHAPTER TWO	Nineteen Sixty-Two and the Busmen	36
CHAPTER THREE	The Building Workers and the National Agreement	72
CHAPTER FOUR	The Power Workers	99
CHAPTER FIVE	The Maintenance Dispute	150
CHAPTER SIX	The Banks and the Teachers	184
CHAPTER SEVEN	Conclusions and Temptations	218

Appendices

APPENDIX 1	Employment Characteristics	248
APPENDIX 2	Industrial Relations in the Republic	250
APPENDIX 3	Trade Union Membership in Ireland	252
APPENDIX 4	The National Wage Rounds	253

Acknowledgements

I am deeply in the debt of quite a number of good friends of mine, in trade unions, in management and in government, for information, guidance and opinion. I should perhaps acknowledge them by name, but, since this is anything but a neutral commentary, I feared that, despite disclaimers, my own views might be attributed to them. They will know on reading this how profound my indebtedness is to them.

While some early material for this book had been gathered before the summer of 1972, the fact that I was appointed about then the Player-Wills Research Fellow in Trinity College Dublin made possible its early completion and indeed its present range. I thank the President and the Executive Council of the Teachers Unions of Ireland for giving me leave of absence, and the Department of Education for facilitating it.

Finally, in a very special way which they will understand, I am grateful to my friends in the Institute of Public Administration, T. J. Barrington, James O'Donnell, and in particular, Jonathan Williams, who so quickly and skilfully piloted the book to publication.

C. McC.

October 1973

CHAPTER ONE

Introduction

THIS is a study of Irish society at odds with itself. It is primarily a study of some major strikes and industrial disputes which took place in the nineteen sixties. The object, however, is not to write a history of the industrial disputes of the last decade; rather is it an attempt to identify such common characteristics as we can, and by identifying them, gain some insight into industrial disputes and into Irish society. The object also is to give an account of the Irish trade union movement. While a description of the trade unions by reference to numbers and structures is useful, it represents only a small part of the truth. The attempt here is to give a picture of the trade unions in action, and to see this activity in the context of Irish society as a whole, particularly in the context of the social and economic developments of the sixties.

We shall be concerned essentially with the Republic. However, Northern Ireland will appear in our discussions from time to time, not only for the practical reason that the Irish Congress of Trade Unions serves the whole island but because the two states are bound together inextricably by the very nature of our modern society.

What can be said of the disputes that we examine here? They were damaging to the economy; indeed at times we feared for the fabric of our society. They occurred at all social levels. We shall see in dispute busmen and building workers, skilled workers in the electricity-generating stations and unskilled workers in the great peat bogs, bank officials and bank managers, school teachers and school managers; and we shall see thousands of workers of all descriptions thrown out of work by the pickets of the maintenance fitters or by the interruption of electric power. And through it all, we shall see the major single characteristic of Irish industrial disputes – their very protracted character. Indeed it is this characteristic, rather than the number of disputes, that put Ireland high in the international league table of man-days lost through strikes. When disputes drag on, bitterness grows; and since strikes in Ireland tended to be protracted, it was inevitable that they should also be bitter. But there are some who say that the bitterness in Irish disputes was deeper and darker still; that while there was much in Irish industrial relations that created tensions and difficulties, it did not explain adequately the industrial chaos that we experienced. All this raises some basic questions about Irish society itself, which our study may help to answer.

When this study was begun in the summer of 1972, we had already entered the period of industrial peace under the national agreements. However, we were hardly aware of it at the time, seeing it as a fragile thing against the background of our turbulent past. But the habit of industrial peace has grown in the last year or so, turning our thoughts in the summer of 1973 to the shape of the new national agreement rather than to the management of industrial disputes. But it would be far too sanguine to expect that the days of strikes are over, or that the passions that gave the sixties their special character will not arise again.

II

This, therefore, is also a profile of the nineteen sixties in Ireland which, in truth, was a decade of upheaval. We are probably as yet too close to it to recognise its uniqueness. It was a period of national adolescence. The old structures of society were breaking down, the second Vatican Council had shattered the timeless authoritarian image of the Roman Catholic Church. New attitudes were being painfully developed and new structures and institutions to reflect them. Television mirrored and magnified all that we did. Adolescence, if it is a time of blundering, is also a time of hope, which forgives and almost justifies the blundering. And up to the 1969 maintenance strike, those in the middle of events saw no malice in the disputes but rather the painful inadequacies of men and institutions caught up in the whirlwind of the new affluence and the new expectations. Later, we shall contrast the sixties with the decade that went before, but first let us try to catch something of the quality of the society in which all this occurred.

We are a small island people who in the fifty years since our independence have been much concerned with our national identity. In recent years, because of our growing affluence and openness, and also because of the appalling events in the North, we have begun to question the assumptions that lie behind the idea, with its demand for homogeneity and uniformity of culture. But for the last fifty years, no idea has been more dominant:

it has been the centrepiece of our education policy; it caused us to engage in the astonishing experiment of attempting to change the spoken language of the people; many of our economic decisions were based on the idea, and politically the whole republican movement, including the IRA, seek validation of all they do by reference to it. In its more extreme form, it rests on the belief that Irish people, being culturally confused, cannot give their society adequate purpose and stability, and consequently, the promotion of cultural and (some would insist) political uniformity comes before economic and social planning, and indeed all else.

All this can be related, on a more superficial level, to the old economic argument that England was the source of all Irish ills, and that her expulsion would result, by that fact alone, in an improvement in social and economic conditions. When the creation of the Irish Free State in 1922 had not any marked effect economically or socially (although there was an improvement in national self-respect), people tended to look deeper for the cause of the *malaise*. First, they looked to the unification of the country, which had been sundered in 1922 when the six north-eastern counties were retained as part of the United Kingdom. They looked to it not merely because it made good sense economically, but because of a conviction that some deep national principle was involved. Our history books did not help us here. European historians, conscious, for example, of the dreariness of the Italy of the sixteenth century, of the Cinquecento, after the high promise of the Renaissance, attributed much of this despondency to Italy's failure to form a unified state; more than that, indeed, to foreign domination as well. This point is usually selectively put in Ireland. Equally, the unification of Germany is offered as the starting-point of her modern greatness. What is not recognised is that the unification of Germany, or rather the hegemony of Prussia, was in many ways a decline to the more barbaric in European life, which had its own terrible consequences in recent times; or that it was a divided Germany in the sixteenth century that saw the great blaze of the Reformation; and that even in the eighteenth century, well before its unification, Germany pushed forward the very frontiers of European thought.

The fact seems to be that as far as society is concerned, in its vigour and in its capacity to achieve, political unity is neither here nor there. But just as the historians of the Risorgimento attributed past disasters to the absence of unity, so our leaders held as axiomatic that independence and national unification were preconditions for economic and social progress. There is now, of course, a growing belief that while economic interdependence between north and south is necessary, we need not rush our fences with regard to political unity. It is a belief that has gained considerable impetus in the last few years, years in which political attitudes have changed with great rapidity. Yet it may well be that this is still quite a sophisticated view, and those who have a passionate commitment to nationalism continue to take the same view as the contemporary historians of the Risorgimento.

But it was not only a divided country that troubled the nationalist mind; there was also a divided culture, which many considered to be an anterior problem, stemming from what they saw as a kind of rape of the Irish soul when the English language was imposed by England, and the Irish language all but eliminated. The answer here was to restore the Irish language and also to restore the simple peasant folk ways which were regarded as the essential part of the Irish heritage.

This approach takes a particularly narrow view of Irish history. While the eighteenth century undoubtedly saw a wretched, ruthless attempt to destroy a native culture, there were substantial parts of Ireland which were unaffected because they were never really Gaelic. Large towns such as Cork, Waterford and Wexford were probably never Irish-speaking to any great extent at any time in their history. And Dublin itself was a great Scandinavian metropolis before it became a Norman centre and finally the home of that talented subculture, the so-called Anglo-Irish ascendancy of the eighteenth and nineteenth centuries. The fact is that Ireland, like every other society, is a mixture of a number of cultural traditions. Extreme nationalism, however, tends to adopt one subculture to the exclusion of others.

In Ireland, until late in the nineteenth century, the real power rested with the ascendancy of which I have just spoken, very much a minority group, talented, cultured, wealthy and Anglican by persuasion. This was the subculture of Swift and Sheridan, of Goldsmith and Burke, of Wellington and George Bernard Shaw. The last hundred years have seen its gradual eclipse, and in its place other subcultures have become dominant. In the Republic, a subculture sprang up which made the Irish language and a romantic peasant culture both its special badge and its special objective. In the last decade, since Ireland has caught the excitement of industrial development and affluence, the peasant culture, as an objective, tended to evaporate, and even the Irish language and its revival became much less significant. Nonetheless, these are still the identifying marks of a subculture which has been overwhelmingly dominant in the Republic, and which views itself as being the only valid Irish culture, the others being at best only partly Irish.

The subculture is confessionally a Roman Catholic one. This is not surprising in a country where up to very recent times a substantial part of the economy was based on agricultural small holders and the little towns that serviced them. It seems clear now that, as Europe became industrialised and town centred, the Roman Catholic Church failed to respond adequately, lost touch with the rapidly growing proletariat of industry, and clung to the countryside and the traditional ways. While one would in no way wish to understate the remarkable steadfastness of Irish people to Catholicism in the centuries of persecution, nevertheless, the social and economic conditions of Ireland were typically those in which Catholicism continued to flourish, until the great revolution of the recent Vatican Council.

The subculture, then, was powerfully reinforced by Catholicism and understandably by the other major institutions of society as well. National teachers – that is teachers in primary schools – have for many years traditionally come from the homes of small farmers and small shopkeepers (actually from quite a limited number of counties in the south and west of the country). When one views the country as a whole, this is quite a small socio-economic group, yet an astonishingly large number of primary teachers spring from it, and all our education, whether urban or rural, is strongly influenced by their cultural values. Since all primary education in Ireland is in practice denominational, this socio-economic group also influences the institutional Catholic Church in Ireland; it is remarkable how many of the Catholic bishops are the sons of national teachers.

Political representatives have a similar background, coming not so much from the farmers perhaps as from the small shopkeepers and publicans in the rural towns. In 1967, small shopkeepers and publicans provided 34 per cent. of the Dáil deputies and twenty per cent. of the ministers, although they represented only 3.2 per cent. of the population as a whole.[1]

The civil service gives a very similar appearance. I speak here of what is known as the general civil service, that is to say the general clerical and administrative grades, but not of the vastly greater number in the specialised grades, from engineers to postmen. I do so because, although the population of the general grades is relatively small, the persons in these grades give the civil service its character and indeed its leadership. The influence of the Gaelic subculture becomes clearer when we recognise that recruitment to the civil service is by competitive examination among secondary school students, and the highest posts are filled more often than not by promotion from below. In 1922, when the state was founded, quite a number of junior officers in the Irish civil service found themselves unexpectedly promoted to high office when certain of the higher civil

---

[1] F. B. Chubb, *The Government and Politics of Ireland* (Oxford University Press, 1970), p. 95. Actually, the farmers did poorly enough. In 1967, they formed approximately a third of the population and provided only 24 per cent. of the Dáil deputies.

servants opted either to retire or to transfer to the British administration. This tradition has been carried on and, while there is some recruitment of young university graduates to the administrative grade, the substantial majority of leading posts are filled from below, from among those who went straight from secondary school into the civil service as clerical officers or junior executive officers. Very many of these young men came from the same socio-economic group of small shopkeepers and small farmers, and since within the general grades a virtual closed system had been created, they carried with them – relatively undisturbed into the very highest offices of the land – many of the convictions and prejudices of their background.

In parliament, in the civil service, in the Catholic Church, in the official culture, we saw after 1922 the growing dominance of this subculture, which regarded itself as being exclusively Irish, and whose views were reinforced by the romantic campaign to revive the Irish language and the Gaelic culture, which became the special objectives of Irish policy from the nineteen thirties onwards. The earlier Anglo-Irish subculture was given a special place in the early ministries of the twenties, but in the thirties it became eclipsed politically, an eclipse to which it contributed itself by what appeared to many to be an opting out from the modern Ireland. It still had substantial wealth, it still had Trinity College, it still had extensive farmers and businessmen among its members, but it was viewed by many, and viewed itself, as being somewhat out of the mainstream of modern society in the South. In a word, it never made any real attempt to declare itself to be an entirely indigenous part of Irish society. Its attitude to itself was not unlike that of the diasporic group, as Arnold Toynbee calls it, the group which, while committed to its local society, is not dominated by any notions of exclusivity and sees itself with a wider loyalty and a wider vision, although in the case of the Anglo-Irish community this may have sprung from nothing more perceptive than a tradition of service to an empire.

In government, the ascendancy gave way to a republican Gaelic culture; in ecclesiastical matters, the Roman Catholic Church became in practice the established church; in business, the Anglo-Irish group continued – with, however, diminishing influence as the years went by. Those who joined them in the nineteenth century, and who are now dominant both in business and the professions, are the Catholic *bourgeoisie* (for the want of a better term), hard-headed, middle-of-the-road people, good churchmen rather than pious Catholics, and very similar to the Catholic *bourgeoisie* of France of the Age of Enlightenment and Revolution, so well described by Bernard Groethuysen. They are important to this study because they influence strongly the federations of employers and industrialists. In recent times, because of our comparative affluence, this has become a growing subculture, fed from rural rather than from urban society, from the farms rather than from the workshops; in Ireland, as elsewhere, there has been little upward mobility from the skilled and semi-skilled urban occupations.[2] The sympathies of these urban groups, therefore, would tend more and more to lie with the Gaelic subculture.

Having sketched in this broad cultural picture, we come to a subculture which is of particular relevance to trade unionism in Ireland and therefore to our study. This subculture is quite different from the Anglican—and the Gaelic; it is the subculture of the city working class, its small tradespeople and its shopkeepers. In particular, Dublin is its home; and to some extent Cork. In Dublin, it has inherited from its rich history a conviction of superiority, a conviction that one mile west of Inchicore, the bog begins. This is the subculture of the 1913 strike, of the O'Casey plays, and of the Irish trade union movement, whose origins lie within it. Let us therefore turn to consider the tradition of trade unionism – indeed of radicalism – which expressed itself in particular through this urban subculture. It is a tradition which has little place in our official histories, although there are few Irishmen who are not conscious of it.

The rebellion of 1798 is regarded in the Gaelic subculture as a uniquely Irish event, although we see in it the birth of republicanism and we revere Wolfe Tone. In modern Ireland we rarely recognise that the republican movement in 1798 was closely associated with a wider Jacobin movement in Britain at the same time, a movement which had such a profound influence on British social thinking. This radical tradition had also a profound influence in Ireland, where Tom Paine's *Rights of Man* had in its time enormous sales.[3] This was the tradition that proclaimed that every man was capable of reason and of a growth in his abilities, and that a deference to distinctions of status was an offence to human dignity. It was the tradition of self-education and of the rational criticism of political and religious institutions; the tradition of conscious republicanism; above all, the tradition of internationalism. "It is extraordinary," says E. P. Thompson, "that so brief an agitation should have diffused its ideas into so many corners of Britain."[4]

During the nineteenth century, the principle of social equality between all the classes made little headway in Ireland, but neither did it in England,

[2]Bertram Hutchinson, 'Social Status and Inter-Generational Social Mobility in Dublin' (The Economic and Social Research Institute, paper no. 48, Dublin, October 1969).

[3]E. P. Thompson, *The Making of the English Working Class* (Pelican, Harmondsworth, 1968), p. 117.

[4]ibid., p. 201.

probably because of the shift of emphasis from political to economic rights under the new socialism. Equally, in Ireland, apart from the north-east, free-thinking made little headway. But the tradition of self-education remained, the tradition of conscious republicanism and the tradition of internationalism. These traditions too were to be found right through the nineteenth century in the small traders and craftsmen of the cities. Even the recourse to a folksy Gaelic past had a quaint forerunner in the Saxon trythings which were established by the Jacobin movement in England in the last decade of the eighteenth century.

Social radicalism, therefore, could not be dismissed, as some in the Gaelic culture tended to do, as the influence of one or two people such as Connolly in 1916, and Tom Johnson in the early Dáil when it adopted its explicitly socialist programme. The wider tradition was solidly based, although, after 1922, it remained in the shadows, beyond the limits of the Gaelic tunnel vision. But the trade union movement, in its own powerful commitment to tradition, holds quite firmly to it, and in doing so, corrects to some extent the narrow and rather turgid official view of our southern society.

III

But, of course, the Roman Catholic Church was the overwhelming influence in modern Ireland in its formative years, and from 1922 up to the present decade one gains a picture of a church not only dominant but triumphalist and a government respectfully cautious and occasionally supine.[5] Apart from its immense moral authority, in practice it controlled and administered both the education system and the hospital system.

While of course there was always dissent, nonetheless up to the nineteen sixties, the solid and overwhelming reality of the Roman Catholic Church in Ireland carried with it, in the minds of a great majority of the people, an unquestioning commitment to the existence of God, and consequently a purpose in all things. Since the second Vatican Council, and since the social changes which have taken place in Ireland during the nineteen sixties, this unquestioning commitment to the idea of God and purpose has changed.In a word, God has become contingent, and men are no longer prepared to regard the meaningless events and frustrations of this life as having purpose hereafter. This is not so much a growth of unbelief, as a growth of the notion of the contingent God, which in Europe, in a much earlier generation, wrecked the Cartesian view of reality and which led ultimately to the existentialism of our own time.

The effect of all these changes was much more powerful in Ireland

[5]J. H. Whyte, *Church and State in Modern Ireland* (Gill and Macmillan, Dublin, 1971).

than elsewhere in Europe (with the possible exception of Malta) since Ireland was almost an enclosed garden of luxuriant ultramontane practices. In other countries, men had to live in a pluralist society side by side with other Christians or with men of no religious belief; we had turned our backs on the North, and apart from resounding declarations by our politicians, it was culturally no part of us. There was therefore an immense homogeneity of religion. The changes of Vatican II, the greater emphasis on personal responsibility and openness of structure, were timely and necessary. In Ireland, they first appeared to be alien and irrelevant, and although they have had a profound effect, nonetheless, the older attitudes still dominate many people's minds. Let us glance at some of them.

One must recognise the extraordinary spiritual wealth of the Roman Catholic Church, the manner in which it cultivated fortitude and deep spiritual perception when it was understood and lived. Its ancient liturgy, particularly prior to Vatican II, moved through a stately procession of great feasts, calling Christians to penitence or to joy. But the very organised strength of the liturgy can diminish personal morality, since everything, even penitence, had an orderly and liturgical character. Personal responsibility for one's own acts (so much a consequence of the Protestant ethic of personal judgment) became shrouded in ceremonial or in canonical jurisprudence, where one's conscience could be assuaged either by ceremonial penitence or by some clever logical distinction of a canonist. (This, I believe, is how Catholics who are members of the IRA, and who are still convinced and practising members of the church, can set their consciences at rest while pursuing a campaign of appalling atrocity against a civilian population). Furthermore, in order to understand the greater reality, the church has urged men to look beyond the immediate appearance of things. This is necessary to any adequate understanding by a man of his place in the world, but, crudely understood, it can encourage men to deny the reality that they perceive, almost as if it were a matter of religious discipline to do so. Perhaps the uncertain grasp of reality which is evident in much Irish political and social thinking comes from this and contributes further to the diminishing of personal responsibility for one's own acts.

Despite the escape hatch which this might have offered for the occasional IRA militant, the prevailing quality which it produced in Irish society was quietist; people generally were spiritually dependent and perhaps morally immature. Ireland, like Italy of the Cinquecento, had little of the prophetic about it, and turned to personal pietism; this indeed has been particularly characteristic of Irish religiosity. Inevitably, therefore, Irish society was vastly conformist. This conformism, I have no doubt, was greatly reinforced by the influence of rural values in the life of the

Catholic Church (we have already noted how closely they are related), and a peasant subsistence economy (with all its conservatism) continued in many parts of Ireland up to quite recent times.[6] In such an ecclesiastical society there is little place for the prophet, and, as in *The Brothers Karamazov*, the Inquisition must reject Jesus if he comes once more among men, so that they may not be disturbed from the certainty which the church has provided them. The role of the prophet fell rather on our writers and the men of intellectual dissent. They were novelists and poets, and, more often than not, because of the hostility of a conforming society, they became emigrants or drunkards or both.

Since Vatican II, the Catholic Church in Ireland has changed very much, some would say bewilderingly so, but nonetheless that was the mood in which most Irishmen and women grew up. Perhaps this helps to explain, too, much that is second-rate in Irish life, that has its own special dreariness. It is characteristic of second-rate people to place emphasis on forms and procedures, where decisions are predictable and where a person of some genius would be regarded as capricious. This has been much in evidence up to recent years both in the church and in the public service.

Romantic nationalism I believe to be a Christian heresy, with its ritual, its music, its saints and its sacrifice. Although in its extreme form it is condemned by Roman Catholic leaders, it seems to flourish in a society of Christian values. Unlike traditional Catholicism, it is, however, distinctly Palagian in character. Pelagius was an urbane Englishman who, in the early days of Christendom, held that men were self-sufficient and needed no special intervention from God. While this might have been all very well for a man of even and gentle temperament (and Pelagius himself rarely spoke, his ideas being propounded by a talkative Irish companion), it does not help where passions are strong. Pelagius challenged the traditional Christian position – that is, the view that men should do their utmost – but always with a tranquility which comes from being certain that ultimately God will find a way. There is something of this in the Marxist position where the final achievement of socialism is in any event inevitable. But no such tranquillity can exist for the Irish nationalist. He is entirely Pelagian. If things are not achieved now and in his terms, then he has no confidence that he has made any valid contribution to anything. There is so very often a gap between a man's best efforts and the objective that he has set his heart on. To a Christian

---

[6]Damien Hannan, 'Kinship, Neighbourhood and Social Change in Irish Rural Communities' (*Economic and Social Review,* Dublin, 1972). Professor Hannan, speaking of the west of Ireland, sees it as continuing right up to the end of World War II. This experience, in my view, would be general throughout rural Ireland.

or to a Marxist, this can be faced with some tranquillity. To an Irish nationalist, it will appear to be insupportable; and the more it continues, the more frustrated he becomes. In this time of growing affluence, when the old certainties have wavered into contingency, the Pelagian idea of self-help seems to make very much more sense, and this too may help to explain not only the development of the entrepreneurial spirit in Ireland but also the vehemence of some of our recent strikes.

But there are other attitudes in Ireland which have been influenced by the Roman Catholic Church and which are often accepted as axiomatic, even by those who consider themselves quite independent in their thinking. Here I refer in particular to the conviction of the church that there cannot be unity without union, that is to say, there cannot be a common movement, a common spirituality, a common way of life, without a common institutional structure to hold it together. This is of enormous significance in Roman Catholicism since it is the justification for the papacy. It lay behind the final break between Rome and Byzantium in the fifteenth century. The Byzantine position is put well by Alexander Schmemann, an orthodox theologian:

> The [Byzantine] Church recognises only unity and therefore cannot recognise any 'union'. The latter implies a lack of confidence in unity, a denial of the unifying fire of grace which can make all that is 'natural'– all historical insults, limitations, gulfs, and misunderstandings – nonexistent, and can overcome them by force of the divine power.[7]

The Lutheran Reformation was greatly reinforced by political motives, just as the Byzantine schism was, but nonetheless, running underneath it lay the same concept of a unity which did not require an explicit union to give it form, indeed which saw in such a union a denial of the validity of the unity itself. In Ireland, however, there is a strong conviction that there cannot be unity, there cannot be common endeavour, there cannot be a great movement, whether national, spiritual or economic, without some physical union to give it purpose and direction. Otherwise, it is seen as something of a sham, something which has no real respectability since ultimately it could not be effective. The idea that the creation of a common institution might in fact damage the unity would be quite alien to Irish thinking. Our present institutions, all of them heavily centralised, reinforce the Irish view and, I believe, support powerfully as well the conviction that Ireland cannot go forward as a nation until a

[7]Alexander Schmemann, *The Historical Road of Eastern Orthodoxy* (Harvill Press, London, 1963), p. 254.

union is achieved of north and south. In a more domestic sense, it also supports the conviction that the trade union movement cannot go forward unless it is also bound in one union, and this indeed has been the logic of at least some of the efforts to reform the structure of the trade union movement. It has only been dimly grasped that the creation of such a union might have the effect of diminishing the reality of the movement itself, since it would put in question its quality as a movement – the curious impalpable thing to which many people give a fundamental and unwavering loyalty – and attempt to replace it with a single institution which, however one looks at it, must be less than the movement itself.

But although these problems of the church were also essentially the problems of our whole society, they remained almost a closed system, where the ecclesiastical specialist dealt with them in a mannered way. Irish people were unable to deal with them with any sophistication since, even among educated Irishmen, there was no current idiom for theological, or even for philosophical, discussion. There is still no chair of theology in the National University of Ireland, which was the university attended by Roman Catholics (Catholics were forbidden to enter Trinity College up to a few years ago). Not only that, but laymen were discouraged, although not overtly, from reading philosophy in the National University. One way or the other, there was up to recent times almost no laymen to express the growing anxiety regarding purpose which the sixties had introduced and which contributed very considerably to a new impatience which many felt both with regard to their economic condition and with regard to the structure of society.

IV

In speaking of centrality of government, we are leading up to the major political difficulty in Irish society, where local institutions are agencies and not governments and where the people are, in the political sense, inarticulate. Of course, this cannot be attributed to the Catholic Church, although its own style reinforces it; its origins lie deep in Irish history. There are many who claim that the frustrations caused by this system contribute greatly, not perhaps to disputes themselves, whether industrial or not, but to the difficulty in resolving them. If the chalet of a German landowner is burned by local people, or if a Swiss businessman is threatened in a rural area (and these things have happened here), it is often because the local people had no way of communicating with these visitors before they set up in the area, no way of expressing fears or resentments, or indeed sound reasons for opposing them. There are no local democratic institutions in Ireland, that is to say institutions by which a small local community can govern itself in those matters appropriate to it and give expression readily to its views in an organised manner. The local priests of the parish did in the past offer political and social leadership, but this was always somewhat inappropriate, and is now seen to be merely another form of representation to a central authority. There are local politicians, but they are singularly ineffective in local matters. The county councils, or county borough councils of which they are members, are distant from the local community and, in any event, the member finds that he has little power as against the manager, in whom is lodged the substance of administrative authority. Even at that, the number of councils is small in relation to the population. There are thirty-one county councils and county borough councils, but even if one adds the very restricted and insignificant town councils and similar bodies where they exist, one gets a total of 115 bodies in all, and consequently an average of 25,000 in population to each elective body.

But this gives a far better picture than the reality. Dublin city, the capital, has had no elected borough council for some years. The members of the council were removed from office by the central authority because it refused to strike a rate which was regarded by the manager and the central authority as adequate.[8] This was one of the few significant functions which the elected body possessed. The astonishing part of this débâcle is that Dublin people have shrugged their shoulders and accepted the situation. It is an indication of their grasp of the reality that in Ireland the elected local government representative possesses no real power; power is exercised by the manager, who is an official responsible ultimately to the central authority. Although there are some other outlying authorities in the Dublin area, the same manager and his assistants are responsible for the administration of the whole area, and a recent recommendation of a government white paper is that there should be one all-purpose authority for the whole Dublin area, an area containing almost one-third of the whole population of the country – that is to say, very nearly a million people.

But even if the ratio of one authority to every 25,000 people is accepted, it contrasts very badly with local administration in other countries. The continental average is very much lower than this.

> In France, with 38,000 communes, it is 1,300; in Switzerland, 1,800, in West Germany 2,400. In Scandinavia it ranges from 5,000 in Denmark to about 9,000 in Norway and Sweden. While crude averages of this kind tell us little about individual authority sizes,

---

[8]In the summer of 1973, the members removed from office were appointed as Commissioners by the Minister for Local Government, a move which, in practice, restored the council.

they at least prove the point that local authorities with more comprehensive functions can operate effectively for areas and populations that would be regarded here as quite inadequate. The tendency in Britain and in the Scandinavian countries is to reduce the number of authorities, but nonetheless they remain very numerous in comparison with Ireland.[9]

There are, then, no local community councils or district councils springing from the need of people to provide their own local government. There are no local institutions by which people can express their views, despite the efforts of some voluntary groups of a developmental or social character. If institutions are the voice of a society, then Irish society is largely dumb.

One can put all this in another and indeed in a more immediate way. There is a kind of hopeless conviction in Ireland that even if one could articulate one's problem, there is no one there to listen. This is how many people from the unskilled worker to the bank official see it. The complaint is not so much that there are faceless men, but that the men who command power regard you as faceless. This is what becomes unbearable.

There is a danger of exaggeration here, since, in modern society, all men are subject to such stresses. Nevertheless, the argument is a compelling one. If, it is argued, men find that their circumstances are insupportable, and if there is no remedy from an authority which is indifferent and remote, then they become frustrated to the point of violence. In this regard, one can point to Northern Ireland, where all the unrest began in a demand for civil rights, indeed for basic self-respect, a demand to be seen and heard and recognised as people. France, too, which in its centralised system of government approaches us rather closely, saw in 1968 a revolutionary movement of surprising vigour and tenacity. Although in the Republic we have been spared physical violence, we have experienced what some claim to be a form of violence – the bitter, protracted, dogged strike, disruptive of the industry concerned and not infrequently of the economy. Some see in it something of the agonised cry of the inarticulate man; and they see a situation in which, even where articulation becomes possible, it is not relied on. There is little trust in civilised communication and its effectiveness.

Whether this picture is an exaggerated one or not, there is no doubt that our whole social and political climate fosters centrality, and it is not surprising that we should find it among trade unions and employer organisations. The Federated Union of Employers, for example, followed

[9]*More Local Government. A Programme for Development* (Institute of Public Administration, Dublin, 1971), p. 11–12.

a policy during the sixties aimed at centralising negotiations. The trade unions are reluctant to allow any power to pass out of the hands of the central executives, even when it becomes clear that the real problem may not be capable of being perceived, far less resolved, by those at the centre.

V

However, when we come to consider the character of our strikes in the last decade, we must recognise that strikes in their modern form tend to be anti-society in any event, without being revolutionary either in purpose or in character, and consequently it might be misleading to see in them a general protest against the manner in which our society is organised and the centrality of its institutions. When a strike occurs today in a large undertaking (and these are the strikes that dominated the sixties), then it can no longer be seen as a knockout contest between and employer and his workers, in which society is only peripherally involved. The general manager and the directors of the Electricity Supply Board or of the transport authority, CIE, are not affected in their incomes by a strike, nor perhaps in their reputation either. The damage is caused to the public, whether a particular public or the public in general, and the contest is a moral one – one in which both sides are attempting to hold out against the distress and the anger of those, manifestly innocent, who are affected by the dispute. But I do not believe that the public here is seen as the organised society of authority, but rather unorganised groups of ordinary people who have been pulled willy-nilly into the mêlée.

To the observer, the position may look worse than it is – and at times very frightening – since trade unions (and sometimes employers) on the whole have not made any great effort to communicate to the public the reasons for the damage and the inconvenience. This may be because of the personal inadequacy of the officials concerned, but the major reason probably is that strikes are usually carried on in a climate of public disapproval. Those carrying on the dispute find themselves in a dogged, desperate fight, for which they receive little support or sympathy, except from within the group itself. This has been very marked both in the case of the lengthy strike of bank officials that brought banking business to a standstill in 1970, and in the strike of maintenance workers throughout industry, the damaging effects of which persisted for a very long time. In the first case, as we shall see, the Irish Bank Officials Association were reluctant to make any statement; it was, they claimed, a private dispute between the banks and themselves, although in fact the whole commercial life of the country was in peril. Despite occasional statements, the bank directors were clearly of the same view. Equally, in the case of the strike of the maintenance workers, no statement of a coherent character was published at any time by the striking unions. This dispute had got itself into such a complex mess that this is perhaps not too surprising, yet one would have expected some effort at justification at some stage in the dispute. The unfortunate fact, of course, is that it is not the understanding of the public that a union seeks but its pressure to force a solution. It does not expect approval, but only recognition of the inconvenience and difficulty it can cause. Its silence, therefore, in a dispute, often caused by a sullen helplessness, should not be seen as something more sinister.

There is a further reason why we should treat with caution the idea that the strikes in the sixties indicated something revolutionary in our society. While some of the strikes were mass movements of protest (this was the case in Bord na Mona, in the Dublin city bus services, and in some respects in the Electricity Supply Board), there were others which appeared to be initiated by a small leadership group without any general pressure from the membership. This was the case in the building strike in Dublin in 1964, when the industry was offering good and well-paid work, and where many of the workers, returning from their summer holidays, were astonished to find themselves on strike. Furthermore, in the maintenance dispute, which concerned key workers scattered throughout industry, the problems of communication were immense, and it is difficult to see how any general movement could be identified. Of course, when the strikes became protracted, feelings ran very high, but this is quite a different matter; the strikes did not find their origin in any general feeling of unrest.

There is a more compelling reason still. When we examine these disputes in depth we shall find in each one a uniqueness of character. It is difficult to discern any background of general bloody-mindedness in the community which finds its expression in this way. The strikes themselves arose from circumstances peculiar to each of the industries, and often resulted in changes which make the possibility of a strike occurring again somewhat remote. This applies even to the Electricity Supply Board, where the tensions and difficulties have by no means worked themselves out, but where the end is clearly in sight.

Nevertheless, the strikes have a number of alarming aspects which cannot be readily explained. In the first place, while the silence of the unions in dispute is explicable, it also demonstrates that men do not look to the public for equity. One hurts the public, one manipulates it; one does not appeal to it. This is not an isolated phenomenon. We shall meet it again and again, among tradesmen, among busworkers, among teachers, among bank officials, among all groups of the community. It is almost as if men were determined rightly or wrongly to win their point of view, the only limit being the extent of their power to inflict damage on society. This mood is a dangerously easy one to grow into, where an industrial situation grows worse day by day and month by month, where no possible solution seems in sight, and where frustration among the workers is growing dangerously high. I have experienced it myself. If men are upbraided because of it, they say that they have no alternative, that normal negotiation brings one nowhere; or rather, that it is effective only when the situation has been softened up by industrial action or by the threat of it. Otherwise, no one will listen, because the workers are faceless men. In many of the disputes this mood ran very deep. But the very essence of a civilised society is its ability to provide equity, whether the person seeking it is weak or strong. This we assume to be the character of our Irish society, yet these industrial disputes seem to demonstrate that, in at least one very extensive and important area, equity has no place.

But by far the most alarming – and, to many, inexplicable – aspect of many of the disputes has been the use of the picket and its effectiveness. The sacrosanct nature of the picket is at the centre of many of the strikes that we shall examine. It is the especial characteristic of Irish strikes and the most mysterious.

> But there is a sort of unthinking picketing and observance of pickets which is peculiar to Ireland, and which militant labour movements in other advanced industrial countries neither have nor want..... Recent disputes in the ESB have been unreasonably extended and aggravated by this.[10]

It reached its most pernicious form in the chaos of the maintenance dispute. The Economic and Social Research Institute is attempting to gain some insight into its operation: why a handful of men, without notice or explanation, can mount a picket and have it recognised by thousands, instantly and completely, to the point of refusing to carry out the instructions of their union leaders to pass the picket line and do their job. In Northern Ireland, such total observance is neither expected nor given. It is a special characteristic of workers in the Republic. Furthermore, it is the special characteristic of certain groups of manual worker (not all, by any means); it is not at all a characteristic of the clerical worker, who, while he will observe a picket, will normally do so only when the union instructs him.

[10]*Final Report of the Committee on Industrial Relations in the Electricity Supply Board* (Stationery Office, Dublin, 1969), p. 35.

What then is in some blue-collar industrial workers in the Republic which makes them observe a picket so totally? Perhaps it is essentially a matter of group solidarity. Certainly, when unions whose leadership was close to the workers, such as the National Busmen's Union or perhaps the Electrical Trades' Union, instructed their members to pass pickets, the men did so. But it is always a highly dangerous business for any union to urge its members to cross a picket line, no matter how close the leadership is to the men. In other words, while solidarity explains a great deal, there is also a sense in which the picket line has a sacrosanct character in its own right. Perhaps the highly structured society of the rural west, which Professor Hannan described, also existed in the centres of industry, although it was not as clearly identifiable. In other words, perhaps it all derives from an overwhelming desire to conform to group standards, even when they are abused, and known to be abused, by selfish men. While, of course, this would be resented, the group standards would nevertheless be maintained, if this were possible at all.

There are two objections to such a proposition. The first is that the total observance of the picket line is not so much a feature of rural Ireland as it is of urban Ireland. This, however, I believe to be irrelevant. It merely means that picket lines are not part of the group culture in rural Ireland, although they are in industrial Ireland; if they were, they would be observed in much the same way. The second objection is more difficult to overcome. The dominance of the group began to die in the fifties in rural Ireland, and must have been dying in industrial Ireland at least as late as that, and perhaps earlier. Yet the reverence for the picket line seems to have grown rather than diminished, finding its most vigorous and extensive form in the strikes during the sixties. This, then, is a major phenomenon in Irish industrial disputes which we shall describe in the pages that follow, even if we cannot altogether explain it.

When we come to consider strike statistics, we must recognise how unreliable a guide all these figures are. In 1970, for example, over a million man-days were lost due to strikes – the highest number, with the exception of 1937, experienced since the foundation of the state. But *Trade Union Information*[11] for April 1971 makes an important point in regard to it:

> The number of days lost through strikes is, of course, a minute fraction of all days worked by employees. Taking the number of employees at work in the Republic as 750,000 and the number of working days in the year as 240 (i.e. 365 less Saturdays, Sundays and 21 days leave), the total days worked in a year is in the region

---

[11] *Trade Union Information*, no. 160 (Irish Congress of Trade Unions, Dublin, April 1971), p. 6.

of 180 million. The number of man-days lost through industrial disputes in 1970 was just over 1 million or about one-half of one per cent. of the total. This loss of 1 million man-days through strikes last year may be compared with the loss of over 18 million days in 1969 through illness (based on claims for disability benefit by insured workers) and an estimated loss of nearly 16 million days through unemployment in 1970.

What is of far more importance is that over three-quarter of a million of those man-days were lost in one dispute, that of the commercial banks, which did great damage to the economy.

Nor indeed are international comparisons of much help. There has been much talk of the international league table of man-days lost, but it is extremely difficult to draw any firm conclusions one way or the other. It is not possible to establish from the figures the prevalence of strikes in the various countries, or the number of workers involved as a proportion of the whole working force. Professor O'Mahony says:

> International comparisons in regard to work stoppages are not, however, of much consequence. Such data relating to economic growth and the incidence of work-stoppages in different countries as it has been possible to assemble do not reveal any close relation between the absence of work-stoppages and the speed of growth ..... This may seem surprising at first sight, but it must be remembered that not only are the data of a very restricted coverage but that strikes (to which the statistics refer) are restricted by law in some countries but not in others. Strikes may not, of course, be a good indication of the usual state of industrial relations or else good industrial relations may not be necessary for growth. This last supposition however is hardly tenable at the level of the individual firm. It may also be that the statistics present a distorted picture of the position because most of the strikes may be concentrated in relatively few industries or even firms, e.g., those which are not growing – indeed their lack of growth or their decline may be one of the factors causing disputes.[12]

An examination of the Irish position itself, however, can give us some indication of trends. Professor O'Mahony, writing in the early years of the nineteen sixties, remarked on an international tendency for strikes to decline, and continued:

[12]David O'Mahony, *Industrial Relations in Ireland: The Background* (The Economic Research Institute, Dublin, May 1964), p. 28.

While the number of man-days lost in the Republic from 1954 to 1961 due to work-stoppages.....is certainly fewer than during the preceding eight years from 1946 to 1953, the picture presented of the whole period since 1923 shows no definite trend one way or the other. It would, therefore, be premature as yet to include this country among those in which the strike is withering away. At the same time, it is worth noting that there is a greater reluctance on the part of the trade unions to engage in strikes than before.[13]

Unfortunately, this trend did not continue; indeed, it reversed itself, and during the nineteen sixties the figures leapt up as the following two tables show:[14]

	1954-1961				1964-1971		
Year	Number of strikes and lock-outs	Days lost ('000)	No. of workers involved	Year	Number of strikes and lock-outs	Days lost ('000)	No. of workers involved
1954	81	67	8,294	1964	87	545	25,200
1955	96	236	11,841	1965	89	552	38,900
1956	67	48	4,420	1966	112	784	52,200
1957	45	92	4,059	1967	79	183	20,900
1958	51	126	12,043	1968	126	406	38,900
1959	58	124	9,305	1969	134	936	61,800
1960	49	80	5,865	1970	134	1,008	28,800
1961	96	377	27,437	1971	133	274	43,783

In the thirty-nine years from 1923 to 1961, there were only four years out of the total where there were more than 500,000 man-days lost in strikes. Since 1964, this number was exceeded in five out of the eight years.

There is yet a further interesting comparison between the sixties and the earlier periods. Professor O'Mahony points out that in the period 1953 to 1960 "the number of working-days lost in Ireland and the United Kingdom are almost identical but there are considerably more separate stoppages here".[15] This is in very great contrast to the nineteen sixties. *Trade Union Information,* discussing the period from 1964 to 1970, summarised the position as follows:

[13]O'Mahony, op. cit., p. 27.
[14]O'Mahony, op. cit., p. 27. Also, *Trade Union Information,* no. 160 (Irish Congress of Trade Unions, Dublin, April 1971).
[15]O'Mahony, op. cit., p. 28.

A feature of the strike statistics for this country is the fact that a very small number of strikes account for the great bulk of man-days lost through disputes.... 29 strikes representing a mere 4% of all strikes over the period, accounted for 83% of total man-days lost.... By far the greatest loss of man-days occurred in the following strikes: banks 1970 (787,000), maintenance craftsmen 1969 (629,000), construction industry 1964 (419,000), banks 1966 (323,000), printing industry 1965 (315,000), paper mills 1966 (153,000). These six strikes involved a loss of 2,626,000 man-days or 60% of all man-days lost through disputes in the seven years 1964 to 1970....4% of the strikes in the seven years accounted for 47% of the workers involved in all strikes and 83% of the total man-days lost.... The high placing of Ireland in the (international) table is due to the relatively long duration of a very small number of strikes.[16]

While figures relating to strikes must therefore be treated with reserve, particularly when international comparisons are attempted, nonetheless they point to the overwhelming importance of the small number of extensive and protracted strikes. Of these, the following are dealt with in this study: the dispute of the Dublin busmen, the 1964 dispute in the building industry, the series of disputes in the Electricity Supply Board, the Bord na Mona dispute, the dispute of maintenance craftsmen, the dispute in the banks, and the dispute in education. While this does not cover all the extensive disputes of the sixties, it covers a substantial majority, and deals with all those in respect of which there was a subsequent independent evaluation.

VI

We have already referred to the extraordinary changes in every aspect of Irish life which characterised the sixties. To those of us who lived through the changes, their radical character may not be immediately evident, but they did in fact represent an upheaval, not only in our economic condition but in all our social values. If, in this chapter, we approach the changes from an economic and industrial point of view, it is because it is more relevant for our study that we should do so. But the social and political changes have been immense and perhaps might be briefly reviewed first.

We have already spoken of the changes in religious perceptions, so fundamental to the way many Irishmen regard themselves and society. In politics, too, the changes were considerable. The fifties saw two interparty governments alternating with the traditional elderly Gaelic

[16]Op. cit., pp. 2, 3, 6.

conservatism of Eamon de Valera and Fianna Fáil. In contrast, although the Fianna Fáil party was in power during the whole period of the sixties, there were sharp political changes. Seán Lemass, when he became Taoiseach, brought to government in Ireland a vigorous, entrepreneurial economic leadership which it had never experienced before. The elderly members of the party began to drop away, and young men, full of a glossy promise, moved into the major ministries. By the mid-nineteen sixties, we were boasting that we had the youngest cabinet in western Europe. Towards the end of 1967, Seán Lemass retired, and the vigour and drive seemed to go out of government. Nevertheless, in the spring election of 1969, the Fianna Fáil government under Jack Lynch was confirmed in power and all seemed set, in a favourable economic climate, for continuous development into the seventies.

A year later, all was in shambles. Events in the North had shattered our complacency. In January 1969, we had seen the attacks on the civil rights marchers at Burntollet bridge; we had seen a hasty general election in the province and O'Neill's resignation soon after; and then, during the summer of 1969, extensive rioting, stones, petrol bombs, CS gas, no-go areas, gunmen in the streets and eventually the calling in of British troops. Everybody in the Republic was in a state of confusion, torn between the traditional loyalties of kith, kin and religion, and the horror at the breakdown of law and order; torn between a tradition which had romanticised the gun and the freedom fighter, and the appalling implications of violence in our own time. And then, in May 1970, in a manner which seemed to shake the very institutions of our state, two ministers were dismissed from office on suspicion of gunrunning and another resigned in sympathy with them. One of these was the Minister for Finance, Charles J. Haughey, who many believed was the government within the government, a source of real power within the state. Another was the Minister for Agriculture, Neil Blaney, an immensely influential organisation man. The decade therefore ended with many people fearing that we were on the brink of revolution. It was not until early 1971 that the IRA appeared on the streets of Belfast and Derry. In 1969 and in 1970, there was in the North what appeared to be a beleagured Catholic Gaelic people, and, in the South, a republican government standing idly by, in the phrase of the time. In the event, Jack Lynch's steadfast holding to peace has been seen to be his greatest achievement. But in 1970, all was in confusion.

Let us now retrace our steps and consider the economic and industrial developments of recent decades, and in particular the contrast between the fifties and the sixties.

The first round of wage increases[17] following the war, in 1946, was of course substantial, recovering what had been held back under the wages standstill orders. Before the second round emerged in 1948, the Labour Court had been established under the chairmanship of R. J. P. Mortished. The Court relies on a moral, not a legal, authority to support its recommendations, and Mortished gave it this during his period of office until 1952. The reports at the time showed a drive and a dominance much in contrast with the more prosaic, service-type reports of recent times. When the second round began to emerge, the Labour Court gathered under its auspices both the Irish Trade Union Congress and the Congress of Irish Unions on the one hand, and the Federated Union of Employers and its associated organisations on the other. They hammered out a maximum of eleven shillings a week and a statement of principles which recognised a number of equities, including the compensating of workers for the rise in the cost of living. This held broadly until 1950, when, despite the efforts of the Labour Court to secure another general agreement, the settlements were individual ones and showed some diversity. By 1952, however, the idea of a national agreement became prominent again and the Congress of Irish Unions (but not the Irish TUC) concluded an agreement for twelve shillings and sixpence a week for men, which became the general pattern; women got substantially less. This fourth round pattern held until 1955, and there was a lengthy period of stability. Leo Crawford, writing in 1954, remarked on how free the country was of industrial disputes.

The real push came in 1955, when restraint was abandoned and the unions sought not merely compensation for the rise in the cost of living but a restoration of 1939 standards. There was a great diversity in the increases given, ranging from eleven shillings to sixteen shillings and sixpence. Immediately after, Ireland plunged into the economic doldrums and was to remain so until 1958. When pressure for a wage adjustment mounted in 1957, after the inevitable span of two years, the two trade union congresses (now united as the Provisional United Trade Union Organisation), conscious of the need for restraint, negotiated a national settlement which pinned increases to ten shillings a week.

At last, Ireland began moving into a period of development. 1958 was hailed as a year of promise. This was how *The Irish Times* in their *Irish Review and Annual* for 1958 headed their survey, which began: "A bewildering succession of new developments marked the year 1958 in the Irish economy. New events and new ideas crowded the scene, and a new spirit, very different from the dejection of 1956 and most of 1957,

---

[17] See also: David O'Mahony, 'Economic Aspects of Industrial Relations' (The Economic and Social Research Institute, Dublin, paper no. 24, 1965).

motivated the actors." This sounds a little highly-coloured; but *The Irish Times* was usually sober. There is no doubt that there was promise in the air. The white paper on economic expansion had been issued following the publication of *Economic Development* by T. K. Whitaker, the Secretary of the Department of Finance, marking the first steps in economic planning. There was talk of the Common Market, and of wider horizons. Expectations began to rise, but now began the tumbling movement through the seventh and eighth rounds in which we see the beginnings of the problems that beset us throughout the sixties, not only in regard to wage movements themselves, but also in regard to the relations between clerical and manual workers; we see stress growing between them, and the critical role of the Electricity Supply Board.

The seventh round in the later part of 1959 brought to manual workers, in individually negotiated settlements, increases ranging from ten shillings to fifteen shillings. This, however, did not determine the pattern as one might expect. The Labour Court in its fourteenth annual report[18] says:

> During the latter half of 1959, clerical and salaried workers obtained percentage increases corresponding to those obtained by manual workers, but during the early months of 1960 certain large groups of clerical and salaried workers negotiated settlements which provided for increases substantially greater than those negotiated under the 1959 wage movement. As a consequence of this many groups of clerical and salaried workers who had concluded wage agreements in 1959 put forward new claims for salary adjustments. A number of settlements were reached during 1960 and in most cases they provided for a general revision of the salary scale structure with widely varying increases at different points of the scale.

We shall see later that the clerical workers in the Electricity Supply Board were a key group in this movement.

But the general awakening also caused workers to seek shorter hours, a five-day week and other fringe benefits; and by the middle of 1961, not alone had these been achieved in many cases, but a further wage increase of up to 14 shillings a week had begun to emerge. This was the point at which electricians both in the Electricity Supply Board and in private industry pressed their claims to a crisis point, and the Labour Court, conscious of the 14 shillings-a-week-pattern, recommended that the electricians should get the same amount; they made a similar recommendation for the building trade. These were rejected and the strike of electricians drove up the amount to twice the figure recommended. This

---

[18]Labour Court, *Fourteenth Annual Report* (Government Publications Office, Dublin).

became the new target for all others, and by the end of 1961, wage increases for men were ranging from twenty shillings to twenty-five shillings a week. As for clerical and salaried workers, the system of revising salary structures continued, resulting, the Labour Court says,[19] in further large numbers of clerical and salaried workers receiving improved salary scales. Not surprisingly, it was a period of considerable unrest. The Labour Court reported sadly[20]

> The year was remarkable for the number of occasions on which groups of workers resorted to strike action in an effort to force their claims for increased wages and improved working conditions. In very many instances the strike action was taken or threatened before the Labour Court was afforded an opportunity of either arranging a conciliation conference or investigating the matters in dispute, even in cases where the action of the workers threatened the disruption of essential undertakings.

The sixties, then, began in a mood of rising expectations, of increased confidence in our ability to develop; it began with a taste of affluence in our mouths for the first time and a heady feeling for the future; but it began as well with a swirl of stress and tension in industrial relations. It was a time of unparalleled economic expansion.

> With very little doubt the 1960's have been the most successful decade in the recorded economic history of Ireland. The population decline has been reversed and living standards raised. Also there has been an impressive transformation from a basically agricultural economy, with industry serving a relatively static protected local market, towards an internationally competitive industrial economy.[21]

This was the decade of national planning. The first tentative programme which ran until 1963 was followed by the second programme which took up some of the ideas of French indicative planning, necessitating substantial participation by all concerned; and consequently the trade union movement was caught up, not only in the National Industrial Economic Council, but in a large number of other bodies as well. These were the years of new institutions and the glow of responsible participation.

"It appears," said The Economic and Social Research Institute in 1967,[22] "that the economy was growing along a tolerably steady course

---

[19]Labour Court, *Fifteenth Annual Report* (Government Publications Office, Dublin).
[20]*idem*, p. 4.
[21]T. J. Baker and J. Durkan, *Quarterly Economic Commentary* (The Economic and Social Research Institute, Dublin, December 1969).
[22]'The Irish Economy in 1967' (The Economic and Social Research Institute, Dublin, paper no. 39, August 1967).

until the end of 1963 [when] an unstable boom was allowed to develop in the early part of 1964, and to continue until the middle of 1965. The unprecedented size of the ninth wage round was a major factor in causing this boom because of its effects on both private and government consumption." Perhaps it was. The round itself was the result of an agreement nationally concluded between the employers and the Irish Congress of Trade Unions; it was seen at the time as a model of progress and order, and, if it was large, Lemass was prepared to tolerate it because already he was making a bid for an incomes policy. But the summer of 1964 saw the building strike which almost wrecked the national agreement. Personal consumption continued to rise, and, although the national agreement inhibited any further wage increases, there was pressure for other benefits. By June 1965, there were strikes and the threat of strikes, and the newspapers fell to preaching at the workers, distressed to find not only busmen on strike and Dublin transport paralysed, but, rather grotesquely, the gravediggers on strike as well, with prospects of corpses being left unburied as men refused to pass the pickets. There was growing pressure for some form of industrial legislation, which, it was believed, would resolve the situation. Lemass had indeed talked about it, but it was easier said than done. In July 1965, the government introduced measures to damp down the economy and in the dying days of 1965 there was issued the white paper on a free trade area with Britain and an even more urgent demand for greater competitiveness.

The protracted talks between the Irish Congress of Trade Unions and the employers in search of a further national agreement broke down, and in January 1966 the ICTU attempted to take the steam out of the situation by recommending a maximum of £1 a week increase; later, this was endorsed by the Labour Court and became the tenth round. This was the fiftieth anniversary of the Rising of 1916, and perhaps because of this and the feelings of national solidarity, there was a very genuine desire to get on top of our industrial difficulties. The Congress representatives on the National Industrial Economic Council joined in a far-reaching report on a possible incomes policy but the industrial situation seemed to get worse rather than better. The newspapers were full of the news of strikes, in the sugar confectionery industry, in the deep sea docks, in CIE, in the paper mills. Bank officials went on strike in May and remained out for three months. And then, electric power was put in jeopardy through a strike in the Electricity Supply Board. Panic-stricken, the government rushed through legislation which attempted to meet the crisis by imposing legal penalties; in the event, they were not required. Towards the end of 1966, Dr Garret FitzGerald, in his economic comment in *The Irish Times*,[23] said flatly: "The growth of the economy has virtually come to a halt in the past twelve months contrary to the plans and expectations of the government."

Yet, in fact, economic activity had begun to revive in the second half of 1966. It quickened in 1967, and 1968 was a boom year during which national output rose at perhaps twice the normal rate. However, the government were unable to anticipate this at the time, and in 1968 they decided to abandon the second programme – which was designed to run until 1970 and which was falling woefully behind its targets – and launch instead a third programme, to run from 1968 to 1972. In this way, they avoided the embarrassment of demonstrating how substantial the shortfall was, and since this kind of programming is, among other things, an exercise in national self-confidence, there was probably some sense to it, although there was much barbed comment at the time.

During 1967, there emerged a new and important phenomenon, the two-year comprehensive agreement, and throughout 1968 this pattern developed, constituting the eleventh round. The agreements provided men with increases of the order of £1.75 to £2 a week in two or three phases, women receiving 75 per cent. of the men's increase.[24] This idea of a termination date (the inevitable result of a term agreement) was to have two consequences: it tended to invite negotiations for a further increase when the term ended, and it created a wide span of different termination dates, extending, indeed, over an eighteen-month period, which was to make the negotiation of future national agreements inordinately difficult. Strikes continued to trouble the economy, but the climax in the decade was reached in the dispute of the maintenance craftsmen early in 1969. This dispute, unparalleled in the bitterness it generated, was settled when, after a six weeks strike, the employers capitulated completely and conceded an increase of £3.50 per week for a forty-hour week over a period of eighteen months. This began to spread throughout industry, rising, as it did so, to £4 a week or more. This was the twelfth round.

The banks were in trouble again; so also were the teachers; and so also, in a most serious way, was the Electricity Supply Board. The pace of economic growth slowed. National production had risen by 7.9 per cent. in 1968, which was the highest we had ever achieved. In 1969, it was 4 per cent. and in 1970 it had dropped to less than half that figure. In December 1970, a national agreement was concluded which was the most sophisticated yet achieved, coming into operation only when current

[23] *The Irish Times,* 13 October 1966.

[24] *Trade Union Information,* no. 158 (Irish Congress of Trade Unions, Dublin, February 1971).

agreements ran out, and offering increases in two phases (the first being £2 a week, the second being 4 per cent.) with in addition a cost of living automatic escalation clause. This was the thirteenth round. A national agreement on similar lines was negotiated in the summer of 1972, reinforcing as well the growing stability in industrial relations.

There was very great economic development during the nineteen sixties, despite our industrial difficulties; a consequence of this was a substantial growth in affluence and in self-confidence. But employment figures over the period were disappointing, despite the remarkably comprehensive programme for full employment produced by the National Industrial Economic Council. Total employment increased by only one per cent. over the decade. However, there were very great internal changes. Employment in agriculture declined very considerably, while in industry there was a sharp rise. Employment in services increased only slightly; this was surprising, but the reason offered is that there was substantial underemployment in the services sector in any event. Emigration, however, fell steadily throughout the decade until now it has almost ceased.

The nineteen sixties was a decade very different indeed from the fifties. During that period, not only were the various increases small in size compared to the sixties, but those in the bargaining field were not conscious of any continuous pressure between rounds as they are now. Some attribute this to the fact that the agreements are now for fixed terms which, as we have said, create expectations on the dates of termination. This may be a factor, but pressures had begun to mount well before term agreements began to emerge. In any event, expectations are much greater now; and most important of all, the tempo of the rounds is increasing, which, in view of the high level of the amounts sought, is a dangerous inflationary phenomenon.

During the nineteen fifties, trade unions were inhibited in their activity by the existence of the two congresses. Their interest lay in politics in a much more extensive way than in the sixties, since the Labour Party participated in the two interparty governments of 1948-51 and 1954-57. Above all, however, the fifties was a time of gloom, of pessimism, while the sixties (until perhaps 1969) were always full of promise and of rising expectations. Finally, during the sixties the question of industrial disputes, of strikes and pickets became a central problem in industrial relations and indeed in economic development. The overwhelming success of some strikes, however irresponsible, and the fear of strikes from other groups, have no doubt contributed to the high level of the settlements in recent years. Professor O'Mahony[25] was reflecting fairly the mood of the fifties when he wrote: "The truth is that we are in danger of attributing an importance to strikes which, in fact, they do not possess, and of assuming that the unions are very much stronger than they really are." Things have changed very much since then.

VII

Finally, in this chapter, let us consider briefly the institutions which have grown up in the field of industrial relations in Ireland, their development and their present character.

It is useful at the outset to distinguish between disputes about rights and disputes about interests. When we speak about rights in this context, we speak really about their interpretation and application; standing behind are the rights themselves, conferred by law or by custom, or, as is frequently the case in industrial relations, by agreement. These are not in question. What is in question is their application in a particular instance. This idea is a familiar one since it underlies the operation of our courts of law. On the other hand, there are the disputes about interests – disputes where the parties fail to make a bargain, for example, at the conference table and where industrial action, as it is called, results. Of course, in such circumstances there is also much talk of rights – a right to a living wage, or a right to fair treatment – but, while these may at times be compelling, they do not rest on any agreed statement or understanding between the parties. It is in this context that we speak of a dispute about interests.

In recent years, the emphasis in Irish industrial relations has changed markedly from disputes about interests to disputes about rights. This was inevitable as national agreements became more dominant, limiting the area in which bargaining occurred and directing attention instead to the manner in which agreements would be implemented – in other words, to the question of rights. But it is important to remember that in its early years, and indeed until quite recently, the Labour Court in Ireland was concerned primarily with disputes on interests, not on rights.

The Labour Court, probably the best known of our industrial relations institutions, was established under the Industrial Relations Act of 1946[26], the object of which was to avoid industrial conflict as the standstill orders of the war period were removed and pent-up claims put in peril the return of free collective bargaining. The act, which had the approval and support of both sides of industry, encouraged employers and workers to regulate their own relations primarily between themselves, but, in the

[25]O'Mahony, op. cit., p. 34.
[26]O'Mahony, op. cit., p. 4ff. See also Appendix 2.

last resort, with the assistance of the Labour Court. The act therefore provided for the registration of agreements freely negotiated, for the establishment of joint industrial councils, and above all for a conciliation service to assist the parties to reach agreement. But the central institution was the Court itself which oversaw these activities, and in addition itself investigated and reported on industrial disputes. For this purpose, there is now[27] a chairman, two deputy chairmen, and six other members, three appointed by the employers and three by the trade unions so that the Court can sit in three divisions. But, in its decisions, the Court must rely on a moral, not a legal, authority. It has no power to enforce; essentially it has power only to recommend. This, on the face of it, may appear to be small substance indeed on which to build such a large structure, yet in the bargaining field, in the field of conflicting interests, there is really no law to implement or rights to enforce; and this was the very area to which in the past much of the work of the Court was devoted. Therefore, although the institution is known as the Labour Court, it differs very much from a court of law, and differs very much as well from the labour court system as it is known in West Germany, for example, where labour relations have a strong legalistic character and where labour courts at federal, land or local level, are prominent both in the interpretation of contracts and in the application of labour law. There, lawyers preside in the courts, while in the Irish case, the trade unions in 1946 opposed the appointment of a lawyer as chairman and ensured as well that the right to be represented by counsel or by solicitor was very limited. Furthermore, while the Court has the power to summon witnesses and examine under oath, in practice, in order to maintain its voluntary and persuasive character, these powers are not used.

The great debate over the years was whether the Labour Court should be given powers similar to those in West Germany. This may have missed the point, since one would have had to develop first the practice of industry-wide and national agreements, that is to say the private law which the Court would enforce. In very recent times, where the national agreements have produced just such a situation, unions and employers seem willing to accept a Labour Court ruling on questions of the application of the national agreement, and there is little pressure for compulsory powers. There remains the question of the banks, where, as we shall later see, both employers and employees appear to wish to discount the national agreement and settle outside it. It was for this reason that the Minister for Labour, Mr Michael O'Leary, decided to introduce a bill in Dáil Éireann on 9 July 1973, the effect of which would be to impose penalties

---

[27]The size of the Court has been increased recently.

on the banks if they gave increases to their employees in excess of what the Labour Court considered to be warranted under the national agreement. The question, however, once again turns on a conflict of interests rather than a dispute on rights, since the implicit challenge of both the banks and their employees was to the application to them of a national agreement which, when it was negotiated, was seen as a voluntary agreement affecting only the parties (and these did not include the banks), and which only later developed some of the characteristics of public law. It is very doubtful indeed whether the reinforcing of the national agreement by penalties will be extended to other than the banks. Already in the summer of 1973, there is restlessness among some unions, although the move was made in their interests as much as any other; but if it were to be extended, and if the Labour Court were to be given the right to impose penalties, then the Court would move much closer to the West German model.

Before we leave the question of rights, it is necessary to remark on the two rights commissioners who were appointed by virtue of section 12 of the Industrial Relations Act of 1969. These are essentially industrial ombudsmen, not dealing with bargaining matters but, by and large, with rights as we have defined them here, although in practice the service is largely based on good sense and fair play, is very informal, and has little legalism associated with it.

Section 4 of the 1946 act excluded from its provisions state employees generally, and, in the early fifties, a conciliation and arbitration system was introduced in the civil service. In the years that followed, similar systems were established for other state employees. In the case of the civil service, the arbitration board (whose chairman was independent and appointed by agreement) made decisions on conflicts not of rights but of interests, on disputes regarding salary claims and related matters, and by custom these decisions were accepted by both sides. In one early case, in 1952, the government temporised about implementation, and the vehemence of the civil servants' response not only secured future government acquiescence but made the idea of rejection of an award highly unlikely in their own case as well. It is only in quite recent times that the question has been raised about the good sense of leaving to one man a decision not of equity but of industrial bargaining. However, for twenty years or more, the system has not been challenged in its substance; perhaps, as we shall see, one reason for this is the skill the civil service unions developed in using it. There are other negotiating systems outside the state service, particularly in large employments such as the Electricity Supply Board; some of these we shall meet in the course of this study.

During the nineteen sixties, as we shall see, there were a number of instances of damaging and extensive disputes arising not out of conflict of interest but apparently out of conflicts of rights, conflicts of interpretation and implementation; these raised the whole question of the powers of the Labour Court, and whether in these circumstances, if in no other, it should be given judicial and penal functions. The problem was particularly marked in the disputes arising from the 1964 national agreement, which ended in considerable stress and recrimination. We shall examine in some detail the background to all this, but it is important to recognise that we were, during the time, in a period of transition, and many workers, and their representatives, did not really see clearly the cutting edges of the agreements which they had concluded; the whole thing was unfamiliar. On the other hand, the employers had expectations of an exactitude of performance so explicit that any departure from it was seen as a threat to the whole. But the real difficulty lay in the woeful inadequacy of our institutions.

In contrast, in the national agreement of 1970 and again in 1972, the Employer-Labour Conference fulfilled the role not only of general supervision of the agreement, but also that of interpretation. The Employer-Labour Conference was established first in 1963, but in recent times, under the impetus of the national agreements, it has developed into a major institution in wage and salary matters. It has an independent chairman, appointed by agreement, and consists of representatives of trade unions and employers only, although the government, latterly, is represented in its employing role. But what of the Labour Court in all this? The national agreements were not concluded under its auspices, as some might have expected. It is of course given an important role under the agreements, but the Employer-Labour Conference continues significantly to deal with questions of interpretation and also with general problems of implementation such as the varying dates on which the agreement terminates for different groups of workers.

The relationship between the Labour Court and Employer-Labour Conference is a complex one, and this we shall explore in a later chapter, taking up as well the relationship of both with other institutions in the field of incomes policy.

Industrial relations, like all other relations, are subject to the normal process of the law, and it is desirable, therefore, in this discussion of institutions, to look briefly at the manner in which the courts in Ireland have approached industrial disputes. We are in some difficulties here

INTRODUCTION

since there is so little scholarship[28] in the law in Ireland, and in particular in the law as it affects trade unions.

The origins of Irish labour law lie in the British system, and there is a temptation to see it largely as a variation of that system, which has quite a rich literature. However, this is too facile a view. The Irish Constitution represents, in the first place, a distinctly different concept of society; and secondly, its legal implications are so fundamental that it is quite inappropriate to see it merely as a complicating factor in an essentially British legal construct.

The contrast with the British system and, in particular, the development of the Irish system of law in the matter of industrial relations can best be seen if we explore the trade union distinction between judge-made law and the law as enacted by parliament. This distinction is the key to the great trade union campaign which resulted in the Trades Disputes Act of 1906. For thirty years after the Trade Union Act of 1871, the trade unions had been secure in their legal charter, but in the first years of the new century, there were in particular two decisions, Quinn v. Leathem (an Irish case) and the Taff Vale judgment, which shattered their legislative security. The trade union campaign that followed rested not on strikes nor on further expensive litigation, but rather on the seeking of a political solution through parliament. The change in government in 1906 was seen therefore as a victory for 'the democracy' and the 1906 Trades Disputes Act reversed the decisions of the law lords. Here, then, parliament was supreme.

This also of course is the broad pattern still, but, in this country, in matters which bear on constitutional rights (and this covers a number of important trade union cases) the Irish Constitution of 1937 in practice places the courts above parliament, much in contrast with the British system. Of course, the object of the Constitution was to guarantee personal rights even as against parliament, but in matters of interpretation, the courts necessarily had the final word, short of a constitutional referendum.

What made this of particular interest in Ireland was the marked cultural difference which existed between the lawyers who, in a somewhat whiggish way, tended to be concerned with individuals and their rights, and parliament which was troubled by problems of social integrity and

---

[28]Bernard Shillman's *Trade Unionism and Trade Disputes in Ireland* (Dublin, 1960) is a useful practical guide. See also R. F. V. Heuston, 'Trade Unions and the Law' in the *Irish Jurist* 1960, vol. IV, p. 10ff., where there is a good discussion of the 1906 act, dealing with both Irish and English cases; and J. B. McCartney, 'Strike Law and the Constitution' in the *Irish Jurist* 1964, p. 54. Most important of all, is the judgment of the Supreme Court as delivered by Walsh J. in Becton Dickenson and Company Limited *v.* Patrick Lee and Ors. in 1973, where the law in a number of important areas is reviewed and clarified. It is as yet unreported.

development. As industry began to develop in the nineteen thirties and trade unions began to become important, the government clearly wished them to play their part in an integrated way within the state; consequently, in later years it legislated both for their protection and performance. In article 40 of the Constitution we find the guarantee to the citizens to form associations and unions, and in the Trade Union Act of 1941 we find provision for the licensing of bodies to carry on negotiations. As far as legislating for performance is concerned, we had, as we have already seen, a beginning in the act of 1946 which established the Labour Court. It was this same integrated view of the state, strongly reinforced by nationalist feeling, which tempted the government, also under the 1941 act, to exclude British-based unions.

All this was much in contrast with the traditional view which the law had of trade unions. Fundamentally, they were seen as tortious bodies, more often than not engaged in tortious activities but exempted from penalty in certain circumstances. This view was exemplified in particular in cases decided in the fifties and early sixties, and reached its climax in the Educational Company case[29] which the trade unions saw as the turning of the constitutional guarantee on its head; certainly, there appeared to come from the courts a marked dislike of those corporate constraints which trade unions tend to exercise. Heuston, in his article in the *Irish Jurist*, remarked that the Irish courts tended to be stricter in the matter of certain statutory definitions than the English courts; and, furthermore, there was a great readiness to employ the injunction in industrial disputes. The tradition of the law is much the same in both countries, but in Britain the political and social reality of the trade unions at a very early stage moderated the traditional position. If we are to judge from recent decisions, there may well be some moderation in Ireland as well, but we must bear in mind in all this how mannered and traditional the education of Irish barristers is, how tenaciously tradition is adhered to, and how barristers and judges subsequently work all together in the common, club-like, somewhat archaic society of the Four Courts. Whatever the reason, prominent trade union officials with a strong commitment to good order in society were sometimes distressed to find themselves treated in the courts as persons of questionable repute.

This too may go some way to explain the great chariness with regard to the law which trade unions manifested in the face of pressures for reform during the period which we shall review here, and why the legislation of recent times became, in the event, more a matter of housekeeping than of radical change. Of course, in the Irish trade union

---

[29]Educational Company of Ireland *v.* Fitzpatrick (1961), I.R. 345.

conferences there were echoes of the great debates in Britain following the Donovan Commission Report[30] and a certain fascination with the Conservative government's Industrial Relations Act of 1971. No doubt we were conscious that, whatever the difficulties and stress in Britain, the introduction of such legislation would be far more difficult here, while at the same time feeling a certain satisfaction that, for the moment at least, the success of the national agreement made the question unnecessary.

VIII

In the chapter that follows, we shall begin by considering the character of the Irish trade union movement. We shall establish the background events of 1962 and 1963 and then we shall examine the first of the disputes, the strike of the Dublin busmen. In the subsequent chapters, we shall follow the same pattern, outlining the major industrial events of the period and setting them as a background to the disputes. In a final chapter we shall deal with some of the major topics associated with the disputes, particularly those concerned with strategies for the future. Inevitably, I shall write with more awareness of the trade union point of view than the employers', although I have tried to maintain a reasonable balance.

---

[30]*Royal Commission on Trade Unions and Employers' Associations* 1965–68 (The Donovan Report), Cmnd. 3623. See also the British Labour government's white paper, *In Place of Strife,* Cmnd. 3888.

CHAPTER TWO

Nineteen Sixty-Two and the Busmen

I

THE fifth annual conference of the Irish Congress of Trade Unions took place in Killarney in 1963. In its annual report and in its discussions, it reviewed the period from July 1962, and this we shall take as the starting-point in our survey. The fifth annual conference meant, of course, the fifth conference since the amalgamation of the two bodies into which the movement split in 1945, the original Irish Trade Union Congress, and the Congress of Irish Unions. There was still in the air a certain sensitivity about the split, and an anxiety to continue to cement the organisation. Perhaps it was for this reason that the president, Jack Macgougan, himself from Belfast, brought the annual conference that year to the deep Gaelic south, to Killarney.

Here is immediately revealed the special character of the Irish trade union movement, with its range of unions both Irish-based and British-based, many of course confined either to the Republic or to the North, but others representing workers throughout the whole island, and consequently confronted with two governments and two administrative styles. Apart from this complexity, the student of trade unionism will recognise in Ireland a situation very similar to that in the United Kingdom, where a large number of workers is represented by a small number of large unions; but where, on the other hand, a small number of workers is represented by a great number of unions, up to eighty or more, some claiming a vigorous independence. It is because of this that we shall hear from time to time of the problem of the multiplicity of trade unions, as it is called. There is no clear trend towards the industrial type of trade union, that is to say, one union for a whole industry, although there are one or two examples of such a structure. On the contrary, general unions in Ireland, as in Britain, tend to develop by spreading into further industries and further occupations; there does not appear to be any deeper penetration in the industries and occupations already organised. The system, therefore, has a sloppy look to it, which invites reorganisation from tidy minds. Ruaidhri Roberts,[1] about the time our survey begins, summarised the position as follows:

> We have therefore at present in Ireland a few local unions, mainly skilled unions, a few Irish national craft, occupational and industrial unions, a large number of Irish branches of British craft unions, a few of them large, many of them very small, and a small number of large general unions, both Irish and British, which between them organise more workers than all the other unions put together.

We shall, in the material that follows, deal with the Republic, bearing in mind, however, that the pattern is broadly similar in the North. Unions varied greatly in size, as we have seen. Some were tiny, not only civil service grade associations, but some craft unions as well.

> At the other extreme are the large general unions – the largest of which is the Irish Transport and General Workers Union with about 150,000 members or not far short of 50 per cent. of all the trade unionists in the State. It may be noted that despite the multiplicity of very small unions, the nine unions having more than 5,000 members each cater for three-quarters of all organised workers.[2]

Let us continue to focus, then, not on the island as a whole but rather on the trade union movement viewed from within the frontiers of the Republic. Professor O'Mahony does this very clearly, but even in setting it out, one becomes conscious that the figures themselves distort the reality of the movement by a kind of crisp polarisation, which did not reflect much that was done in common. Nevertheless, his presentation is important, particularly to an understanding of earlier decades:

> Of the 123 unions operating in the Republic, 94 have their headquarters in the Republic and the remaining 29 have their headquarters in Britain. Only 3 of the 94 unions having their head-

---

[1] R. Roberts, 'Trade Union Organisation in Ireland' in the *Journal of the Statistical and Social Inquiry Society of Ireland* (Dublin, 1958–59), p. 94. See also Appendix 2.
[2] O'Mahony, op. cit., p. 11.

quarters in the Republic have members in Northern Ireland but all 29 British unions have members in both parts of the country. Thus 91 unions have members in the Republic only, and 32 have members both in the Republic and Northern Ireland.[3]

It is very difficult to compare the level of unionisation in Ireland with that in other countries. The figures we have are for non-agricultural employment, and if they are high, it may merely imply a low level of industrialisation, or perhaps more recent industrialisation. Further, the figures in each country are not always compiled in the same way. Subject to all that, Ireland is highly unionised, comparatively speaking:[4]

> The proportion of the employee labour force who are in trade unions in Ireland is just over half (52%): the proportion for the Republic is 56% and for Northern Ireland, 48%. This is higher than in Britain where the proportion is 43% or in the Netherlands (36%), Japan (34%), West Germany (32%), USA (25%) or France (23%) but lower than in Sweden where 56% of employees are in unions.

Over the decade of the sixties there was considerable growth. The total trade union membership, that is north and south, increased by 58,000 between 1960 and 1970, the total membership in that latter year being very nearly 650,000, three-fifths in the Republic and two-fifths in Northern Ireland. Of the Republic, *Trade Union Information*[5] says:

> The membership of unions with head offices in Ireland increased between 1960 and 1970 by 44,200 (15%) and the membership of unions with head offices in Britain by 14,600 (36%). Notwithstanding the relatively faster rate of increase in the membership of British-based unions over the decade, the proportion of the total trade union members who were in British based unions rose only slightly from 12% in 1960 to 14% in 1970.

We shall see in the sixties as well the growing importance of the white-collar workers, who gradually abandoned their claim to privilege as the salaried classes, and threw in their lot with the trade union movement:

> Between 1966 and 1970 the membership of general unions rose by 12,700 (or 6%) while the membership of white-collar unions increased by 10,500 (or 13%) and the membership of other (manual

[3]O'Mahony, op. cit., p. 11. The figures are for 1960.

[4]*Trade Union Information* (Irish Congress of Trade Unions, Dublin, August 1967), p. 2.

[5]*Trade Union Information* (Irish Congress of Trade Unions, Dublin, June 1971), p. 3.

workers') unions by 4,100 (or 5%). The biggest relative increase in membership both in the 1966-68 and in the 1968-70 periods were those recorded for white-collar unions.[6]

But the influence of the white-collar worker had become even stronger than this. While by 1970 the exclusively white-collar unions represented almost a quarter of trade union membership, "....it is estimated on a very rough basis that upwards of 40,000 members of general unions may be regarded as white-collar workers so that the total number of white-collar workers in membership of unions is in the region of 130,000 or just one-third (34%) of total trade union membership".[7]

II

But figures, for all their conceit, can confuse as well as clarify, and in this case they give an impression of almost perverse fragmentation. Yet by 1960, the trade union movement had an underlying unity which had been achieved with great difficulty during the fifties. In order to understand it, in order to round out this skeletal frame of numbers, it is necessary to look briefly at the past.

As with Britain, the early trade unions were craft unions, and although they have now lost their dominance, the traditions of trade unionism in Ireland have their roots in them. Up to 1850 or so, they were local unions, and therefore – as some would describe them with hindsight – Irish. In fact, they reflected the tendency throughout these islands to form local unions which maintained among one another some degree of correspondence and reciprocity while retaining their local character. Then came the period of amalgamations. It was described[8] in the chauvinist forties as "....the invasion of this country by the large English unions which quickly absorbed many of the small local associations in Dublin and the provinces," but it is doubtful if it was seen in that way at the time. By 1894, the great majority of Irish trade unionists belonged to unions with head offices in England; but about this time as well the Irish Trade Union Congress was founded, marking in this way an autonomous concern with Irish affairs while still maintaining the tradition of international solidarity. This then was the craft tradition. The other tradition lay with the general workers. In the early years of this century, the general unions came to Ireland with the object of organising the dockers, the labourers and the transport workers; and so began the turbulent career of Big Jim Larkin. There arose at this time the despairing

[6]ibid., p. 3.
[7]ibid., p. 2.
[8]*Report on Vocational Organisation* (Stationery Office, Dublin, 1943), p. 182.

militancy of the city workers, of Belfast in 1907 and of Dublin in 1913. This period saw the emergence of the Irish Transport and General Workers Union, by far the most populous union in the country. This was the second tradition in which Irish trade unionism has its roots, the tradition of the urban labouring classes. In the years that followed, the Irish Transport and General Workers Union spread throughout the country taking the tone of the Gaelic subculture, its members increasing tenfold in four or five years under the influence of nationalist fervour; but its origins lay in urban misery.

The nineteen twenties was a period of dissension and decline. The craft unions were heirs to Paine's republicanism as well as his internationalism, and this republicanism began to enter the exclusive service of a Gaelic culture. Large groups of craft workers broke away to form exclusively Irish-based unions. Sometimes, the British union no longer continued in the Irish Free State, but in many cases the Irish-based and British-based unions continued side by side, creating many complex problems which continue to trouble us to the present day. It would be wrong to assume that all those who remained in the British-based unions were not committed republicans. On the contrary, there were many who saw no difficulty whatever in combining militant Irish nationalism with international trade unionism, and indeed imported into the British trade union tradition some of the sad songs of murdered Irish heroes. But if this was so in Dublin, and if the members of the British craft unions there were often Catholic republicans, the members of the same unions in Belfast were working class Protestants, of a distinctly different tradition. While the trade union leadership in the North could be radical or socialist, the rank and file members were often loyalist to a man.

In the great general union, the Irish Transport, Larkin's return from the United States in the early twenties was marked by a bitter split between him and William O'Brien; and in 1924 Larkin broke finally with the union he founded, forming instead the Workers Union of Ireland. The personal enmity between O'Brien and Larkin, and between quite a number of their associates, dominated the trade union movement in Ireland for a quarter of a century until the late forties. The decline in membership of the trade unions during the nineteen twenties could be attributed in part to these difficulties. It was due, probably in much larger part, to the economic disruption following the civil war, and also to the recession of the later years. With the programme of industrialisation of the thirties, things began to improve, and after the war, the period of steady and continuous expansion in membership began. But right throughout these dark years, there was, in Donal Nevin's words,[9] much personal animosity and distrust. The clash between Larkin and O'Brien and the traditions they represented was not by any means the only source of dissension. In the Free State where, as we have seen, the vast majority of members were in Irish-based unions, the Irish unions and the British unions worked uneasily together. There was a clash in the thirties between the Irish Transport and General Workers Union and the Amalgamated Transport and General Workers Union[10] which had its echoes in the busmen's dispute in the sixties, and there were implications of British invasion and domination. The Report of the Commission on Vocational Organisation, which was established in 1939 and which reported in 1943, expressed[11] the mood of very many at the time:

> National sovereignty and national security require that the control of trade unions in the country should be in the hands of Irish nationals. We hold that it is extremely dangerous that persons outside the jurisdiction of the State should have ultimate control in such an important matter as the trade disputes of its citizens.

This too was the period of corporatism. The Commission we have just referred to was established in response to the spirit of the time, and, in a long report, recommended in detail a system of vocational organisation for the country. Even those staunchly in the liberal tradition, while condemning Nazism and Fascism (as indeed the whole Commission did) could say: "We agree to the principle of vocational organisation, because the general trend of economic and social development impels us inevitably towards a system based upon it."[12] Also, for many reasons, not least that the Bishop of Galway was chairman, it had the steady glow of Catholic social teaching about it. Seán Lemass, however, dismissed it brusquely as of no account, and, in rapidly changing times, its impact evaporated.

But the mood of corporatism gave considerable impetus to the idea of One Big Union, the dream of Robert Owen, which was so powerfully advocated by James Connolly and which was urged very strongly by the Irish Transport as early as 1921, when they were prepared either to attempt an OBU themselves or to support the Irish TUC in achieving it.[13]

[9]Donal Nevin, 'Industry and Labour', in K. B. Nowlan and T. D. Williams (eds.), *Ireland in the War Years and After 1939–1951* (Gill and Macmillan, Dublin, 1969), p. 96.
[10]This, in the United Kingdom, is the Transport and General Workers Union, "amalgamated" being an Irish identifier.
[11]Op. cit., p. 366.
[12]Op. cit., p. 477. Reservation by Louie Bennett and Seán Campbell.
[13]Ruaidhri Roberts, op. cit.

In 1936, Mr Lemass, who was then Minister for Industry and Commerce, informed the Congress that if they were not in a position to reorganise the trade union movement, then the government would have to take a hand. This, at least, was the formal position, although the suggestion may not have been entirely a surprise to the Irish Transport. Congress, in response, appointed a commission of inquiry to consider and report on the trade union movement in Ireland. It reported in 1939, but without a majority recommendation. Five of the twelve members recommended a radical recasting of the whole trade union movement into ten industrial groupings; five others stated that this was much too far-reaching, that the various unions with their separate and varied traditions could not and should not be assimilated in industrial unions in this way. This latter view prevailed at a special conference called to discuss the report, but the majority who rejected industrial unions was a small one. Some of the Irish-based unions joined with the British unions in rejecting the idea; but the Irish Transport and the other Irish unions had mustered an immense showing in favour of radical reform and there was some suggestion that if the positive rather than the negative proposal had been put to the conference, it might conceivably have carried the day.

In 1941, the government, true to its promise, introduced the Trade Union Bill. Among other reforms, it proposed that a tribunal should be established by the government which would declare the majority union in a job to be the only recognised union, but in a manner which favoured Irish-based unions. There was uproar, particularly from the Dublin Trade Union Council, also with its hackles well up because of the Wages Standstill Order. James Larkin by then was a member of the Dublin Council. His union had been consistently refused membership of the Irish TUC "... because its record as a cause of disruptive action against the trade union movement and promoter of libels against officers of affiliated unions and of Congress itself would make its admission a disintegrating instead of a harmonising element within Congress"[14]. His acceptance by the Dublin Council had resulted in fact in the withdrawal from the council of the Irish Transport. Larkin flung himself into the campaign against the Trade Union Bill with a flamboyant vigour, burning a copy of the bill before a huge crowd in College Green.[15] But the Irish Transport was sourly mute about the whole affair. William O'Brien was president of the annual conference of the TUC in 1941, and he claimed that the trade union movement had only themselves to blame, because of the failure of the 1936 commission to provide an agreed

[14]Donal Nevin, op. cit., quoting the annual report of the ITUC.
[15]Donal Nevin, op. cit.

answer. But he was implacable in his continued hostility to the British-based unions: "No matter what the proposals in the measure were, there would be an outcry from the superfluous unions which we want to see eliminated – or, to use an expression in fashion in some quarters 'liquidated'."[16] Larkin had been excluded from the Congress for many years; at this conference he was a delegate not from his own union, which had been refused membership, but from the Dublin Trade Union Council. There was much acrimony throughout the conference, particularly about the origin and purpose of the bill. It was, in fact, enacted, although the section dealing with the tribunal was later declared unconstitutional by the Supreme Court.

The Labour Party had, in the early years of the century, sprung from the womb of the trade union movement, and the two continued to be closely intertwined both in their leadership and in their policies. Because Larkin was readmitted to the party and nominated as a candidate for the 1943 general election, the Irish Transport disaffiliated and some five Labour deputies associated with the Irish Transport resigned from the party alleging communist influence, and formed a new National Labour Party. Early the following year,[17] the *Catholic Standard* was to reveal the 'Story of the Red Coup in the Party.' The 1944 general election was disastrous for Labour, and in 1948 when there was an opportunity of joining in an interparty government, the two Labour parties, more hardheaded in these matters than the unions, established a common front. This political row, based not only on a straight conflict of personalities but also on a driving difference in ideologies and traditions, set the scene for the rift between British-based and Irish-based unions which in 1944 tore the Congress apart. Late in 1943, the British TUC extended an invitation to the Irish TUC to attend a world trade union congress in London. The executive committee was sharply divided on the issue, but decided that in the interests of Ireland's neutrality, they should decline. At the 1944 annual conference, Sam Kyle of the Amalgamated Transport, genuinely committed to the idea of world trade union solidarity, put down a motion regretting the decision. O'Brien told the delegates that this, if passed, would be the first step to the breakdown of Congress. Kyle's motion was adopted by 96 votes to 73. This vote, however, represented something of even greater significance, a swing in power on the executive committee of Congress from the Irish-based to the British-based unions. The 1944 annual conference elected[18] nine executive committee

[16]Irish Trade Union Congress, *Forty-Seventh Annual Report,* 1941.
[17]17 March 1944.
[18]The real problem here was that the British-based unions used the system of block voting not only to win Kyle's motion, but, much more important, to elect a somewhat unrepresentative executive. The present ICTU elects by a proportional representation system.

members from British-based unions and six from Irish-based, the very reverse of 1943. The new executive committee, as was expected, appointed representatives to the London conference in February 1945. The Irish Transport and fourteen other Irish-based unions declared that the Irish TUC was controlled by the British trade unions, and on 25 April formed the Congress of Irish Unions. Manifestoes crashed out from both sides, the TUC calling to its aid the international traditions of the trade union movement, while the CIU declared that the Irish people were masters of their own destiny. Both had recourse to the writings of James Connolly. Now, in the new situation, the TUC accepted the Workers Union of Ireland, Larkin's union, into membership.

Yet in a few years, all began to change. William O'Brien retired in 1946, and in 1947 Big Jim died. On the day that his funeral moved through the bitter, snow-filled streets of Dublin, his son, Young Jim as he was called, wrote an open letter to the newspapers asking for unity among all workers and all trade unionists. This, indeed, was to be the theme of the fifties and its great achievement.

The fifties, for the trade union movement, was the decade of reconciliation. In 1953, the first tentative talks began, followed by the establishment two years later of the Provisional United Trade Union Organisation. This body, over the next three difficult years, drafted the constitution for a new united trade union congress, the Irish Congress of Trade Unions, which was established in 1959. Roberts says:

> The new Congress, apart from restoring unity in the trade union centre, differs from the Irish TUC of 1944 by developments designed to secure (1) control by the Irish membership, (2) provision of the more extended service required by the Irish membership, (3) special provisions for Northern Ireland, (4) provisions designed to secure better inter-union relations.[19]

This is a sober description of a remarkable achievement, not only in overcoming the personal dissensions of the past but in overcoming as well great structural difficulties. Roberts's own contribution was considerable but the substance of unity was created by John Conroy, now general president of the Irish Transport and General Workers Union, Jim Larkin, now general secretary of the Workers Union of Ireland and, in the case of the Amalgamated Transport and General Workers Union by Sam Kyle, whose continuous goodwill towards unity was reinforced by his successor, Norman Kennedy.

Without in any way lessening the achievement, it must be recognised as well that there was in the country a strong movement towards unity.

[19] Ruaidhri Roberts, op. cit., p. 102.

The nationalist war-time sensitivity had given way to problems of economic growth; Lemass and the government were pressing for unity (although probably only in terms of the Republic) but, apart from this, there were quite a number of important Irish-based unions which had remained in the Irish TUC, forming the bridge between Irish and British-based unions. While their affiliated membership represented about a third of the total ITUC affiliation[20] (much more of course if the Republic alone were considered), they were often significant in Irish affairs. There was the Irish National Teachers Organisation, whose national position was unquestioned; there was the Post Office Workers Union, whose general secretary, William Norton, was leader of the Labour Party. Other unions covered bakers, insurance workers, civil service engineering workers, vocational teachers – all Irish-based. So strong became the movement for unity that, when the final proposal was put to the two congresses in February 1959, the opposition came from some of the British-based unions of the ITUC, scared of losing all their Irish members both north and south. Things were not helped by a Sunday newspaper report some weeks before the conferences, claiming that the new constitution insisted that unions must break their branch and office links with Britain. Ruaidhri Roberts,[21] at the opening of the ITUC special conference, vehemently denied this:

> As most of you know, this is completely and absolutely untrue. There is no clause requiring that British branch and office links must be broken. From the point of view of the unions with headquarters in Britain the most important and most significant feature of the ICTU is the fact that it recognises the position of British unions in Ireland, recognises the desire of the Irish membership of British unions to retain their branch and other links with British headquarters, and provides accordingly that these unions shall have the right of affiliation to the Irish Congress of Trade Unions. They have that right without any condition concerning breaking with Britain either now or at any future date. The only conditions they are subject to are conditions with which most British unions with members in Ireland already conform.

But some of the British-based unions, often represented by English head office delegates, while subscribing to the idea of unity, raised legal and other difficulties, so much so that Jim Larkin[22] roughly questioned their original commitment to the idea of unity talks:

[20]See Irish Trade Union Congress, *Sixty-Fifth Annual Report* 1958–59.
[21]ibid., p. 63.
[22]ibid., p. 80.

In 1953 after a long and tortuous series of negotiations we went on record with this statement '....that the conference should have in view the objective of the Irish Trade Union Movement being wholly Irish based and controlled....' That was embodied in our Annual Report and every one of the unions whose representatives spoke to-day endorsed and accepted that principle. Are we to go back on it? We have now a draft constitution carried out on that basis; first that it shall be Irish-based and controlled; second, that it shall apply to the whole of Ireland; third, that there shall be no breaks in their industrial links with their brothers across the channel. Isn't that what you sent us to get? Why then would you repudiate the instructions given by our affiliated unions. Is it unfair to say of some that they are now being presented with unity which they never expected to be realised?

On the other hand, many of the British-based unions stood solidly for unity, and in the ITUC the proposed constitution was adopted by 148 votes to 81.[23] John Conroy, who had led the CIU into unity, became, on its establishment, the first president of the Irish Congress of Trade Unions, to be followed by Jim Larkin, who took office at its first annual general meeting later in 1959. He was succeeded the following year by Norman Kennedy of the Amalgamated Transport. Thus ended fourteen years of division.

We have recognised at the outset that there was in the healing of this split the deeper common tradition of the trade union movement, pulling all the diverse elements together, the Gaelic subculture, the Dublin working class, the Belfast artisan, the clerical and professional groups of the quasi *bourgeoisie*. In this, it demonstrated that it can validly span subcultural boundaries in a society so often bent on eliminating cultural diversity instead of recognising it. Later, the Irish Congress of Trade Unions, because of this character, was to make a valid and substantial contribution during the political difficulties in the North, particularly when rioting threatened to spread in employment in 1969, and in the years since then, its call for reconciliation and for peace has become more vigorous and more compelling.

Although the problem of national sentiment had been met, what of Marxism, that great bogey of the fifties? The unification of the trade union movement brought ideological uncertainty to many trade union councils, and well into the sixties there was still, among those of us in the Gaelic subculture, a whispering of Marxism in the corners of the conference rooms, a sense of quick anxiety about the possibility of a

[23]ibid., p. 81.

communist *démarche*, although how this could take place in the overwhelming Catholic climate of the time, it is difficult to see. The anti-Marxist socialism of many of the Northern officials and the radicalism of some of those in the Republic made any polarisation on the old lines within the trade union movement unlikely. Nor did it appear to have any disruptive effect. Conroy's courtesy to all men and all opinions helped calm hostility from the conservative centre, and, in any event, the continuing respect which Conroy, Larkin, Norman Kennedy and others had for one another gave the Congress stability.

III

But how important was Congress in this year of 1963, and to what extent did it represent the trade union movement? Certainly, numbers were impressive. Almost all trade unions were affiliated to it, the only significant exceptions being some of the white-collar unions, most of whom were to join during the decade. The fact remained, however, that ninety per cent. of all trade unionists in Ireland (perhaps half a million) were in unions affiliated to Congress, ninety four per cent. in the Republic and 85 per cent. in the case of Northern Ireland.[24] At the same time, Congress was by no means the governing body for the movement. Its position was not dissimilar to that of the British TUC, and in considerable contrast to some of the European trade union centres. We have already seen, in the debate in 1939, how strong the desire was to see a powerful centralised trade union structure, not unlike that of Sweden at the time and of West Germany after the war. This view was held not only by William O'Brien and the Irish Transport, but by quite a number of officials in the more radical tradition, relying often on the views which Connolly so explicitly expressed. But equally powerful was the desire of many unions to retain their independence. Consequently, while at a time of national crisis they might demand to know what leadership Congress was prepared to give, they were very sensitive about their independence, and very hostile to any suggestions of centralising authority. However, the executive council of Congress was composed of the leading trade union officials in the movement, and consequently, despite its weak constitutional position, when the executive council spoke with a united voice, it carried with it the support of the trade union movement as a whole. Some indeed would urge that when Congress is inadequate, it is an inadequacy that springs from its leadership, not from its constitution. When we come to consider the executive council, therefore, we can be confident that, if it does not always represent the trade union movement in Ireland, it very adequately reflects it.

[24] *Trade Union Information,* various numbers.

The position of president of Congress is a curious one. He holds office for one year only, and during that time is regarded as the principal officer of the trade union movement: the political, elected head, as it were, in contrast to the officials – the joint secretaries as they were in 1963. The position has been variously seen as a tribute to an official of long service, as a recognition of the importance of a large union or of a particular group of workers (craft workers perhaps, or the white-collar group), and also, of course, as an attempt to choose somebody for the leadership which he could offer. In the various men selected, it has been a bit of all these things. Some of those who held office during the sixties made a very distinct personal contribution; it was an office of opportunity very much more than of specific function. From the foundation of the ICTU to date, there was never a contest for the presidency; the vice-president has in all cases been the sole candidate. Up to the mid-sixties, the vice-president emerged by consensus, and the practice was that there should be only one agreed candidate. Since that time, however, a contest has taken place every year. The original consensus had a substantial point to it since it provided a means by which the office of president could alternate between the two broad interest groups, sometimes seen as the old TUC and the old CIU unions, sometimes seen as British-based and Irish-based, and sometimes as simply north and south. It was an arrangement which was only partly formulated, since the personality of the person chosen was the overriding factor.

In any event, it brought to office in the year 1962-63 Jack Macgougan who was at that time Irish officer of the National Union of Tailors and Garment Workers, an English-based union with membership north and south. He had been president of the old TUC in his time, and had considerable experience of labour politics in the North. He was friendly with Norman Kennedy, and represented the careful, constructive, socialist trade union tradition which had done a great deal to restore unity, and which later was to succeed in gaining recognition of the Irish Congress of Trade Unions from the government of Northern Ireland. Like many of the men at that time, he was conscious of the need to establish the trade union movement – and consequently the office of president – as an all-Ireland one. For example, although he was a northern Presbyterian, he had readily fulfilled the traditional duty of the president of the Irish Congress of Trade Unions, to give the major speech outside the General Post Office in Dublin on the occasion of the annual trade union commemoration of James Connolly, the trade union leader who was one of the signatories of the 1916 proclamation of independence and who was executed for his part in the Rising. As a president, Macgougan contributed stability and firmness. Let us look then at the executive council whose meetings he chaired.

In 1962, the council consisted of nineteen members: a president, a vice-president, a treasurer and sixteen ordinary members. (In 1970, the number of ordinary members was increased to twenty). All were elected at the annual conference by the delegates voting in accordance with the proportional representation system; the delegates themselves were appointed by their unions – the number of delegates being related, but not in proportion, to the size of the unions. We have already noted the election pattern in the case of the president and vice-president, but also, for some curious reason, there has never been a contest for the position of treasurer, which has always gone to the Irish Transport and General Workers Union, probably in recognition of the fact that it is the largest union in affiliation, and because of the limit placed on the number of executive members any one union may have. The Irish Transport can elect automatically, by reason of its size, two ordinary members to the council, the maximum it is permitted. (For some time, it was limited to only one ordinary member, but now it may once again elect two). The Amalgamated Transport and General Workers Union affiliated for 50,000 members (an underestimate of its strength), that is to say about a third of the affiliation of the Irish Transport, and could comfortably elect one member to the executive council. The Workers Union of Ireland, with 20,000 members, was the only other union which could automatically elect in this way. All the others, attempting to elect to the remaining twelve seats, had to depend on support from other unions; inevitably, the larger unions, particularly the Irish Transport, carried substantial influence.

The Irish Transport, therefore, had three members on the executive council for that year of 1962-63: John Conroy, their general president, who was treasurer of Congress and indeed remained treasurer for most of the sixties; Fintan Kennedy, then general secretary of the Irish Transport and later to become general president in succession to Conroy; and finally Dan McAllister, a Northern Ireland branch secretary who organised dock workers. Conroy, with Jim Larkin, was a dominant voice on the executive council, apart from being the clear authority in his own union. He was a strong supporter of the programmes of economic development of the period, conscious of the fact that this was the only way by which wages and employment could be improved on a broad front, and he gave an unwavering commitment to the policy of Congress participation in national planning. Inevitably, in these mature years of the Irish Transport, he was concerned with good organisation and the recruitment of able officials. Fintan Kennedy, whom we shall meet later as president of

Congress, was the son of Tom Kennedy, a general president of the Irish Transport during some of its difficult years.

The other powerful voice on the executive council of Congress at the time – and indeed until his death – was Jim Larkin, the son of Big Jim. To many people, he represented radical trade union dissent and, as a result, he was distrusted politically. During this period of economic reconstruction, he was always somewhat unhappy about the various institutions of economic planning, whether the Irish National Productivity Committee, the Employer-Labour Conference, or the National Industrial Economic Council. Indeed, it was he who proposed the abandonment of the Employer-Labour Conference in 1962 in rather obscure retaliation for a government statement on wage restraint. Some believed that his uneasiness with these institutions stemmed from a radical commitment to a different sort of society, in respect of which they were merely palliatives; others believed that, being more sensitive than most to the views of the ordinary worker, he was daunted by the difficulty of retaining their loyalty while becoming identified with planning councils which smacked of the establishment. But he was formidable, intellectually and personally, had considerable insight into industrial disputes, and was frequently consulted by unions in difficulties. Since his death, his brother, Denis Larkin, has taken his place both as general secretary of the Workers Union of Ireland and also as a member of the executive council of Congress. In contrast to the previous leadership in the union, Denis Larkin has emerged in the early seventies as a trade union figure very much in the tradition of John Conroy, and in 1972, under his leadership, the Workers Union campaigned in favour both of a comprehensive national wage agreement and entry to the Common Market, in circumstances where the new leadership of the Irish Transport was reluctant on the one, and vehemently opposed to the other. This indeed was a dramatic reversal of the traditional positions under Jim Larkin and John Conroy, and as they existed in 1962.

The other major voice on the council was that of Norman Kennedy, although in the year which we are now reviewing, 1962-63, he had become seriously ill and had attended only a small number of meetings. He was, as we have already seen, the Irish officer of the Amalgamated Transport and General Workers Union. The union, a few years earlier, when it came to the business of building a new head office in Ireland, decided to do so in Belfast rather than in Dublin, largely because most of their members were in the North, but perhaps because of the uncertain future of the British-based unions in the South. Norman Kennedy consequently had moved to Belfast, and although continuing as senior officer for both north and south, largely confined himself to

Northern Affairs. The union in the South was dominated by Matt Merrigan, who in contrast with Kennedy's more mature socialism, had a radical Dublin working class approach. Although Kennedy was explicit in his leadership, one gained the impression that the southern branches of the union acted with a substantial autonomy, even if they did not theoretically possess it. Kennedy was largely instrumental in bringing about the recognition of the Irish Congress of Trade Unions by the Northern Ireland government the following year, and later became a senator in Stormont. We have already noted the arrangement between the Amalgamated Transport and the Irish Transport concerning spheres of influence, and throughout the sixties there was no tension between these two large unions, both operating north and south and both recruiting the same type of worker.

In the leaders we have dealt with up to now, the different traditions of Irish trade unionism are represented, although with personalities such as these, one must be very tentative in venturing categorisation. Conroy and Fintan Kennedy were influenced by the Gaelic subculture, but also by the Dublin radicalism which sprang from James Connolly. Larkin represented the more traditional working class radicalism of Tom Paine, combining progressive socialism with free-thinking and religious toleration. He combined this, just as Paine did, with a recognition of the freedom of entrepreneurial activity and the freedom of the trade union to combat it. Perhaps it was from this that came the strong trade union advocacy which he represented for state planning in economic matters, combined with an almost entrepreneurial freedom for trade unions. This too was the old Irish TUC position, particularly after the split, and was the position held by many of the northern trade unionists. Norman Kennedy would give it his broad support, and so would Macgougan.

Against this background, then, let us glance briefly at the other members of the executive council at this time. In the Gaelic tradition was William J. Fitzpatrick, the general secretary of the Irish Union of Distributive Workers and Clerks, a large union of 14,000 or so – mostly shop assistants – with a conscious commitment to Gaelic cultural activities. Despite the union's stability, it seemed to be continuously beset by industrial disputes, perhaps because of the nature of the industry. Fitzpatrick, a year or two before, had a difficult year of office as president of Congress, when the country experienced a good deal of industrial tension. In the Dublin craft tradition were Nicholas McGrath of the printing union, the Dublin Typographical Provident Society (now the Irish Graphical Society), who had at that time only 1,500 members and who secured his place on the executive probably through the support of unions generally in that trade; and Matt O'Neill of the British-based

Amalgamated Society of Woodworkers, a union with a large Irish membership of over 16,000, very influential in the building industry, although O'Neill himself was moving towards retirement.

In the basic tradition of the Dublin working class was Jimmy Dunne, later to become an outstanding president of Congress. His union was the small (5,000 member) Marine, Port and General Workers Union, which represented among others the rather turbulent Dublin dockers. Jack Cassidy of the Irish-based National Engineering Union, with 3,000 members, owed his place to support he received from the Irish Transport (among others), as also did Jim Candon, of the 5,000 member Irish National Vintners, Grocers and Allied Trades Assistants, strongly representing Dublin barmen. He was very much in the same tradition as Willie Fitzpatrick.

The public service at the time was represented in particular by William Bell of the Post Office Workers Union. This was the union that had, up to recently, William Norton as general secretary. Norton had become a major political figure, leader of the Labour Party, minister of state under two interparty governments, and Tánaiste, or deputy Prime Minister. Bell, his successor, conscientiously tended the union and took little part in politics. His union was a small one, 6,000 members, but very large in civil service terms. At that time, the number of civil service trade unions was not great, but in all probability most of their support went to Bell for election to the council. Dominick Murphy, of the British-based Transport Salaried Staff Association, had just under 4,000 members. He was a Labour senator, and secured his support for election to the executive council on a fairly broad clerical and professional basis. He was later to become a president of Congress. The 9,000 member Irish National Teachers Organisation was represented by Miss Mairead Skinnider, a powerful voice for both women's rights and the Gaelic tradition; she had fought with Countess Markievicz during the 1916 Rising. She, however, made no special trade union contribution, being concerned essentially with the cause of primary school teachers.

When we turn to the North, we find that, apart from Macgougan and Norman Kennedy, there were also Andrew Barr and Harold Binks. Barr's members were almost altogether in Northern Ireland. He was Irish officer of the National Union of Sheet Metal Workers and Coppersmiths, which was affiliated to Congress for less than 2,000 members. He was an avowed Marxist and was later to become chairman of the Northern Ireland Communist Party. He represented a small but very vigorous tradition in Irish trade unionism, which was particularly influential in the North. At the annual conferences of Congress, the Marxist point of view was urged very strongly by certain Belfast delegates, prominent among them being Barr, Betty Sinclair, secretary of the Belfast and District Trades Council, and Billy McCullough of the Theatrical and Kine Employees, also of Northern Ireland. Barr at the time was somewhat distrusted both by his socialist northern colleagues and by the southern trade unionists who were in the Gaelic tradition; but his popularity grew over the decade, both as hostility to Marxism declined and as his personal capacities became clear, until eventually in 1972 he ran Denis Larkin very close in the contest for vice-president, gaining the support, among others, of the Irish Transport and General Workers union.[25] Harold Binks of the Clerical and Administrative Workers Union had approximately 3,000 members and stood somewhere between the radicalism of Barr and the conservative socialism of Norman Kennedy. Paul Alexander of the National Boot and Shoe Operatives was in fact Irish officer of a northern union and president of an Irish-based one, a situation which arose from an early effort to find a solution to the Irish-British problem.

Finally, I myself was vice-president at the time, and would become president the following year. My union, the Vocational Teachers Association, was a small one, and I owed my position on the Congress executive council initially to Willie Fitzpatrick and subsequently to the support of a number of unions, principally the Irish Transport and General Workers Union. It was Conroy of the Irish Transport who had ensured my nomination and election as vice-president.

While this is helpful as an indication of the character of the trade union movement at the time, Congress itself depended primarily on its executive officers, the joint secretaries Leo Crawford and Ruaidhri Roberts, and the research officer, Donal Nevin. The amalgamation of the two congresses in 1959 provided for the continuation of the two general secretaries as joint secretaries of the new body, although, as I understand it, the two men themselves would have been happier had a decision been made to appoint one as general secretary and the other as his assistant. In any event, the arrangement worked out very well until Crawford's retirement in 1965 when Roberts became general secretary. It worked because the two men sprang from two quite different traditions in the trade union movement: Crawford the hardheaded shopfloor bargainer and trouble-shooter, and Roberts much more concerned with economic problems, the development of trade union structures, a trade union education policy, and in a word the role of the trade union in finding a socialist solution. The first offices of the joint congress were on the first floor of an auctioneer's premises in Merrion Street in Dublin, with twin office suites on either side of the stairway, one being the preserve

[25]In 1973, in a very close contest with Norman Kennedy, he was elected vice-president.

of Ruaidhri Roberts and the other of Leo Crawford. There was no room large enough to accommodate the full executive council which met in the head office of the Irish Transport, then in Merrion Square. This gives some idea of the size of the office, and business was normally carried on against the noise of the Dublin traffic if the windows were open, and in near suffocation if they were not. In 1964, Congress moved to a house in Raglan Road, an area that once had some Victorian grandeur, and which can still boast of cherry blossoms and broad avenues.

Leo Crawford, as well as being general secretary of the CIU, was also president of the Plasterers' Union, more properly the Operative Plasterers' and Allied Trades' Society of Ireland, a very small union of 2,000 members, but significant because of its influence among the craft unions in the building industry. It was an entirely Irish-based union, and like a number of the Dublin craft unions at the time, it was militant, volatile and contained leading members who were strongly republican, or strongly socialist, or both. Crawford drew his strength, therefore, from a background of 'real' trade unionism, which in Ireland at that time – and still, to some extent – was identified with militant craft unions, particularly in the building industry. The significance of these unions was further enhanced by their reputation at the time of being the pacemakers for general wage increases. Crawford, also from his CIU days, commanded the friendly support of the Irish Transport and General Workers Union, particularly that of John Conroy. Ruaidhri Roberts, on the other hand, represented the wider intellectual tradition of the trade union movement and was as happy in the north as in the south. Despite this intellectual background, there was nothing of the academic about him, although at this time, probably because Crawford specialised in the field, he took little part in the rough and tumble of trade union disputes. Despite his background in economics, he made little contribution to the National Industrial Economics Council when it was established; but he was largely responsible for the firm grip which the Irish National Productivity developed. He was a considerable strategist in organisation matters, and was the architect of many of the plans for trade union reform. Donal Nevin was research officer at the time, coming in this capacity when the Congresses amalgamated. Later, on Crawford's retirement, he became assistant general secretary of Congress. He had acted as Congress representative in a number of important economic bodies during the fifties, but he reached his full effectiveness in the National Industrial Economic Council and particularly in its general purposes committee. Much of the growing sophistication of the Irish trade union movement in economic planning matters during the sixties can be attributed to Nevin.

This gives a fair picture of the Irish trade union movement in 1963, a movement of diverse cultural background and diverse social aims. In the Republic, its voice was still that of the Dublin craftsman, impatient and perhaps truculent, spearheading the cause of the general worker and indeed the clerical and professional worker as well. This was the time of major influence of the separate centre for clerical and professional workers, the Irish Conference of Professional and Service Associations, but the various public service and professional unions were gradually looking to the Irish Congress of Trade Unions as the really effective national body. While the trade union movement in the Republic rested on a broad Gaelic republican tradition, it was, as we have seen, sensitive to and influenced by quite radical Marxism, not really because of the glamour of some Marxists in the North, but rather because its own hagiography – in regard to James Connolly in particular and to Jim Larkin to some extent – made it open to such views. In the Republic, however, while Connolly was revered, the vast majority of members tended to discount his teaching.

IV

"One might say that trial by combat was impressive and dramatic, but trial by jury is more likely to be just." This statement by Ruaidhri Roberts, when he addressed the 1963 annual conference of the Irish Congress of Trade Unions on its second day, summarised the tone of the annual conference that year, and indeed the approach generally of the trade union movement at the time. This was a period of growing economic confidence, and the trade union movement responded accordingly. True, there had been a bubble of unrest in the Dublin city bus services because of the proposed introduction of one-man buses, but the year had been dominated by broad economic policy questions. The government had issued a white paper which had attempted to bring wage increases into line with productivity. This had caused a sharp backlash from the trade union movement and the withdrawal of Congress from the Employer-Labour Conference, a bi-partite national negotiating body. The Taoiseach of the time, Seán Lemass, continued to woo the trade unions, and a short time later offered to establish the National Industrial Economic Council, a national planning advisory body on which government, employers and trade unions would be represented. This was accepted by the conference on the recommendation of the executive council, and with poor grace, they decided to return as well to the Employer-Labour Conference.

Congress recognised the need for participative planning. Although, in January 1963, the talks between the European Economic Community and other countries, including Ireland, which had applied for admission to the Community, had been discontinued, the trade unions were fully aware of the need for greater competitiveness and greater productivity. Barry Desmond – later to become a member of Dáil Éireann – helped in the organising and running of trade union advisory bodies, and Congress played a major role in the campaigns of the Irish National Productivity Committee. But with thoughts of efficiency ringing in the air, it was inevitable that the trade union movement should be caught up in it all. Lemass had been urging a better trade union structure based on legislation; he was almost prepared to allow the trade union movement to write its own law, but he felt that law was necessary. He was conscious of the panic which had been created by a national strike of Electricity Supply Board electricians a year or two before, and also of the bad impression which might be created abroad by the inter-union dispute in the newly-established Potez factory in Galway. The trade union movement, on the other hand, was almost panic-stricken at the idea of the intervention of positive law; but it recognised only too clearly the defects of its own structure. The Dublin city bus dispute, where the men in large part rejected the official trade union leadership, had made them anxious and uncertain.

In 1962, Congress had established, in view of all this, a committee on trade union organisation. It was as important a committee as Congress could make it, and was given priority over all other trade union committees of the time. The idea was to promote amalgamations and streamline the trade union movement in this way. In view of the achievements of unity, there were high hopes at that time, but almost nothing was realised. The obvious field was that of the craft unions where two, and sometimes three, unions catered for the same kind of worker; but there was the intractable problem of the large British-based union and the small Irish-based union, where a takeover, not an amalgamation, seemed to be the only way out. Amalgamation was eventually attempted between two Irish-based craft unions, the National Engineering Union and the Irish Engineering, Industrial and Electrical Trade Union, but this ran into very heavy weather because of the complexities of Irish law in the matter.

Although no headway was made in amalgamations, the committee on trade union organisation made a recommendation to the annual conference that an appeals board should be established. This was quite radical and innovatory, and, as we shall see, was influenced by the experience of some of the unions in the Dublin busmen's dispute. The problem sprang from the work of the disputes committee which was established by the executive committee to deal with disputes between unions, and which owed a great deal to the British Bridlington Agreement.

The disputes usually concerned the poaching of members by one union from another. Of course, if more than one union were in the job, then a transfer of members could be effected merely on notification, but if the union were the sole union organising that grade of workers, then no other union could accept a transfer of members from it without its consent. Congress, of course, in its constitution subscribed to the principle of freedom of association, but the dilemma was that, if this principle were admitted with no limitation whatever, it could create endless fragmentation, particularly at a time when responsible and orderly negotiation was being demanded. The appeals board was designed to meet the difficulty. The principle of sole organisation was preserved, but if a group of members found themselves dissatisfied with the service which they received from their union (but not with policy), and if they established this to the satisfaction of the appeals board, then they could transfer to another union, even where the first union was the only union in the employment. The appeals board was designed to meet another criticism. The unions were vulnerable to a charge that if they expelled a member, he could, as a result, be excluded from working at his trade or occupation. It had been suggested that workers, in these circumstances, should be guaranteed certain rights by legislation, and Congress was anxious to counter such a possibility by providing machinery itself. The appeals board, therefore, would also hear and judge individual cases concerning the expulsion of members.

The unions had considerable reservations about the proposal. It meant the establishing of a committee which would review the very basic and rather personal business of how they looked after their members. While appeals against expulsion were all very well, appeals against inadequate service were another matter; even if they were wrongheaded, they could still be embarrassing. The conference adopted the proposal after a convincing speech by Larkin, largely because they feared that if they did not, then Lemass and the government could well introduce legislation and take the matter out of their hands. In the event, the appeals board has worked successfully.[26]

This was a time of national spring-cleaning, and Congress, at the same conference, went on to establish a demarcation tribunal to deal with those inter-union rows which above all others bring the trade union movement into disrepute. More than that, there emerged during the year explicit support for the idea of groups of unions acting in consort for negotiating purposes. It was inevitable in the Irish situation that large employers such as Córas Iompair Éireann should experience a multiplicity of unions,

[26] See K. I. Sams, 'The Appeals Board of the Irish Congress of Trade Unions', *British Journal of Industrial Relations*, vol. VI, no. 2, July 1968.

sometimes representing the same grade of workers, and they were not slow to condemn it. It was reasonable that the unions concerned should form a committee and negotiate as a group. The executive committees of the various unions, however, were reluctant to yield any degree of autonomy to the groups, and this, as we shall see, made them at times a hindrance rather than a help.

But enough is enough; there were certain proposals that Congress was not prepared to accept. It had been recommended by a subcommittee of the Employer-Labour Conference that there should be arbitration on certain issues, and that there might be a cooling-off period in disputes. Both these ideas were rejected by the executive council of Congress, and they would, without a doubt, have been resoundingly defeated by the annual conference had they been put to the delegates.

It is clear from this discussion that we have been dealing only with the Republic, since this is our concern, but in any event the affairs of the Republic dominated the conference that year. Northern Ireland received some attention because of the proposed National Economic Council there, and because of the rising unemployment in the ship-building industry. The imbalance is not surprising however. Many of the special problems of the North were dealt with at an earlier conference in Northern Ireland, and the day-to-day affairs were conducted, almost autonomously, by the Congress Northern Ireland Committee, served by the Northern Ireland officer, William Blease.

There were a number of disputes which were noted by the annual conference in 1963: a dispute in Bord na Mona (Irish Peat Development Authority), a dispute in Radio Telefís Éireann, a report on industrial relations in the Electricity Supply Board (the first of a number), a strike in the new firm of Potez in Galway (another inter-union row which had troubled Congress), and finally the Dublin bus strike, which is the first major dispute which we shall examine, and to which we now turn our attention.

V

Transport services in Ireland are the responsibility of a national transport authority, Córas Iompair Éireann. This authority was established in 1945, unifying the activities of earlier companies and authorities, and it was, at the time, the largest single enterprise in the state, with over 20,000 employees, an enormous number in Irish terms where "....industrial relations must be viewed primarily in terms of undertakings employing dozens, rather than hundreds or thousands of workers."[27]

[27]O'Mahony, op. cit., p. 7.

The bus services were one of the charges of CIE, and down through the years it was a service that had been beset by strikes. There is much stress in the work of bus drivers and bus conductors, and a number of large cities have experienced strikes in these services. CIE regarded bus drivers (and road freight drivers) as being the most militant of their employees, much in contrast to the locomotive drivers, for example; and they attributed their greater militancy to the nature of the job – the frustrations of driving heavy vehicles in congested traffic. There was a further, more basic reason for the climate of unrest at the time. The busmen believed that their wages and conditions had fallen behind those of workers generally, and this was made worse by the manner in which the management responded to their demands. CIE was following a vigorous policy of paying its own way, and they tended to give increases belatedly and after hard bargaining. But the busmen were convinced that the Dublin buses were more than paying their way, and were in fact subsidising other aspects of CIE's work, particularly the railways, which were known to be losing money. They were understandably aggrieved.

The vast majority of the busmen were in the Irish Transport and General Workers Union, perhaps 4,000 when one takes the country as a whole, among whom over 2,000 were in the Dublin city services. The Workers Union of Ireland had about 600; and the National Association of Transport Employees had only a handful, since this union was essentially concerned with railwaymen. The relation between the men and the unions is central to the dispute as it developed. The position was particularly difficult for the Irish Transport, representing, as it did, many workers in the railways whom the busmen claimed they were subsidising. To the men, therefore, the vigorous – even militant – approach of the company did not appear to produce a militant response from the union, and their frustration grew.

There was no doubt about CIE's vigorous policies. The management was headed by Dr C. S. Andrews, a man with a reputation for efficient management. He believed that what was required to make CIE pay its way was an efficient, integrated organisation, and he was determined to achieve it. And it was this policy which brings us to the kernel of the dispute: the introduction of one-man buses, as they were called. Buses were normally crewed by two men, a driver and a conductor; CIE, as part of their productivity programme, proposed to introduce a new bus which could be operated solely by the driver. They were intended initially for some provincial services operating out of Dublin and for tours. It is important to mark here a difference of policy between the Irish Transport and General Workers Union on the one hand and the busmen on the other. The union recognised that CIE was a public undertaking, run in the public interest, on the board of which was a retired president of the union. Furthermore, its efficient and economic management was seen to be in the interest of all the workers. In these circumstances, the union took the view that CIE management was there to manage. The union did not wish to interfere with that right; they wished merely to ensure that when changes were made, their members would be protected. They therefore did not oppose one-man bus operations in principle, but instead sought certain guarantees concerning job security, and, conscious of the deep reluctance of the men, sought improvements as well in such things as sickness benefits and pensions, on the grounds that the men should participate as well in the increased productivity. But the men saw the whole thing quite differently; it appears that to them job security was the principal concern, and they were not impressed by the guarantees that they had received. Some have claimed in retrospect that this was exaggerated, and that the important issue was wages; but there is no doubt that anxiety ran deep.

CIE was impatient. Negotiations were very protracted, the unions stickily insisting on fringe benefits as a *quid pro quo*, while the company was not at all satisfied that, even if they agreed to these demands, the men would give their consent to one-man buses. They therefore adopted a policy of progress by confrontation. They declared that they intended to introduce one-man bus operations on 2 May 1962. They recognised that this would result in a crisis, that in the dispute that followed they would have to make concessions, but that nevertheless progress would be made. This apparently was quite an explicit policy at the time: to 'raise the level of reality' by creating such a confrontation. To many of the management of CIE, industrial relations was the science of conflict, not of peace; it was their view that only by conflict could the choices be clearly seen. The Transport Union felt their position was a strong one; the company proposed to introduce one-man buses in the absence of any agreement with them, and consequently they instructed their members not to work without a conductor. They confined their instruction only to those immediately affected by the decision of CIE; they had no desire to escalate the dispute. CIE, however, were determined on a confrontation and when on 2 May six men in Broadstone depot in Dublin refused to work without a conductor, they were instantly dismissed. It seems that a further six men were dismissed by noon, but at that stage reaction was building up alarmingly among the men, and CIE did not proceed further with the confrontation.

That night, the Transport Union called an emergency general meeting of its Dublin members in the Theatre Royal, a meeting which was attended by perhaps 2,000 men, and which began at half-past midnight, so that the late shift could be present. It was a very emotional meeting, not helped by the lateness of the hour. The purpose of the union, convinced that all this should be played in accordance with rule, was to seek from the meeting authority to lodge seven days strike notice. The men, however, were incensed and demanded immediate strike action. This alarmed the union representatives greatly, since not only would their position in the negotiations be undermined, but if they failed to give adequate strike notice, they might be exposed to legal penalties for damages at the suit of CIE. They pleaded with the men to permit them to act in accordance with normal procedure, and they offered to make good the earnings of those who had been dismissed. The men would have none of it. As they saw it, six of their colleagues had been dismissed instantly for carrying out a union instruction, and the only adequate reply was an instant withdrawal of labour. On this note, the meeting ended. The following day, Tuesday, there was a total unofficial strike in the Dublin bus services. The company, the union and the men were therefore in three different camps.

On Wednesday, the men paraded to the head office of the Irish Transport and General Workers Union in Merrion Square. Fintan Kennedy, then general secretary of the union, came to the door but refused to speak to the men, whom he saw as a mob. This rankled very deeply. But it was understandable that the union should be perturbed. These were times of few demonstrations, and the union saw parades of an unauthorised kind, marches on headquarters and emotional meetings as dangerous and disruptive. This is what prompted Fintan Kennedy to act as he did, and what prompted the disciplinary action which the union later took against the ringleaders. The men, on the other hand, were quite shocked to hear themselves described as a mob, or regarded in any way as being undisciplined. A year earlier, during the course of a CIE lockout, the men, in accordance with a union arrangement, marched in a body to Parnell Square where they were addressed by their trade union leaders. This may have been in their minds. In any event, when one participates in a mass movement of people, what one may regard as being orderly and unified – even though exciting – may appear to an outsider as alarming and uncontrolled. Things went from bad to worse. A day or two later, a meeting was called in the National Stadium by Paddy Dooley, the branch secretary, in the hope of securing a ballot vote for a return to work, but there was such confusion in the voting procedure that the meeting was abandoned, and the men chanted "Hang down your head, Tom Dooley." In this impasse, two Dublin priests managed to mediate, and a formula was worked out. Congress was asked to supervise the ensuing ballot, and when the votes were counted on Sunday night, there was acceptance and a return to work. But the problem was by no means resolved.

The agreed formula stated that the dismissed men should be reinstated forthwith. It also stated that the unions accepted the principle of one-man operations, although the company undertook to defer implementation until negotiation on the conditions should take place under the Labour Court. But the men's consent to one-man buses was a fragile one. Later, some of them were to claim that they returned to work because the men had been reinstated; *this* they saw as the substance of the proposal, not the one-man operations. The Labour Court acted with commendable speed, and when proposals from a conciliation conference were rejected by ballot, the Court itself made a recommendation.[28] One-man working, it recommended, should be introduced at once for day tours and private hire, and arrangements should be worked out with the union for an extension of the system. They also recommended bonuses, training for conductors, and an absolute guarantee against redundancy. But the men were very negative and rejected the proposals; however, in a subsequent ballot, they decided not to take strike action if the company merely introduced one-man working in day tours and private hire. The company took what they could from the situation, but when they approached the unions to negotiate an extension of the arrangement, they found them adamant that they must first get improvements in pensions and sick leave and in free and privileged travel. A public hearing was held by the Labour Court towards the end of 1962. They refused to accept the wider claims of the unions.[29]

In April 1963, therefore, CIE decided to extend its one-man bus operations; there was immediately an official stoppage, which lasted for five weeks. This was a national strike involving the Irish Transport and General Workers Union, the Workers Union of Ireland and the National Association of Transport Employees. The mood of the men made the dispute a particularly intractable one. Michael McInerney, industrial correspondent for *The Irish Times*, wrote on 1 April:

> The lock-out strike which is to begin to-morrow morning has some of the ingredients of the 1913 strike and some of its penetrating bitterness. Anyone who meets busmen these days cannot but be deeply impressed by the passion and determination being shown even by middleaged and grey haired men in this dispute. There is a bitterness abroad such as Dublin has not seen for fifty years. The dispute, therefore, may develop into a grave national crisis which could easily have political repercussions.

[28] Labour Court, *Sixteenth Annual Report,* for the year 1962.
[29] Labour Court, *Seventeenth Annual Report,* for the year 1963.

Certainly, the government became concerned and in the third week of the strike the Minister for Industry and Commerce asked Congress to intervene.[30] Somehow or other, Crawford managed to break the deadlock, and the company invited the unions to a direct conference to clear up what they described as misunderstandings. An agreement was hammered out, put to ballot and accepted; and work resumed on 12 May. The union had in fact won their case. True, it was agreed that the limited one-man bus operations could commence on 12 May, but these were subject to the stringent guarantees as before; on the other hand, it was also agreed that the Minister for Industry and Commerce would establish a commission to recommend on sick pay and pensions, and several other benefits were won.

More than that, the company had lost heart with regard to one-man operations and never extended the system very much further. They felt rather aggrieved about the whole affair, pointing out that they had offered all the guarantees that had been asked of them, and furthermore had offered the men a higher percentage differential payment than was offered in similar circumstances in any other European country. But although the unions had succeeded in all this, the dispute had created a crisis in the relations between the men, and the Irish Transport in particular, which was to lead to a breakaway movement and the establishing of a new union of busmen.

Many of the men found it difficult to accept the result of the ballot which ended the dispute in May 1963. They claimed that there were a number of things which reduced its validity, although in retrospect, none of the points they made seem to have much substance. The fact was that many were bitterly disappointed because, while the union may have achieved its objectives, many of the men had not; the one-man bus operations threatened them no less than before. They had no way of knowing that it was no longer an immediate issue. The Transport Union saw all this – probably quite correctly – as a dogged reluctance on the part of the men concerned to accept the democratic decision of the majority. No union could tolerate this, but ballots are crude instruments and can produce a very reluctant agreement because they permit often of no alternatives. There was a further source of grievance with the union. When the unofficial dispute ended in 1962, the men understood that there would be no victimisation. CIE, contrary to its normal practice, did not require the unofficial strikers to reapply for their jobs; but the Irish Transport, adhering grimly to its policy of good order and discipline, reprimanded a number of members for their part in the unofficial action, and suspended

---

[30]Irish Congress of Trade Unions, *Fifth Annual Report* 1963, p. 84.

others from holding office within the union, two for a period of five years. For these reasons, and for others that have been dealt with, many members of the Irish Transport began to look elsewhere.

The question of union membership was a key one, since it was a condition of employment that all busmen should belong to "....one of the trade unions representative of the grades." A year earlier, after the unofficial strike, seven or eight hundred men had applied for membership of the Workers Union of Ireland, the other large union organising busmen. By 1963, however, the Workers Union had fallen out of favour since they refused to pay strike pay to the men who were on unofficial strike after the Broadstone dismissals, and obviously wished to have no dispute with the Irish Transport. In the aftermath of the 1963 ballot, between 1,600 and 1,700 busmen applied for membership to the Amalgamated Transport and General Workers Union, some no doubt remembering the row over membership between the Irish Transport and the Amalgamated Transport in the Dublin United Tramway Company in the thirties. But those days were gone, and the arrangements between the two unions held firm. In all this, we must remember that, apart from trade union propriety, Conroy, Larkin and Norman Kennedy had done a great deal to bring unity to the movement and they were not prepared to put it in peril. They were conscious of the frustrations all this caused, and, as we have seen, they established an appeals board at the following annual conference of Congress. But for the moment, the men appeared to have no alternative but to remain in the Irish Transport Union.

In the Clontarf garage in Dublin, a small group known as the General Purposes Association had been established by the men with the object of providing a modest benevolent scheme, and in the circumstances of 1963, they changed their role and registered themselves as the Dublin City Busmen's Union; they had yet to deposit £1,000 with the High Court in order to be given a negotiating licence under the 1941 Act. At this point, however, the new union received powerful support from the provinces. The anti-Transport feeling there seems to have arisen because of the union's unwavering policy regarding discipline among the members. During the official strike in 1963, certain busmen from Cork and Limerick held a meeting in Parnell Square in Dublin, which had not been authorised by the Union, and the disciplining by the Union that followed was greatly resented. Some men in Cork and Limerick approached the Dublin busmen with a view to establishing a national union, and this they did, the union receiving its negotiating licence in 1964 as the National Busmen's Union. It now claims a membership of something over 2,000 busmen, and the Irish Transport and General Workers Union claims about the same number.

The clash between the unions that followed is outside the scope of this book. Inevitably, it was fought out in a series of disputes that paralysed the transport services, ostensibly for higher wages, but essentially on the question of recognition of the new union. After a while, of course, things began to settle down. Unions on the whole tend to cooperate rather than compete, and although the National Busmen's Union is not yet accepted as an affiliated union of the Irish Congress of Trade Unions, nonetheless, relations are now good between it and the other unions in CIE, including the Irish Transport and General Workers Union.

CIE and the unions were deeply troubled by the strong feelings which lay behind the dispute, and, perhaps believing that they had done all that was expected of them, they began to look for the cause in some deeper *malaise* among the men. Probably at the suggestion in the first instance of Dr Andrews of CIE, the Tavistock Institute of Human Relations was invited to undertake a study which, in their own words, "....was aimed at determining the attitudes toward the work situation and the reasons underlying these."[31] It was a study of morale. The project was sponsored by CIE, the three unions concerned (the NBU was only beginning to emerge), and the Human Sciences Committee of the Irish National Productivity Committee. Dr Hans Van Beinum directed the study. It was carried out during the period October 1963 to September 1964, that is to say, when the dispute was still fresh in people's minds. This was the first experiment of its kind, and there was a good deal of uncertainty about it. John Conroy went along with the idea, principally because he was disturbed at the attitude of the men generally, for whom he had a special regard; this was courageous in view of the fact that anti-Transport feeling was known to be very high. Larkin and the Workers Union had great reservations about the idea from the beginning, and were reluctant in their participation.

It was recognised that such a study could reflect both on CIE and on the trade unions, and in order to overcome this problem, but more important, in order that the study should be a catalyst by which improvements would be made, it was agreed that the survey itself would merely be the first phase; the second phase would be a joint examination of the results and a series of joint measures to effect improvements. The eventual publication (and it was clear from the start that the results would be published) would contain not only the survey, but the steps which both management and unions had taken as a result of it. In this

---

[31]Hans Van Beinum, *The Morale of the Dublin Busmen* (Irish National Productivity Committee, Dublin, 1966), p. 1.

way, improvements would be effected and hostile criticism circumvented. The first phase worked well, but when it came to mounting the second phase – that is to say joint procedures arising from the survey – there was considerable difficulty. The results, of course, were difficult to handle; institutions are often nonplussed when they are confronted with the hard, angular reality of how people really feel. Apart from that, there was a change in senior officials in CIE, and their support began to evaporate. Material from the survey was also leaked to the newspapers; it was referred to publicly by some of CIE management, and versions of it were circulating among the busmen. Eventually, the survey itself was published in 1966 but without any follow-through report as was originally intended.[32]

Not surprisingly, the research team found that morale among the Dublin busmen was low. "The way in which the work situation is perceived is predominantly negative and, without exaggeration, our findings can be regarded as disquieting."[33] It was evident that the relationship between busmen and their job, between busmen and the management, and between busmen and the trade unions all contributed to this low morale. Yet they found a positive attitude to the actual work, a conviction that these were worthwhile jobs, and they felt that this was one real foundation for better relations in the future. The research team explained that the busmen's job contained important elements of stress, principally because the work was organised more as "....a technical system than a socio-technical one", and they devoted a separate chapter to the theory underlying this concept.

In attempting to explain it, Tavistock identified two extreme positions. The first, which they considered to be the traditional way of looking at work organisation, they called the 'rational machine type,' and it was based on such principles as the division of labour and the establishing of homogeneous tasks which minimised the skill required from the operative. It was characterised by rigid controls and close supervision; the human component in the organisation was reduced to a constant, and the dependence of the organisation on the individual was minimised. "In this way of thinking, technical and rational constructions are superimposed on social reality, and when discrepancies are discovered they are regarded as abnormal, deviant or informal."[34] The other position was that taken up by the 'Human Relations School' which originated in the findings of the Hawthorne experiment. In its extreme form, it regards the industrial organisation only as a social organisation.

[32]Op. cit.
[33]Op. cit., p. 89.
[34]ibid., p. 60.

This way of thinking is the counterpart of the engineering approach, and considers the actual job and the technology as extraneous factors, or as background information, and thereby makes the same mistake as it made in the engineering approach by trying to understand and explain a complex reality by means of singling out one component.[35]

But – and this was the basic contribution of Tavistock – the work organisation should be regarded neither as a technical system nor as a social system, but as a socio-technical system, encompassing both the technical organisation and the relations between those who work the system. If Tavistock is right in this, then many work systems would have to be turned topsy-turvy, and the operative would have to be regarded not as a mechanical constant but as a human variable, whose initiative and creativity would provide the basis not only for increased satisfaction to him, but increased productivity to the firm. All this is seminal and will be taken up at the end of our study. But from this, and from related ideas, Tavistock indicated a number of important changes in the work of the busmen, fostering more team work on the routes and clarifying the management structure of responsibility.

There was also a special chapter on the role of the trade union in a modern society, with particular reference to the Dublin busmen.[36] This took up the notion of the privatisation of the worker. By this, Tavistock meant that the worker tended to see himself less and less as a member of a social group (for example the working class) and tended more and more to focus on his personal work problems. "Class consciousness is changing into self consciousness." But the union seemed to have little relevance in such a local world. In the first place, it was no longer important as a shield in the case of unemployment, illness or death; this role was more and more fulfilled by the state. Secondly, the union, now accepted as an economic partner, was full of concern about national affairs. Thus, while the workers experienced a weakening of their commitment to a social group, and focussed more strongly on their local and personal problems, the unions developed in the opposite direction. All this was particularly apposite in the case of a large general union such as the Irish Transport, which, of necessity, is more concerned with establishing a balanced welfare for all than pursuing singlemindedly the claims of any one particular group. This may be the challenge of a maturing society, and developments such as the NBU may be a fall back into primitivism. But the challenge must be met by new structures, and Tavistock saw

[35]ibid., p. 60.
[36]ibid., p. 79.

the answer in the developing of the tiny society of the shop floor, the restructuring of management systems and trade union systems so that the problems would be resolved as much as possible at that level. For a number of reasons, they felt that there were distinct possibilities of making a breakthrough in this area in Irish society.

But was the question of morale of any great significance when all was said and done? There are many now who say that it was not. In evaluating such an opinion we must recognise that there was hostility to the report at the time and still is, not only because it touches on sensitive matters, but also because of its strange vocabulary and its abstract concepts, which seemed somehow artificial and remote. Consequently, the report's deeper and more penetrating criticisms never really got an adequate airing. Yet, even taking account of all that, we still find a settled view in the company and in the unions, that morale had almost nothing to do with the dispute. There is much less industrial unrest now than there was in the fifties and early sixties, and morale is certainly no better; this broadly is the argument which is used. Of course we are in very uncertain territory here, because it is extremely difficult to know what high or low morale means in the absence of either a norm or a measure; and this difficulty was not dealt with at all in the Tavistock report. In this highly subjective area, we found those who said that one could not expect high morale in bus drivers and bus conductors, since their jobs did not admit of high motivation, compared for example to a social worker. This contrasts with the findings of Tavistock, that the busmen had positive feelings regarding their job but were frustrated by the way it was organised. There is one hard piece of evidence which indicates a lower level of morale now than in 1962. The turnover of staff stands now at twenty per cent. per annum, which is higher than it ever was in the Dublin city services; yet this may be an indication merely of the availability of alternative employment opportunities. In all this discussion, the question of morale is seen as standing apart from the question of wages, one-man buses and trade union representation; but this in a large way begs the question, because if morale in this context is that which lies beyond the feelings which these problems generated, then its identification is particularly difficult. The fact is that morale is not influenced as much by the number of problems which we face as by the intensity with which we experience them. Before leaving the Tavistock report, however, we should note that while its deeper ideas did not bear much fruit, a number of very useful management changes flowed from it.

If morale was not the principal factor, what then was the cause of the unrest in 1962 and 1963, and the relative industrial peace which we have experienced in recent years, during a period when strikes generally have been on the increase? First, as the unions would point out, the wage bargaining system has been improved. At the time, wages were depressed and increases laggardly given; and improvements were resisted on the truculent grounds that CIE could not afford it. This is a dangerous response at any time; negotiations become unreal when the man with whom you are bargaining cannot help and when nobody is clear who can. It was an argument which was abandoned very soon after by CIE, and in the more sensible economic climate of the sixties, CIE came to be recognised more as a public service than as a private enterprise, and this was reflected in the wage policy. There was a further development. Since 1963, there have been a number of national agreements on pay which benefited all workers in much the same way. This had the advantage of providing not only equitable increases but providing them promptly. The unions regarded the promptness of the negotiations as very important, and this is a matter which we must bear in mind when we come to consider the contribution which national agreements make to industrial peace.

Secondly, there was the question of one-man buses, and the apparent drive for efficiency at the expense of the men. So many guarantees had been given on this issue by the company that many now take the view that, while it may have been the spark, it did not provide the fuel for the conflagration, and consequently one should look principally to questions such as wages and morale. But everything seems to indicate that it was the central issue; it appeared to strike down into deep feelings of insecurity. Of course the issue did not stand alone; it occurred against a background of wage dissatisfaction, where the men felt discriminated against; it was introduced in a quite ruthless way (or so the men thought) by Dr Andrews, determined on making CIE pay its way; and the union was clearly not prepared to fight the principle, whatever about the business of guarantees and additional fringe benefits. The fact of the matter is that CIE did not press ahead further with its one-man operations, and has not done so in the ten years since then.

Thirdly, let us consider the company and the unions, and whether other approaches and other policies on their part would have helped. To Andrews, and to the company, the unions had validity in so far as they could deliver the consent of their members to a bargain, and when, instead, there appeared to him to be endless and fruitless discussion, he settled on a policy of confrontation, believing that this clarified the issues and made people face up to the reality of their situation. To many, including some trade union officials, there was much that appeared hardheaded and commonsensical in this approach, and there was an impatience with any softhearted efforts to dull the edge of confrontation, whether they came from Catholic priests or ministers of state. Professor O'Mahony saw such an intervention as a weakening of the authority of the Labour Court,[37] but the impatience ran deeper than that. The Irish Transport Union, which was the dominant union, saw it all quite differently. In the first place, as a maturing union they placed heavy reliance on good order in negotiations and good discipline among the members. Their value system derived not from entrepreneurial success, as CIE's did at the time, nor from tribal battles against an ancient enemy, which small unions could rely on; their value system was that of any pluralist society concerned with equity for all and the rule of law by which it could be achieved. They were impressed, in the public interest, by the argument that CIE should pay its way, and they were disposed to accept the guarantees against redundancy in the matter of the one-man operations; CIE's record was good in this regard. Since the men were still reluctant, they offered as an alternative a campaign for improved pensions and sick leave benefits, which they successfully won. This, on the face of it, seemed to be both reasonable and responsible; yet they earned the anger and the rejection of many of their members. There were a number of obvious reasons. The men apparently were not prepared to accept one-man buses under any circumstances, and the ballot results were misleading because the package offered contained elements which the men felt they had to accept; this probably increased their anxiety and frustration. The union as well, by reason of its public policy, was obliged to be a mouthpiece for the company's economic woes; it would probably have been wiser to have had a sharp and direct conflict on wages at an early stage, letting CIE sort out their problems with the government.

But the deeper problem was that indicated by the Tavistock report. The Transport Union was a large national organisation; the busmen had no member on the executive council; this was a matter of chance, but if they had, it could well have made a difference. The men were becoming more and more concerned with a private, even a domestic dispute, while the union was becoming nationally more significant, and bringing to completion as a head office a towering skyscraper near Butt Bridge in place of the old, faded, familiar Liberty Hall. The men who broke away had many complaints about procedures within the union, but they summarised them by saying that they were not free. But is this kind of freedom (the almost tribal freedom of a homogeneous group) desirable, and was not the Irish Transport right in principle, despite its excessive concern with discipline? People are not necessarily right because they are many, and because they feel strongly about a subject. But the

[37]O'Mahony, op. cit., pp. 5, 6.

NBU would reply by saying that a small union, representing a homogeneous group, can offer a personal concern which helps in promoting good order, that as a rule they behave responsibly; and they point to their own record which is undeniably good in the years between. Perhaps the answer lies in recognising that a member requires a form of personal representation, and it does not matter whether this is provided by a large union with comprehensive local delegation or by a small union which retains its identity while cooperating with others. Men sometimes assume that the small union is more likely to provide such a service than a large one, but it seems to be more a question of the adequacy of the service itself than a question of trade union structure. And there, with many questions unanswered, we shall have to leave the busmen for the moment.

CHAPTER THREE

The Building Workers and the National Agreement

THE ICTU annual conference in 1964 met in Belfast. Four years had passed since Congress had last gathered in that city. Circumstances had changed greatly. Four years earlier, the conference took place on the outskirts of Belfast in a large barn-like agricultural hall; on this occasion, it took place in the Ulster Hall, the very hub of Belfast's conference life. William Jenkins, the Lord Mayor of Belfast, formally opened the conference and later gave a civic reception to the delegates. All this sprang from the fact that the Northern Ireland government was now prepared to recognise the Northern Ireland Committee of the Irish Congress of Trade Unions, subject to some changes of rule. The Northern Ireland government had been extremely reluctant to take this step. If the government of the Free State in the forties feared the influence of London-based unions, the Northern Ireland government feared the influence of a Dublin-based Congress, although in practice the Northern Ireland Committee of Congress was virtually autonomous. But, with plans for a national economic council, they now recognised that they would have to secure the cooperation of the trade union movement. It was in these circumstances that Norman Kennedy and others managed to negotiate a breakthrough.

In the Republic, the National Industrial Economic Council had been established towards the end of 1963, and the delegates were not unaware of the significance of the fact that Congress would now have representatives on the economic planning councils, both north and south, where as yet there was no formal recognition by the two governments of their economic interdependence. As president at the time, it seemed to me that it was a period of hope and of progress. In the Republic, manpower services were under discussion, the Employer-Labour Conference had again taken up its work on negotiating procedures, and above all, there was a conviction that we had advanced an important step on 1 January 1964 when we agreed a national wage agreement[1] larger and more comprehensive than ever before, although the rapid rise in prices that immediately followed caused us much alarm. The building dispute which followed a few months later was the first blow not only to this agreement, but to our notions of what was possible in the business of planning income increases on a national basis. Let us consider the events that led to this national agreement and what was hoped from it.

The eighth round of wage increases had been a spontaneous one, and, as we have seen, it was a substantial one as well, with increases for men ranging from £1 to £1.5 shillings. It tumbled through, with considerable industrial unrest from 1961 into 1962, and frequently consisted of two waves, as workers, finding that later settlements were higher than theirs, went back to the negotiating table. Moreover, the campaign for a five-day week and reduced weekly working hours which began in 1960 swept on through 1961 and 1962, sharpening both the unrest and the cost of the round. The expiring round was pinned by the government early in 1963 with its white paper, *Closing the Gap*, although its attempt to moderate wage increases resulted, as we have seen, in an explosion from Congress and the abandonment of the Employer-Labour Conference. Although there was no wage movement during 1963, tension began to increase. The salaried workers were beginning to emerge as a considerable problem. They saw the early wage rounds after the war as cost-of-living rounds merely, which left them free to pursue in addition claims based on other grounds, principally an evaluation of their work. However, because of the comparability principle, these gradually began a cycle of their own, moving forward steadily in addition to the wage rounds. To manual workers, they appeared to be a special and considerable privilege for the salaried people, and were causing growing unrest.

The lead group in the comparability cycle was the clerical grades in the Electricity Supply Board, whose significance we shall examine more closely in the next chapter. In June 1963, when other clerical workers were attempting to move to their level, the ESB tribunal awarded them a further salary increase of seven per cent. They were not mindful of

[1]For background and text, see Irish Congress of Trade Unions, *Sixth Annual Report 1964;* Labour Court, *Seventeenth Annual Report* for the year 1963. See also M. H. Browne, 'Industrial Labour and Incomes Policy in the Republic of Ireland', *British Journal of Industrial Relations,* vol. III, no. 1, March 1965, p. 46ff.

current constraints, but in 1960 the ESB, rashly perhaps, had agreed to an automatic cost-of-living adjustment. The government immediately asked the Board to defer the implementation of the award, which they did until the autumn, but the period of constraint was coming to an end; civil servants were pressing for increases, teachers were threatening industrial action, and by November, the building workers were becoming militant in their demand for an adjustment in wages. There was a further difficulty. The government had introduced a turnover tax for the first time, and Lemass, with a fragile majority in parliament, was sensitive to criticism on its account, particularly as it went right across the board, taxing such things as food and medicine. But despite his uncertain majority, Lemass was determined on governing progressively, particularly as the economy appeared to have picked up remarkably well. He took the unprecedented step of suggesting a general wage increase which would be nationally negotiated. Early in November 1963, Congress received a letter from him[2] to this effect in which he further suggested that the increase—which would be negotiated at the Employer-Labour Conference —should take account not only of the impact of the turnover tax, but also of the economic growth which he confidently expected in 1964. He hoped in this way to see negotiated a wage increase of reasonable proportions, and without the protracted industrial unrest of the eighth round free-for-all.

But he hoped for something more than that. It is clear from his statement in Dáil Éireann on the adjournment debate in December[3] that he saw in such an agreement a beginning—a beginning of an orderly system of national bargaining which would keep wages and expectations within the limits of national production. It was a heady experience to have a prime minister speak in these terms, but he probably considered that the gamble at that stage was small, since the amount of the increase appeared to have emerged. The Federation of Irish Industries and the Irish Exporters Association, both impressive bodies, supported the view that an increase of eight or nine per cent. ". . . would be not only socially beneficial but economically appropriate."[4] Compensation for the turnover tax increase (three or four per cent.) and the benefits of anticipated growth (another three or four per cent.) amounted to much the same figure and this would also have the effect of obscuring the embarrassing ESB 7 per cent. which was becoming established in people's minds. Thus was the ninth round of wage increases launched.

But the executive council of Congress was shocked and annoyed at this

[2]Irish Congress of Trade Unions, *Sixth Annual Report* 1964, pp. 96, 97.
[3]Dáil Debates: 12 December 1963, cols. 1210 ff.
[4]ibid.

initiative, and in its own words, it took the strongest possible exception to the letter. "[It] could not in any circumstances accept direction from any government as to when wage increases might be sought by the trade unions or as to the basis on which claims for higher wages and salaries could be made."[5] It was all the more infuriating for Congress since they had no alternative but to open negotiations. However, they had received an invitation from the Federated Union of Employers some time earlier to review industrial relations generally, and they availed of this meeting on 26 November 1963 to start discussions on a national wage increase.

The Federated Union of Employers had brought into association with them for the purposes of the negotiations all the other major employer organisations including the state-sponsored bodies; the state was not represented, not even in its role as an employer. This very large group met the full executive council of the Irish Congress of Trade Unions, and negotiations were carried out with up to 70 or 80 people present, ranged on both sides of a long table in the Shelbourne Hotel in Dublin. The employers' offer crept up to a 10 per cent. increase with a floor of 15 shillings a week, or alternatively eight per cent. immediately and a further increase of four per cent. in a year's time. Congress were prepared to recommend fourteen per cent. immediately, or alternatively a first increase of twelve and a half per cent., a subsequent increase of five per cent., and a floor higher than fifteen shillings. At this point, discussions broke down. The parties were further apart than the figures indicate. Congress were prepared to regard their fourteen per cent. position as negotiable, but they were not prepared to accept ten per cent., while the employers, alarmed that things had gone as far as they had, were resolute that ten per cent. was their maximum. These, in the circumstances of the time, were large figures and probably startled the prime minister. However, a dilemma had now arisen because undoubtedly the figures would become widely-known and unions would regard the employers' offer as a starting-point for their own claims. Thus, one could anticipate a high wage settlement with none of the industrial peace which was hoped for from a national agreement. Lemass therefore began delicately to stitch things together again. I, as president of Congress, was invited—rather oddly as I thought —to a small diplomatic dinner which Lemass was giving for Jean Rey, and there he raised the idea of his requesting the two sides to return to the conference table. Congress had no difficulty in this; their position was negotiable, but the employers, in consenting to do so, implicitly conceded their position on the ten per cent. They, like Lemass, had probably con-

---

[5]Irish Congress of Trade Unions, *Sixth Annual Report* 1964, p. 97.

cluded that industrial peace and the promise of orderly negotiations in the future were worth the additional cost. The conference resumed on 31 December and agreement was reached the following afternoon, the first day of the New Year 1964. It was for a twelve per cent. increase with £1 floor for male adult workers, and was for a two-year period, with a further six months for review. Those of us who were prominent in the negotiations were often irritated later to hear it described as Lemass's twelve per cent., but in a real sense it was, although he himself was never involved in the direct negotiations.

There was an ominous end to the special delegate conference of Congress in January 1964 which adopted the agreement. The building trade unions abstained from voting on the grounds that the two-and-a-half year period ". . . was anomalous to the building industry where the period of agreements are for twelve months", and because the terms of the agreement would hamper their efforts to secure a forty-hour week. But, for the moment, all went smoothly and the Labour Court reported[6] "The great majority or workers throughout the country had their wages and salaries adjusted without dispute in accordance with the terms of the recommendations in this Agreement—providing for an increase of 12% in basic rates." It appeared, however, that no effort was made to deal with rapid price increases, and within a few months, in a runaway rush, the real increase on the ninth round was very nearly cancelled out.

As pressures built up, there were a number who doubted that the trade unions as a body could hold the line for two-and-a-half years—who believed that an incomes policy was possible only if there was a strong trade union centre, which clearly, and self-avowedly, Congress was not. In these circumstances, the government looked to the Labour Court and there was much talk of reform, of making it a respected and final body of last resort. The executive council of Congress was, in the climate of the time, also anxious to demonstrate a spirit of reform and made two modest proposals to the 1964 annual conference in July. One, which came from the Employer-Labour Conference, suggested that where both parties went voluntarily to the Labour Court, strike action should not take place until twenty-eight days had elapsed from the date of the Court's recommendation—a period which usually elapses in any event; and the executive council also recommended that where a union took strike action, it should not place pickets for a further period of one week in order to give other unions affected by the dispute an opportunity for consultation. But the annual conference would have none of it. In many respects, it was constructive and forward-looking, but a number of unions had begun to

[6]Labour Court, *Eighteenth Annual Report* 1964, p. 3.

fear for their personal freedom of action in view of all that Congress was doing, and they felt it had gone far enough.

II

In mid-August, in the month after this rather self-confident annual conference had concluded, came the building dispute. It had its roots in the national agreement. Sometimes a mood develops at a bargaining conference which seems to compel an immediate conclusion, at the peril perhaps of a complete breakdown, and there was something of that mood at the discussions on 1 January when the employers and Congress eventually managed to reach agreement on the amount of the increase. The actual text of the agreement was hastily drafted, and clause five (which was later to cause all the difficulty) was understood to be an umbrella clause which, while it permitted a complex interpretation (or perhaps differing interpretations), made no attempt at definition. It stated: "This recommendation is made in the context of existing weekly working hours and annual leave entitlements."[7] Ruaidhri Roberts,[8] in addressing the special delegate conference of Congress on 14 January, made the point that the paragraph did not state that negotiations on hours and holidays were barred for the period of the recommendation.

> Such a proposal was in fact made during the course of the negotiations and was thrown out by our side. We did recognise, however, that the employers' side were anxious to avoid a circumstance where a concealed tenth round could be covered within the terms of this recommendation, by a movement, say, next year, to reduce nominal working hours all round and draw extra pay at overtime rates. We could see that employers were anxious that this should not be as it were covered by the agreement. On the other hand, we recognised that on the workers' side there are some cases where some workers have had their hours shortened but others in the same category are in the process of negotiating reduction in hours. There are other cases where negotiations on holidays have been going on long before the FUE-ICTU discussions started, and negotiations on working hours also. We stated our position quite frankly on this question, but it is extremely difficult to draw up a form of words in this recommendation which will say in effect that a general move to increase incomes by cutting working hours is out, but particular negotiations to reduce working hours or increase holidays are permissible, although this is in fact so. Finally, we reached agreement on the statement of fact contained in the rec-

[7]Irish Congress of Trade Unions, *Seventh Annual Report* 1965, p. 205.
[8]ibid., p. 199.

ommendation, which leaves to the parties concerned in any claim for reduced working hours the question of the terms under which it is negotiated.

While this was all very well, the recommendation itself did not provide any institutional means by which these problems of interpretation could be resolved or the working of the agreement reviewed. When the parties left the conference table, that ended their personal formal contact on the agreement and both went their own way. In fact, the FUE bulletin dealing with the recommendation contained a statement to the effect that working hours should remain unchanged during the period, and when Congress wrote to the FUE complaining of this, they were informed by the Director-General, Charles Cuffe, that each side was free to comment as they wished and that Congress had already done so.[9] It was clear that the consensus, on which the agreement was based, was strained to its limits.

We have seen the concern of the building unions with hours of work. Claims had been made apparently as early as March 1963, and in October 1963 the question of a forty-hour week had been discussed between the National Building Negotiating Committee of Congress and the Federation of Builders, Contractors and Allied Employers of Ireland.[10] However, in February, when it came to the question of the ninth round recommendation, the Federation offered certain additional benefits and the recommendation, much to their relief, was accepted. But the unions were restless, and a few months afterwards, some of the craft unions in the Dublin area reopened the claim, which was promptly rejected by the Federation, and in July was referred to the Labour Court. In its recommendation on 10 August, the Court flatly rejected the claim:

> Having regard to the hours at present being worked generally in the building industry in the Dublin area, it is evident to the Court that the effect of reducing the working-week at the present time in this area would be to increase building wages in the area beyond the 12% provided for in the National Agreement of January, 1964.[11]

Nor could they find any special circumstances which would permit a wage increase; they recommended a deferment of the claim and the immediate discussion instead of other possible improvements. But a meeting of the plasterers union in Dublin (poorly attended by all accounts)

---

[9] Irish Congress of Trade Unions, *Sixth Annual Report* 1964, p. 99.

[10] An extended account is given in the Irish Congress of Trade Unions, *Seventh Annual Report* 1965, p. 67ff. See also Labour Court, *Eighteenth Annual Report* 1964, pp. 4, 5.

[11] Irish Congress of Trade Unions, *Seventh Annual Report* 1965, p. 67.

decided early in August that if the forty-hour week were not conceded, they would not return to work when the annual holidays concluded on 19 August, and it appeared that they would be supported in this by the other craft unions. Congress hastily called a meeting of the unions concerned in the National Ballroom in Dublin on 13 August, but already the die was cast.

> At no stage of the dispute, even when Congress called, on 13th August, a meeting at the request of five major building trade unions, to consider the Labour Court recommendation, did any of the representatives of the sixteen unions present express any reservation on the proposed course of industrial action (not to return to work after the holidays) which had already been jointly decided by a small group of craft unions. The Congress became involved when the basic decision to create a dispute had already been taken by a minority of unions.[12]

But this may understate the position. The meeting of the unions in the National Ballroom on 13 August was chaired by Leo Crawford in his capacity as joint secretary of Congress. But he was also president of the plasterers union (the Operative Plasterers and Allied Trades Society of Ireland), and Gerry Doyle, its general secretary, and Donal O'Reilly, a member of its executive committee, were among the most militant at the meeting. In the event, the Plasterers, the United House and Ship Painters and the Building Workers Trade Union (with its affiliate, the Irish National Painters and Decorators) decided to take strike action by not returning to work after the holidays, and the other unions agreed that if these unions placed pickets, they would be respected. Thus began a strike which lasted from 19 August until 14 October.

In view of the fact that the dispute involved 12,000 workers (8,000 tradesmen and 4,000 labourers), it is important to remember how small these Dublin craft unions were. The Plasterers had a total membership of approximately 2,000 and the Building Workers Trade Union had about the same number, incorporating the Ancient Guild of Brick and Stonelayers, the Irish National Painters and Decorators, the Stonecutters Union of Ireland and the Limerick Operative Housepainters Society. The other union to initiate strike action, the United House and Ship Painters, returned a total membership to Congress of 373 but may have been even smaller. But the record of strike pay is even more revealing. The Amalgamated Society of Woodworkers (which merely supported the strike but did not issue any strike notice) paid dispute benefit to about 2,000 of its members, while the militant Plasterers paid only 200, the

[12]Irish Congress of Trade Unions, *Seventh Annual Report* 1965, p. 67.

Building Workers Trade Union also 200, the Irish National Painters 100 and the United House and Ship Painters 40. Indeed, rumour had it at the time that the last-named union made a profit on the strike since its income from the levy was larger than its outgoings. Even the Irish Transport and General Workers Union, with a very small membership among labourers, paid dispute pay to more than all these together, paying in all 700 workers, 300 of whom were in firms of builders providers which later became involved in the dispute. There were two reasons for this: the strike was a Dublin one and, when it took place, many of the men at this boom-time in the building industry found work in towns around the country, but the second reason is of the greatest importance to an appreciation of the dispute. Many of the members of the militant craft unions had indoor jobs in the public service and in industry, and, while not involved directly in the dispute, hoped to gain by it; some of the prominent leaders in the strke came from these groups.

But of the sixteen unions that attended those fateful meetings in the National Ballroom on 13 August and again on 14 August, there were two that could have had a decisive influence, the Irish Transport and General Workers Union and the Amalgamated Society of Woodworkers. The Irish Transport delegates in fact made very little contribution. John Conroy, probably because of his respect for Leo Crawford who was chairing the meeting, impressed on them beforehand that they should follow the general trend. In any event, the Irish Transport was not in a strong position at the time; they were the labourers' union among craft representatives, and even among labourers their membership was very small; fifteen per cent. is admitted, but perhaps the figure was even lower than that. The position has improved vastly since then, largely because of the work of Seán O Murchu who had joined the union as an official about that time. The Amalgamated Society of Woodworkers was in a stronger position by far. One of its delegates at the National Ballroom conference was Archie Jackson, who was an officer of the National Federation of Building Trade Operatives, a coordinating council of all the amalgamated (or English-based) unions, both north and south. Although in Dublin the small Irish-based craft unions were the leaders, in the country generally the typical union was the large, amalgamated union, and Jackson was well-known and respected. He seemed to wish to avoid the strike, but feeling was running in favour of industrial action, and he eventually went along with it too. When he did so, the other amalgamated unions followed. Some believe that if the Irish Transport and the ASW had offered firm opposition to the strike then, and offered as well an alternative leadership, the strike would not have occurred. It is difficult to be sure of this, however, in view of the dominance in

Dublin of the small craft unions, and this after all was essentially a Dublin dispute.

The fact was of course that nobody believed that the strike would last. There had been no major stoppage in the building industry since the nineteen thirties, and this certainly was not a time when the employers were expected to make a stand; indeed six months before, Lemass,[13] had used the considerable buoyancy in the industry as an indicator of what might be expected from the economy generally. The unions confidently expected that a settlement would be made, if not by 19 August, then very soon after. They had completely misjudged the situation.

To many building workers returning from holidays, the strike was a discovery not a decision. Apart from the fact that the crisis had developed during the holiday period, communication in the small craft unions was notoriously bad. Furthermore, the men were confronted by the somewhat grotesque mobile pickets: so short of manpower were the central strike committee, that they had to drive in cars from one site to another, mounting pickets where none existed in order to stop the jobs. But as the strike dragged on week after week, it began to get ugly, as strikes often do, and craft union leaders, having blundered crossly into the strike, now found that they were riding a tiger. Perhaps a good deal of this came from the nature of the work on the building sites. In a recent study, Derek O'Sullivan[14] conveys a picture of small isolated groups, under a form of supervision which was necessarily casual and remote. There was a tradition of good workmanship, but because of a worker's mobility, no loyalty as a rule to any particular firm. Nor had the trade unions much influence or relevance on the site. They were merely the means by which increases were secured, and since the forty-hour week would mean more pay, once it was in the air, it was pursued.

As the strike became intractable, there was much recrimination about the national agreement and charges of bad faith. The unions declared that they had not contravened the agreement, that the claim was peculiar to the building sites where winter hours were a problem, and that the wet time compensation the men received was not enough to meet the loss of pay. Congress supported this view, seeing it as a limited claim arising out of increased productivity on the building sites. The building employers were reluctant to yield. Maurice Dobbin, the honorary secretary of their Federation, was hard in his opposition; it is possible that Lemass, who was friendly with some of the builders, stiffened their resistance to what

[13]Dáil Debates. Debate on the adjournment, 12 December 1963.
[14]Derek O'Sullivan, *A Sociologist's View of the Electrical Contracting Industry in Dublin* (Irish Productivity Centre, Dublin, 1973). While it deals only with electricians, it provides an insight into the other trades.

appeared as an onslaught on all good sense in negotiations; but, above all, the Federated Union of Employers, although a separate organisation, did everything they could to strengthen the resolve of the building employers, since they saw in the building strike a determined and unprincipled effort by some trade unions to wreck the national agreement once they had milked it of all they could; and they believed that the forty-hour week, once conceded on the building sites, would immediately spread to indoor work, and in this way cascade throughout industry. The FUE made it clear publicly that in their view the claim was in conflict with the national agreement; this, Congress emphatically denied, and later published a report of a meeting which it had with the Labour Court on 3 September, where the Labour Court denied that it had interpreted the national agreement as precluding such claims. The Labour Court's position may have been that, while it held against this claim in the past, it did not preclude such claims in principle; in its annual report it is silent on this aspect of the question.

At this point, early in September, both building employers and unions agreed to a Labour Court hearing but, on the day of the hearing, the builders providers, having received a claim for a forty-hour week three days before, closed their premises and locked a great number of employees out of work. The builders providers were prominent members of the FUE and some saw in this much more than a coincidence. All hope of a settlement disappeared and the strike developed a new, and even more intractable character. In retaliation for the lock-out of their members, the Marine, Port and General Workers Union placed an embargo on the release of all building and ancillary supplies from the Port of Dublin. As September drew to a close, it seemed very likely that the building workers would extend the strike to the Dublin Corporation, the Dublin County Council, the Dublin Port and Docks Board, the Dublin Health Authority, CIE, and the Electricity Supply Board. The last was particularly alarming, and Congress managed to head off a strike notice which had been served by the Irish National Painters and Decorators.

Eventually, the Minister for Industry and Commerce intervened in the dispute and appointed Dermot McDermott of the Labour Court as chairman of the conciliation conference. The agreement that followed reduced the hours for the winter period, and an independent commission was appointed by the Minister for Industry and Commerce to recommend on the summer period. When, in December 1964, it recommended that the same reduction should be made during the summer period as well, the FUE were extremely annoyed, pointing out that the winter concession was made because of bad weather and limited daylight; to concede it for the summer was to depart from the national agreement. But willy-nilly, the bargain was struck. The lock-out of the workers by the builders providers had created great resentment, and the dispute in these firms continued for a further four weeks, settlement being eventually reached on the basis of a cash payment in compensation to the workers, and a commission to go into the question of a reduction in the working week. And there the building dispute ended. It was a strike that did a great deal of damage, not only economically but also to the emerging consensu on national bargaining; but some of the die-hard officials of the craft unions will still say with curt satisfaction: "We got the forty-hour week, and we got it for everybody."

But was it really a campaign fought out cynically by the building unions irrespective of the national agreement? The FUE certainly saw it in this light, and reacted harshly and aggressively, deliberately frustrating (as some would believe) a concession by the building employers in early September and causing Dominick Murphy (who was president of Congress during the period) to accuse them later of trying to enforce a standstill on all claims, whether justified under the agreement or not.[15] But if this somewhat exaggerates the position of the employers, the FUE in their turn attributed far more deliberation, far more explicit intent, to the unions than they possessed. It seems clear now that the building trade unions were restless, in that the initiative was taken out of their hands by the ninth round national wage agreement, and were anxious to assert their special position in Dublin. At the worst, they were seeking the forty-hour week for all their members, outdoor and indoor, irrespective of the terms of the national agreement; at the best, they were prepared to negotiate such a claim within the national agreement if they could. However, to a very substantial extent, they drifted into the dispute. The position was very confused. There was the Dublin building group of unions; there was the national negotiating committee; there were the small Dublin craft unions and the large amalgamated unions; there were the general unions with poor membership and little authority; there was ineptitude in negotiation and poor communication even where union membership was small. Indeed when, at the close of the negotiations, certain recommendations had to be put to the men, electoral colleges had to be established in order to try to get a coherent view.

Arising from all this muddle, a joint industrial council for the construction industry was recommended as part of the settlement, and was establised in May 1965 with an independent chairman and representatives of both sides. Clear procedures were laid down in the case of a dispute, and since then relations have been stable. This effectively eliminated the

[15]Irish Congress of Trade Unions, *Seventh Annual Report* 1965, p. 228.

dominant but random leadership of the small building craft unions in Dublin which had exercised such influence on national wage movements. It furthermore fused the interests of the craft and general unions in the industry. It was a major achievement and, in the view of Barry Desmond, who was deeply involved as Leo Crawford's assistant: "It was the final contribution of the powerful influence of such men as Jim Larkin and John Conroy." Despite their noisy self-confidence, the craft unions had a respect for and perhaps at times a fear of these men. Although the trade union movement looked weak and incapable of standing by a bargain, in fact, in the matter of the building industry, it had put its house in reasonable order, and the industrial peace that followed has shown this to be so.

III

"The high hopes," said the Labour Court, "entertained by many at the time of the conclusion of the National Agreement in January 1964, that the Agreement would very substantially reduce, if not altogether eliminate, serious industrial disputes during the period of its operation were unfortunately not realised either during 1964 or 1965."[16] And in this the Labour Court considered that claims for service pay under clause three created more difficulties than reduced working hours, although both were ". . . fought with a tenacity seldom previously experienced."[17] Clause three, even more difficult to elucidate than clause five, said:

> While the majority of claims for increased wages and salaries and proposals for the settlement of such claims shall take place within the context of the terms of this recommendation, it is recognised that special circumstances do exist where the position cannot be wholly related to the terms of this recommendation, but, nevertheless, in these special cases the terms of this recommendation should be fully borne in mind.[18]

Ruaidhri Roberts, in dealing with this clause at the January 1964 special conference, said:[19] "In brief, the normal kind of anomaly claim, or status claim, or other such claim which is being negotiated all the time apart from rounds of wage increases or general movements for wage increases, are not prohibited in any way by the terms of the Recommendation." But when the employers were confronted with claims for service pay, they took an entirely different view.

---

[16] Labour Court, *Nineteenth Annual Report* 1965, p. 3.
[17] ibid., p. 4.
[18] Irish Congress of Trade Unions, *Seventh Annual Report* 1965, p. 205.
[19] ibid., p. 198.

The claims for service pay came from wage earners as a rule—from industrial workers on flat rates of pay—and they sought some recognition of length of service. But the employers declared that this would defeat the whole intention of the agreement which was to hold increases in wage costs during the period to not more than around twelve per cent.,[20] and so vigorously did they resist these claims that a number of prolonged strikes resulted. But the salaried groups, whose annual incremental scales were so vastly superior to the vestigial structures contemplated in service pay, appeared to have little difficulty in continuing their steady progress on what were now described as status claims. The clerical workers in the ESB now sharpened the contrast still more. We have already seen how, in advance of the ninth round, they had negotiated a seven per cent. increase. At the January 1964 special conference, Roberts had pointed out to the delegates that the special circumstances contemplated in clause three of the recommendation could also benefit employers, and he continued:

> If, for example, a recent wage increase has been given, and if it wholly or partly takes into account the increase in the cost of living and productivity since the eight round then we can anticipate that such an employer will claim that special circumstances will apply and will accordingly resist a demand for the full application of the 12 per cent. increase to such workers.[21]

This was understood by many to refer to the ESB salaried workers, but in fact the ESB conceded the full twelve per cent. Not alone that, but while the wage earners were fighting for limited service pay, on 2 April the ESB Tribunal, in reply to a status claim from the clerks, increased their salary maximum by ten per cent.; the Port and Docks Board followed, and all the other salaried groups girded their loins. We shall see in our account in the next chapter of the disputes in the ESB how this resulted in the establishing of the Quinn Tribunal on clerical pay; but if it hitched up higher expectations among salaried groups, it filled the wage earners with a considerable sense of grievance. In May, *The Irish Times* spoke edgily of the white-collar man absorbing status increases in addition to national agreements, and the National Industrial Economic Council, in a report published later in the year, spoke of the dangers of a lack of consensus in this area.[22] It was a conflict which worked itself out in particular within the Electricity Supply Board. The strikes at this

[20]Labour Court, *Nineteenth Annual Report* 1965, p. 4.
[21]Irish Congress of Trade Unions, *Seventh Annual Report* 1965, p. 198.
[22]National Industrial Economic Council, *Report on Economic Situation,* Report no. 11, 1965, p. 48.

time, as we have already noted, were prominent—even dramatic, and *The Irish Times*, conscious of the irony of our modern society, reported on 5 June:

> On Thursday, of course, Major Edward White, the American astronaut, walked in space: yesterday, thousands of Irishmen and women were compelled to take a walk a little nearer home, as the National Busmen's Union staged the first of a planned series of one-day strikes and removed public transport from the streets. In Dublin it rained to add to the discomfort of the home-going crowds.

As the strikes developed and as the economy overheated, Lemass, who had retained power in the general election in the spring, spoke often of trade union reform, asking pointedly if there was any real prospect of national agreements being fulfilled, and national expansion made possible. Towards the end of June, the newspapers carried a call of his for a truce in industrial disputes, a promise of price control and other such measures, but very soon after, on 2 July, the newspapers themselves, which had done so much in highlighting industrial relations, were crippled by a strike of Dublin printers, a few short weeks before the 1965 annual conference of Congress opened in Cork.

If one is continuously concerned with industrial disputes, one can readily get matters out of proportion, seeing only the conflicts and crises, and little of the humdrum normality of most employments. Congress in Cork felt that the whole business of industrial relations could well benefit from a little sobriety and commonsense. They did not believe that matters had got out of hand. If the FUE had been more flexible, neither working hours nor service pay would have become critical, nor would the cost, in their view, have been so very great. Apart from this, the national agreement was holding reasonably well, and despite the dramatic rise in prices, Larkin ably headed off a demand by the Amalgamated Engineering Union that Congress avail of the escape clause in the agreement and initiate a major wage movement. Larkin's speech gave the tone of the movement at the time: the Irish Congress of Trade Unions was now represented on the major planning bodies; a national agreement was an intrinsic part of this national approach and should not be imperilled. "We are not in an economic crisis," said Larkin,

> but we can talk our way into that crisis if governments and employers and perhaps to some extent we trade unionists are not careful of what we are doing. The crisis that we have insofar as certain aspects of our economy are concerned, is the problem of growth of an expanding

economy for which we have not yet developed all the tools that we require to work on a planned basis.[23]

True, the trade union movement had been shaken by the protracted building dispute, but the president, Dominick Murphy, was careful to stress that, judging by the number of man-days lost, our labour relations were not particularly bad, and when he pointed out the special characteristics of our strikes—their long duration, the dominance of small groups, the drift to crisis—he did so with a hardheaded conviction that these things could be remedied. Even in the very sensitive area of the cooling-off period, and arbitration in disputes, some headway had been made, although all that was suggested was that unions should consider including such provisions in future agreements. There was much to report on economic planning, on manpower policies and on industrial adaptation; and Congress, with its representatives on the planning bodies north and south, welcomed with a special enthusiasm the meeting between the two prime ministers, Seán Lemass and Terence O'Neill, and called for the greatest possible integration of the two parts of Ireland on all matters of mutual benefit.

Let us pause at this point and see what changes had taken place on the executive council of Congress. July 1964 saw elected, among others, three men who would become in their time presidents of Congress. There was Bob Thompson of the National Union of General and Municipal Workers, who had his membership entirely in the North of Ireland; he was nearing the end of his career, and his general approach was closely associated with that of Norman Kennedy and Jack Macgougan. There was James Morrow, who was Irish officer of the powerful Amalgamated Engineering Union and whose background was that of the Belfast shipyards; he was based in Belfast, and the affairs of the union in the Republic appeared to be largely in the hands of Tim Keane. There was Stephen McGonagle from Derry, who was probably the outstanding member of the Irish Transport and General Workers Union in the North of Ireland. His special responsibility was for textile workers. He became later vice-president of the Derry Development Authority until his resignation during the political stresses of 1971. Two others appeared on the executive council for the first time that year: Patrick Crowley of the Assurance Representatives Organisation (a Labour senator), and P. J. Malone of the Irish Federation of Musicians; both unions were very small, and both men served only one year of office. In the lottery of the elections to the executive council in 1965, Jimmy Dunne, who was later to become president, and Willy Fitzpatrick, a past president, both lost their seats. The year before,

[23]Irish Congress of Trade Unions, *Seventh Annual Report* 1965, p. 265.

I had achieved something quite unique in being the first outgoing president who was defeated in the election to the executive council (it had no significance other than a miscalculation of voting strength); this year, I was elected back, as were Fitzpatrick and Dunne the following year. To the office of president, the senior office in the trade union movement, in succession to Dominick Murphy, was elected Fintan Kennedy of the Irish Transport and General Workers Union.

IV

Inevitably, there was going to be trouble about the national wage agreement. The demand for an immediate wage increase had been headed off at the 1965 Cork conference, but the cost of living had risen dramatically and some adjustment was essential. The dilemma was of course that the agreement was scheduled to run until June 1966. Congress had in mind an interim increase, but the FUE offered discussions on a new agreement instead, and when the discussions opened in September 1965, it became clear what the FUE intended. Resentful and angry because of their experiences in the ninth round, they were determined to secure, before any offer was made, precise and explicit agreement on such matters as the scope of the recommendation and arbitration in the event of a dispute. Congress helplessly argued that national agreements were more in the nature of understandings than contracts; and the discussions, tedious and fruitless, dragged on until December 1965 when Congress in despair broke off negotiations. At no time was money discussed.

Congress, however, feared the consequences of a general free-for-all in wages. The economy, deflated in the summer, was sluggish and inadequate at a time when the prospect of freeing trade between the Republic and the United Kingdom was putting everyone to challenge. A recent report of the National Industrial Economic Council,[24] in which Congress had participated, sharpened the awareness of the danger of drift in the matter of incomes, drawing attention not only to the peril which this meant for a developing economy, but also to the growing tensions between salaried earners and wage earners, and between employees and self-employed. "The Report," said *The Irish Press*,[25] "comes at a time when unrest through strikes and industrial friction is threatening the competitiveness of Irish industry and ultimately the employment of Irish workers." And the *Cork Examiner*, in a leader on November 24, caught the feeling of the time well:

[24]National Industrial Economic Council, Report no. 11, 1965.
[25]*The Irish Press,* 25 November 1965.

In an effort to promote the image of a stable economy, it is essential to the success of the programme of industrial expansion that labour-management relations should be conducted on an orderly basis with only the remotest chance of disruption by strike action. Not so long ago, that, in fact, was the picture and a great part of the progress made could be attributed to the assurance of employment continuity stemming from the consultations between management and trade unions. For the most part that is still true, but this year particularly, the advantages have been whittled away by a re-emergence of old animosities which have been given effect in official and unofficial strikes and constant rumour of impending industrial trouble. In the result Ireland is losing the reputation for possessing stable conditions, and would-be investors are warned off.

Congress also, despite its desire to play down the significance of occasional disputes, was very disquieted; and when the FUE talks failed, and a free-for-all seemed imminent, Larkin suggested that a special conference should be called by Congress with the object of unilaterally limiting the round to a moderate maximum of 20 shillings a week.

At the special conference of the 20 January 1966, the executive council bluntly informed the delegates that they could not ignore current economic conditions, in particular the very difficult position of the low-paid workers. In suggesting a maximum of 20 shillings a week, they asked for a sense of solidarity and common purpose; and they urged moderation as well in dealing with service pay, reduced hours and other fringe benefits. The proposals were carried by a majority of two to one.

Lemass was in a dilemma. He suggested a maximum increase of three per cent. in money incomes, but at the same time he did not wish to discount the Congress initiative, although he was quite unsure of its effectiveness. He saw both sides in February and pressed them to meet together to work out an agreement. Professor Basil Chubb of Trinity College was invited to act as independent chairman, but by the end of the month the talks collapsed. At this point, the government made an explicit statement to the effect that a three per cent. increase in incomes was as much as could be conceded, although Lemass was careful to convey that this was not necessarily inconsistent with £1 a week aimed particularly at benefiting the lower-paid workers. The employers, however, were full of anxiety, pointing out that the £1 a week was equivalent to a seven per cent. rise in pay, in addition to the many claims for fringe benefits. Demands had now been served on a wide range of industries, often followed up by strike notice. "On the whole, a situation has developed," said the

Labour Court,[26] "in which a very large number of workers are on strike and there is a serious prospect of the number on strike increasing." On 18 February, the Labour Court invited Congress and the FUE to meet under its auspices, and arising from these discussions, the Labour Court itself issued guidelines on 21 April, generally going along with the Congress recommendation of £1 a week, but seeking a deferment of other claims. It did so because it felt that, in accordance with the two-year pattern of wage rounds, an increase was now expected; and in assessing the size of the increase, it held that, if three per cent. were adhered to, there would be serious danger of widespread industrial conflict ". . . [which] could very well have worse effects on the national economy than an increase in wages somewhat in excess of what could be covered immediately by the increase in national production."[27] The government accepted the position, hoping no doubt that after such protracted disputation, claims would in fact be confined to £1 a week. In the event, they were—male workers getting £1, and women workers fifteen shillings. Thus, in a welter of disputes, the ninth round agreement came to an end.

V

The stresses of the period, the tensions between clerical and manual, skilled and unskilled, will become clearer when we deal in the next chapter with the disputes in the Electricity Supply Board and Bord na Mona. It is necessary, however, to fill in first the general development of events up to the summer of 1968.

Clearly, the Prime Minister, Seán Lemass, now believed that a determined effort must be made to bring order into industrial relations, and in particular to resolve disputes in an orderly way. In April 1966, Congress was confronted with proposals to strengthen the Labour Court, and in fact to turn it into an arbitration board with powers to enforce its decisions. These proposals were vigorously resisted by Congress, who wished to see an improvement in the procedures of the Labour Court, but under no circumstances wished to see a complete change in its substance. The government also proposed to outlaw unofficial strikes and to foster negotiation by groups of unions, but Congress was hostile. However, in the power crisis of June 1966, the government, following this policy, enacted the Electricity (Special Provisions) Act with the object of limiting the right to take industrial action in the Electricity Supply Board, but, as we shall see, the dispute was resolved before its effect could be tested. At the end of June, the Trade Union Bill and the Industrial Relations Bill were introduced in Dáil Éireann, but clearly nobody intended to

[26]Op. cit., p. 37.
[27]Op. cit., p. 40.

rush their fences. On 13 July, in the week before the annual conference of Congress opened in Galway, came the creation of the Department of Labour, and with it, the clear recognition by the government of the great significance of this whole field.

The executive council of Congress faced the 1966 annual conference with some anxiety. They had accepted responsibility, in a period of industrial unrest when tempers were high, for declaring that the maximum increase should be £1 a week, and they were now obliged to take some initiative if they were not to be seen as limiting workers' increases rather than helping in securing them. Consequently, they placed before the delegates a five-year programme for improvements in wages and conditions, and in this way tried to give some positive lead. The programme was put forward with a good deal of vigour: "This is our charter; this is your charter," said Fintan Kennedy[28] in his presidential address. "This we shall plan for and work for and fight for." The discussion later on the proposal had some echo of the Chartists about it. This was a year when xenophobia was running rather high since it was the fiftieth anniversary of the Rising of 1916, but the xenophobia took the form, not of hositility to outsiders, but of the need to compete with them and the necessity for all groups to bind together for that purpose. Despite the widespread industrial unrest, despite the alarming ESB disputes, despite the intractable strike in the printing industry, the turmoil in the banks, the disputes in engineering and in paper-making, on the docks and in the local authorities, there was still a conviction that these problems were not insurmountable, if only because, as one people, we were committed to their resolution. As Fintan Kennedy said:

> We, the workers and the trade unionists of this country, are an integral part of economic, social, industrial, political and cultural life. We are the small farmers, the service people, the factory and office workers, the technicians, the craftsmen, the professionals and the traders. In short, we are the nation because we are from, and of, every fruitful part of its being. It behoves us all, therefore, to cherish and nourish our belief in justice so that within our time we may see the fullness of the social emancipation of the Irish people.[29]

But the industrial unrest continued, causing the Minister for Industry and Commerce to meet separately both the ICTU and the Federated Union of Employers to hear their views on the reasons for the unrest. Congress tended to play down the need for any general strategy, seeing in each strike a cause specific to itself. The ESB fitters strike, for example,

---

[28]Irish Congress of Trade Unions, *Eighth Annual Report* 1966, p. 194.
[29]ibid., p. 197.

could be traced to the absence of adequate negotiating machinery, leading to delays and frustration, and to the belief that unless a stoppage occurred, workers' claims would not be taken seriously. In the case of the strike in the building industry, Congress believed that this came from an attempt on the part of the employers to hold a predetermined line, irrespective of the conditions and circumstances of a particular industry. The government, however, believing that a broad strategy of reform was necessary, continued to press for its programme of legislation, and a working party to go into the matter was established between Congress and the new Department of Labour. At this point, however, the push for legislative reform, in its original radical sense, seemed to fade. Perhaps the government recognised that this was not the answer; perhaps too it was not unrelated to the fact that Seán Lemass retired as Taoiseach in November, and the initiative, which the government usually managed to hold in such matters, gradually disappeared.

When the executive council reported to the annual conference in Portrush in May 1967 (the annual conference was early that year, as an experiment), what had emerged was indeed very far from the driving comprehensive legislation which the government originally had in mind. Congress was determined that the Labour Court would not change its character and become an arbitration tribunal; the other proposals seemed largely a matter of reinforcing, tidying and clarifying, with the exception of the proposal on group negotiating licences (aimed at giving groups of unions real negotiating power) which ran into trouble in any event at the conference.

But the tone of the conference was a positive one, despite all the difficulties, despite all the industrial unrest. The National Industrial Economic Council had issued in January a comprehensive programme aimed at full employment within a measurable period; Congress itself had suggested a rights tribunal to deal with specific problems; a proposal on industrial democracy was well received; the idea of a voluntary incomes policy still received support, despite the opposition of English-based unions sensitive to developments in Britain, but the delegates were very hostile to any legislative proposals which might limit their freedom of action, and were suspicious even of those proposals which were designed to assist them to order their own affairs. It was fashionable to distrust the government with a deep distrust, at times more than the employers and with much less reason.

When John Conroy took over as president in succession to Bob Thompson at the end of the annual conference in 1967 in Portrush, the economy was already opening up, moving into the boom year of 1968, and agreements for improved conditions—the new phenomenon of two-year agreements—were beginning to be negotiated throughout industry. But by May of the following year, when Conroy rose to address the 1968 annual conference in Killarney, there was a sourness in the air, and the trade union movement was annoyed and uncertain. If the new competitive mood in Irish industry meant greater opportunities, it also meant casualties for the out-of-date and the inefficient. If industry provided a greater number of jobs, it was also true that the number leaving agriculture was far greater than was expected, and, consequently, the overall employment figure did not improve. On the other hand, expanding industry provided an affluence that was not there before, and the kind of ostentatious expense-account living which Ireland was not used to; it was aptly described by one fastidious economist as a country gulping and guzzling. While the number of strikes had fallen, there was a national crisis because of the unofficial stoppage in the Electricity Supply Board, and a difficult and dangerous strike, also with its roots in unofficial action, in Bord na Mona. An American subsidiary in the Shannon Industrial Estate refused to recognise the Irish Transport and General Workers Union, and the reaction of the workers was both bitter and vehement.

But if the government had lost heart in trying to make any radical changes in industrial legislation, the trade union movement had also lost heart in its efforts to rationalise its own structure, and decided not to reappoint the committee on trade union organisation. Ruaidhri Roberts, a man normally stoic in his acceptance of the vagaries of democracy, said, not without a hint of bitterness:

> In the face of this massive disinterest in better trade union organisation, it is not easy to see a very useful purpose in putting forward new recommendations, or spelling out the old ones in greater detail . . . It may be that what is lacking is motive. If we are not moved by the belief that in the mass organisation of the trade union movement we have an instrument in the hands of workers which they can use to revolutionise the society in which they live; if we are content to let society evolve in another direction, and to compete with each other for the choicer crumbs from the masters' table, then possibly small sectional trade unions, or sections which demand recognition by unions of their selfish acts, are the kind of union which is most suited to our purpose. It may be therefore that the weakness of our interest in unified organisation reflects a weakness in the sense of purpose and direction within the trade union movement.[30]

These words were prophetic and Roberts's worst fears were to be realised in the débâcle of the maintenance men's dispute a year later.

[30]Irish Congress of Trade Unions, *Tenth Annual Report* 1968, pp. 246, 247.

But as is inevitably the case, there was much criticism of Congress as well, much criticism of its lack of leadership and its lack of authority. Perhaps some missed the rough edge of Leo Crawford who had since retired. But this criticism was not confined to the leadership of Congress. Many unions were themselves undergoing a crisis of confidence. Members in frustration were turning on their own officials and on their own structures. The reports of the National Industrial Economic Council, the adaptation of industry, the seminars on industrial democracy—all these were too remote to have much effect on the rank and file. There was no further discussion of the charter of planned improvement over a five-year period; unions under pressure from their members were looking for what advantage they could get, and certainly the situation was not helped by a decision of the government to increase substantially the allowances paid to members of the Dáil and the Senate, and the members of the judiciary.

This was John Conroy's swan song. He proposed to retire from the executive council of Congress, and from the office of president of the Irish Transport a year later. He was one who had had high hopes in the early sixties, and the present trouble weighed heavily on him. He was deeply disturbed by the growth of unofficial strikes. "It may well be," he said,

> that there are sections and small groups of members in affiliated unions who are selfish and only concerned with securing more and more for themselves; often they are small groups, but nevertheless, as key workers in an industry, they use and abuse their trade union membership by using and abusing the picket line to secure for themselves and secure for themselves alone, extra and special rates of wages and/or special conditions of employment. Such actions cannot in principle, morally or otherwise, be justified. There can be no doubt whatever that the lightning, unofficial and selfish strikes of recent times cannot in justice be defended nor condoned. Nevertheless, injustice, failure to pay a living wage and procrastination in negotiations has provided the excuse and the opportunity for groups of workers to exploit the particular situation for their own selfish ends.[31]

He was sensitive to the charge that the trade union movement no longer retained the confidence of the members; in such circumstances, he urged that structures should be changed in an orderly way, or even that officials should be removed if they no longer held the confidence of the members; but there was to be no further splintering and weakening of the trade

[31]ibid., p. 232.

unions. He made a last bid for working class and trade union solidarity by a highly-coloured condemnation of those ". . . who held the money-bags."

> Looking a little further afield we see the European international ghouls and jackals who accumulate wealth and who enjoy every luxury life has to offer by buying and selling money as a commodity . . . At home in Ireland, the hooded crows in Dublin's Foster Place, Dame Street, College Green, and in the other secret dens throughout the country, are listening in and cogging as best they can from the copybooks of European and American financial manipulators . . . Oh, too, to sit in at a secret meeting of the Taca Club,[32] the Conservative Club, the Royal Hibernian Club, the Grand Orange Lodge, and some other of the disguised Tory clubs. I am sure it would be most revealing and educating for one of the plain people to see how the boys, orange and green, royal and republican, find understanding and common ground in procuring and dividing within their limited circle, the loot collected from the toil and sweat of the workers[33].

Conroy had a sophisticated appreciation of national economics; he was a shrewd contributor to the general purposes committee of the National Industrial Economic Council which he attended regularly. His concern for the underprivileged was unwavering, but his understanding of the administrative difficulties associated with income distribution was also considerable. This language of his, therefore, must be seen as metaphorical, a true expression of his feeling, but couched in a manner which he hoped the workers would respond to, leading as well to their accepting his urgings for discipline and commonsense.

VI

Before we go on to deal with the disputes, there are one or two points which should be made about the period from 1965 to 1968. In the early nineteen sixties, for the first time, we experienced economic growth, but we seemed unable to absorb it into the economy. There are some, recently, who have said—perhaps thinking also of the boom of 1968 and the disputes and difficulties that followed—that we are unable to tolerate a growth rate of more than three or four per cent.; once we achieve this, we seem as a society to burst asunder. High wage demands are made; high expectations are evident; high price increases occur, and there follows a rapid overheating of the economy; deflationary measures are introduced, perhaps more vigorous than they need be; and the econ-

[32]A fund-raising organisation for Fianna Fáil.
[33]ibid., pp. 236, 237.

omy is crushed back once again. Such pattern-weaving can be a very uncertain guide with regard to the future, but there is no doubt that it summarises the broad character of the sixties.

The answer to the problem was evident enough right from the outset: there must be a reasonable relationship between income increases and national production; and Lemass's answer was to try to secure a commanding position regarding incomes—beginning by suggesting wage increases to the trade union movement in the autumn of 1963. The agreement of 1964 was unique, and increases in wages and salaries were introduced rapidly, and without industrial unrest. But the price was very high, not so much in the absolute amount of twelve per cent. over two and a half years, but in the level of expectation for the future which this created. It would be immensely difficult to get people to think once again in terms of three or four per cent. But there was a greater difficulty in the approach of the government at the time; this was the absence of any convincing policy regarding prices, probably because Lemass saw it as a residual, which it may have been; but in trade union politics it was of the first importance. The balance was redressed by the Report No. 11 of the NIEC which received a full-dress debate in Dáil Éireann in June 1966, and the National Prices Commission has been established in more recent times; nevertheless, the trade union movement has been in continuous difficulties about this matter, vulnerable to a charge from the more anxious of its own members that the government's proposals for an incomes policy amounted to nothing more than a policy in restraint of wages.

But the 1964 policies, as we have seen, ran into further difficulties. The building strike was a serious blow to any idea of national bargaining; and we found great difficulty in handling the growing tensions between wage and salary earners, and between skilled and unskilled. All this put in question the capacity of the trade unions to govern themselves, and when unrest began to grow in 1965, Lemass turned, as the employers had urged him to do, to devices by which workers could be disciplined in the kind of action they might take—in other words he thought of legislation—while the trade union movement attempted to meet the problem in a more piecemeal way, resolving industrial unrest, for example, in the building industry by an industrial council, and resolving the problem of inflationary pressures by voluntarily limiting claims to £1 a week. There was then during the period continuous discussion about some national strategy to reduce industrial unrest, so that one might achieve an orderly growth in incomes. That such a strategy was possible was certainly believed by the government, and they devised a statutory programme to give it effect. It was also accepted by many employers, and in retrospect, it seems to me that many trade unionists also believed in a comprehensive strategy to deal with industrial difficulties, but played it down publicly, fearing that it would lead to statutory interventions, and giving emphasis instead to comprehensive but voluntary trade union reform. But perhaps there is no such grand strategy; each dispute may have its own solution, peculiar to itself. Perhaps then we should consider the creation of an institution that would provide, as it were, a sophisticated fire-brigade service, dealing with each dispute and each dispute situation as unique, and requiring a unique solution. Some such idea was, as we shall see, in the minds of the Fogarty Commission. In such a view of things, both the reorganisation of the trade unions and the introduction of more explicit procedures for dealing with disputes would be seen as secondary, springing from clearly understood needs, and not as primary reforming devices introduced in the face of reluctance or even hostility.

Whatever about the truth of this, the NIEC in particular recognised that there was an anterior problem which lay in the question of social self-discipline. A social consensus means necessarily that a number must forego what they might achieve if they consulted their own interests only. While such a consensus may have existed to some extent in the acceptance of the 1966 recommendation of £1 a week, and perhaps in some earlier agreements, the fact is that the measure of consensus does not appear to have been high, and the arrangements generally too fragile to hold against a determined drive by some special interest group. The common sense of keeping wage claims within reasonable limits was reconsised, but it was also recognised that this would only work if everybody played according to the rules; and the rules unfortunately did not mean a great deal at times. In particular, strong feeling was regarded as a good enough reason to discount any rule or any agreement, whether the feeling was well-based or not; and the willingness to suffer for one's beliefs (irrespective of their justice or even of their sense) was too often taken to be *de facto* justification. Some would say that this was characteristic only of the minor turbulent leaders (at branch level, or at firm level, for example) and not of employees generally. But it was very evident in the disputes we examine here, and certainly such feelings gain ready support from rank and file members who are more likely as a rule to follow vehement rather than balanced leadership. Later, we shall examine to what extent this view must be modified in the light of the national agreements of 1970 and 1972, but it fairly reflects the sixties.

All in all, perhaps too much was expected if not attempted; and there is much wisdom in Professor Meenan's judgment that the issues involved were as much social as economic: "Neither employers nor trade unions could be wholly blamed for a failure to cope with forces that lay as much outside their control as outside their experience."[34] In these circumstances, perhaps the most fruitful suggestion was that made by the NIEC, first in their Report No. 13, and then later and much more explicitly in their Report No. 18 on full employment.[35] The report, published in early 1967, was particularly concerned with the long duration of the major strikes: the adverse effects on exports, on our reputation abroad and on the general climate of industrial relations; recognising how complex the problem was, they recommended a system of impartial inquiries conducted, at the behest of the Minister for Labour, by a small expert team who would be assisted by a representative from the ICTU and from the FUE. The report of the inquiry would be published if both parties to the dispute agreed. This suggestion has been partially implemented. The NIEC had suggested panels of experts from whom the inquiry teams could be drawn, but these were never established, and regretfully, therefore, we have not the institutional continuity which they implied. Nonetheless, five disputes were examined and reported on broadly in accordance with these arrangements. Only the first, however,—the inquiry into the ESB dispute which was inaugurated in April 1968—provided for a three-man team, with consultants from the ICTU and the FUE. The Bord na Mona inquiry, which was established in June 1968, was essentially a one-man inquiry, as also was the inquiry into the banks dispute which began in November 1970. The inquiry into the maintenance men's dispute, which was instituted in March 1969, was also conducted by one man, but he was assisted by two nominees each from the ICTU and the FUE. We shall deal with all these disputes in the chapters that follow; it was decided not to publish the report of the inquiry into the EI dispute in Shannon,[36] the fifth inquiry commissioned by the Minister. Professor Michael Fogarty conducted the inquiries into the ESB dispute and into the banks dispute; Mr Con Murphy[37] conducted that which inquired into the maintenance men's dispute and was a member of the team that inquired into the EI dispute in Shannon; and Mr Charles Mulvey conducted the inquiry into the dispute in Bord na Mona. No matter how perceptive and conscientious these reports have been, I am personally of the view that they would have been much improved by the balancing of experts which was contemplated by the NIEC, by the continuous monitoring by ICTU and FUE representatives, and by the continuity and the accumulation of experience which a panel of experts implies.

[34]James Meenan, *The Irish Economy Since 1922* (Liverpool University Press, 1970), p. 328.
[35]National Industrial Economic Council, *Report on Full Employment*, Report no. 18, 1967, p. 102 ff.
[36]This was conducted by a three-man team, all industrialists.
[37]He also conducted inquiries into docks working in Dublin and Limerick; these are unpublished.

CHAPTER FOUR

The Power Workers

I

DURING the nineteen sixties, the Electricity Supply Board acquired a reputation for being particularly strike-prone. The management were in dispute with almost all their employees at various times, clerical and craft, professional and general. Two commissions of inquiry were established to investigate the Board's industrial relations. Acts of parliament were passed to limit the trade union activities of its employees, which resulted in strikers going to prison. Here then was an industry, essential to the well-being of the country, ravaged by unrest and likely to put in peril not only employment elsewhere but services essential to basic well-being and even to survival. Yet for the first thirty years of its existence, the Electricity Supply Board was a peaceful and highly regarded employment. "Whereas in over 30 years of the ESB's existence down to the end of the fifties," says the Fogarty Report,[1] "it experienced only eight strikes, none of which interrupted supply, on a national scale, from 1961 to December 1968 there were . . . thirty eight strikes, and widespread breakdowns of supply occurred in two of these." Since that report was written, there were a number of further stoppages culminating in the highly significant unofficial strike of the shift workers in 1972.

The story of how this dramatic change came about is a fascinating one, since it involves all the industrial stress of the period: the anxieties that attend technological change, the demand for new management styles, the virtual disappearance of the status security of a highly-structured society, the great social tensions as the categories of employment were more and

[1] *Final Report of the Committee on Industrial Relations in the Electricity Supply Board* (*the Fogarty Report*), Dublin, 1969.

more put in question—categories such as skilled and unskilled, clerical and manual, salary earner and wage earner, with all their implications of a class structure. Unfortunately, neither committee of inquiry, neither the Gleeson inquiry[2] of 1961–62 nor the Fogarty inquiry of 1968–69, deals with the events of the period other than for the purpose of exemplification, since both were concerned rather with the state of industrial relations in the ESB than with the disputes and their genesis. However, the broad outline of the events seems clear enough, and conveys a picture not of a number of individual and separate disputes, but rather of an evolving industrial situation, in which the disputes are all to some extent related, one to another.

The Board was established in 1927 under the Electricity (Supply) Act. It was one of the first state-sponsored bodies in Ireland and was a remarkable success. While its main object was to provide electric power, it also had a contracts and sales division, and in this way was involved in the ordinary private enterprise world of the electrical contracting industry—a highly significant link in a number of the disputes. So extensive was its development that, by the end of the sixties, it had 10,000 employees spread throughout the country. True, these employees were represented by a complex range of up to thirty unions, but even in industrial relations the Board was for many years considered to be very sophisticated; there were two tribunals, established by statute, designed to resolve conflicts, one for manual workers which was set up in 1942, and the other for salaried employees, which was set up in 1949. As for the private contract work, there was a National Joint Industrial Committee established as early as 1931, and in this the ESB played a considerable part, up to its withdrawal in the mid-sixties.

The ESB, therefore, for many years had considerable status as an employer, and their clerical grades in particular did well, comparing more than favourably at times with the civil service and the local authority service. We must remember that up to the nineteen fifties, in a country which was indifferently industrialised, there were few large employers of clerical workers, and the ESB was unique in that the clerical workers there were seen to be in a power-producing industrial complex, while the others were in essentially service employments. This supported the view that many had at the time that the clerical employees in the ESB were the lead group in the whole salary field. It was among them that the difficulties began. It was 1958, the year of promise, as *The Irish Times* called it.

At the time, the vast majority of the clerical employees of the Board

[2]*Electricity Supply Board Commission of Inquiry (the Gleeson Report)*, Dublin, 1961.

were members of the Amalgamated Transport and General Workers Union, which also organised manual workers. A number were also members of the Irish Union of Distributive Workers and Clerks. These unions joined with the other salaried grades in the Electricity Supply Board to form a negotiating group known as the ESB Salaried Staff Conference, negotiating separately from the manual grades, and, as we have seen, with its separate tribunal for the resolution of disputes. This distinction was fundamental, even though the Amalgamated Transport had both salary and wage earners in membership.

The difference between salary grades and wage grades was far more profound than merely monthly or weekly payments. The salaried employee had a status within the Board of quite a different character. Not only had he a far better deal in income, in pensions, in sick-leave and so forth, but in social matters—even in his canteen lunch—he was the salaried official, and the other was the worker. Yet up to the mid-fifties, the manual workers in the ESB did not appear to feel any great sense of injustice or deprivation on that account. Some say that this was because, up to then, the clerical workers and the skilled tradesmen had broadly the same income when one made allowances for the many different forms of payment, the difficulty arising only with the growing practice of giving percentage rather than flat increases. But there was very much more to it than that, and it probably reflects the highly structured society which existed in Ireland at the time. It parallels, in an urban context, the changes which Damien Hannan has marked in the rural areas since 1951,[3] to which we have already referred.

The salaried employees were in turn affiliated to the Irish Conference of Professional and Service Associations, which in 1958 carried substantial weight as the spokesman for clerical and professional employees. The phrase 'clerical worker', with its egalitarian overtones, was not yet in use. The Conference had in membership the civil service organisations, particularly the executive and professional grades, which in the early nineteen fifties had gained formal negotiating machinery with the government. There was also the Irish Bank Officials Association, militant and uncompromising, with salaries unusually good for Irish conditions. There were the teachers, also with a militant background, and certain other groups such as local authority officials and Guinness salaried employees.

1957 saw the the sixth round of wage and salary increases—a flat increase of 10 shillings a week for everyone, including those on salary scales. This followed a number of rounds where, while percentage in-

[3]Damien Hannan, op. cit.

creases were given to salaried employees, the percentage was reduced as a rule at the higher levels of the scales. All this resulted in a narrowing of the band of incomes, a compression in relative terms of the higher salaries, and the movement of the wage earner to an income closer to that of the salary earner—despite what some wage earners may have thought. The salaried man at the time saw himself as being different in kind from the wage earner—more responsible, owning his own home, more prudent in his expenditure, and committed to expenses not experienced by a wage earner such as sending his children to secondary school, and if possible to the university. He achieved this, as he saw it, by good management, and yet he saw a wage earner, with none of his personal commitments, pressing close to him in income, and spending money with little of his social responsibility. This feeling of class distinction, so prevalent in the fifties and perhaps the early sixties, has now almost altogether evaporated in the more egalitarian society of today, but it was a powerful force at the time. It was particularly marked in the discussions of the Irish Conference of Professional and Service Associations, which was almost a middle class club defending its privileges, and which, because of that, earned the implacable hostility of Jim Larkin.

In 1957, the flat increase of ten shillings a week (which, whether it had trade union blessing or not, was seen by many as an attack on differentials) was applied by the Board to its manual employees; the salaried staff conference had submitted a claim, however, for fifteen per cent. which they offered to forego until the following year, if the ten shillings were paid. This the Board refused to do; the claim went to the appropriate tribunal, and indeterminate discussions dragged on for about three months. Eventually, the salaried employees decided on strike action. They were militant and very angry, but at the same time they were deeply conscious of the danger of interfering with power supplies; there had never been a radical stoppage in the Board up to then, and this was uncharted territory. Consequently, although they placed pickets on the Board, they invited the manual workers to pass the pickets and continue working, their object being to limit the effect of the strike. The pickets lasted only a week; the tribunal issued a recommendation that the ten shillings a week should be awarded to the clerical grades, and the dispute ended in a welter of recriminations. The manual workers resented having been asked to pass the pickets, were contemptuous of the half-hearted campaign, and suspected, in any event, that the clerical employees were too class-conscious to seek their help. As for the clerical employees themselves, the leadership was under attack from two sides, from the right, who took the view that in any event no strike should have been mounted in an essential service, and from the left who believed that the strike, once it was decided on, was conducted far too timidly. There was a belief as well that the Amalgamated Transport, having many manual employees in membership, would not pursue the interests of the clerical employees in a sufficiently singleminded way, and, arising from all this, a new union for clerical employees in the Board was established in 1959, the ESB Officers Association. At the present time it has in membership approximately 1,500 employees, while the Amalgamated Transport is left with only 350 salaried people, mostly in the technical field. The Distributive Workers continue to have a small membership.

The possibility of a strike in the ESB was now in the air, with all its dramatic implications, and it was realised in the summer of 1961. This was the key dispute of the decade, starting the three movements characteristic of the period, the bid by the wage earners for parity with the salary grades, the bid by all other salary grades for equality with the ESB, and the devastating taboo of the picket line. The strike was a strike of electricians both in the ESB and in private industry. However, it was conducted against the background of the seventh round of increases in which salaried workers had made dramatic advances. We saw earlier[4] that the seventh round began mildly enough in 1959 with increases of ten to fifteen shillings a week for wage earners and seven per cent. for salary earners, which gave approximately the same result. Then almost immediately came the second wave, which appeared to benefit salary people only. Apparently,[5] one of the assurance companies extended the maximum point of the scale of its clerical grade, but this was taken elsewhere to be an immediate increase of twenty-five per cent., and in the scattered negotiations that followed, the key settlement was that for the ESB basic clerical grade whose maximum went from £895 a year to £1,050. Some say that the new chairman of the Board wished to restore the good will lost in 1958; some say it was a result of compelling arguments by the unions, but the fact remained that, not only were the increases very large, but the ESB clerical officer had broken through the magical barrier of £1,000 a year and all the other clerical grades were in full cry after him.

In the ESB, skilled grades such as electricians were particularly resentful, comparing their increase with that of the salaried official, and becoming more conscious now of irritating differences in status; a point sourly remarked on at the time was that they saw the clerical people breezing out to mass on a holy day or to the shops from time to time, while the

[4]See page 24 above.
[5]*Report of Tribunal of Inquiry into Rates of Remuneration Payable to Clerical Recruitment Grades in the Public Sector of the Economy* (*the Quinn Report*) (Stationery Office, Dublin, 1966), p. 7.

electricians were obliged to check in and check out. It was difficult for the electricians in the ESB to negotiate an increase for themselves because of the practice of the Board to 'follow the down-town rate.' This needs some explanation in the complex events that followed. At the time, the Board employed approximately 400 operations electricians, engaged in the supply of power, and approximately the same number of contracts electricians whose work was related to that done in private industry generally. In practice, this latter group received increases in accordance with rates negotiated for the industry generally under the National Joint Industrial Committee, of which the ESB was a prominent member (and indeed supplied the secretariat), and then subsequently the related rate for the operations men was negotiated. Thus, the ESB tied itself to following the rates for industry generally; but there was an advantage here, since, if there was a dispute with regard to the down-town rate, only the contracts men would be involved—not the operations men, and consequently, electricity supplies would not be affected. To many at the time, however, all this appeared to be in the background; it seemed that the essential dispute was with the private sector, the electrical contracting industry, and that the ESB was pulled into the dispute because of the frightful threat of a total failure of power, which was thereby created.

In the summer of 1961, a demand was made on the private electrical contractors and also on the ESB by the Electrical Trades' Union (Ireland). This was one of the major unions organising electricians, the other being the Irish Engineering, Industrial and Electrical Trade Union, which was one of the first to break away in the nineteen twenties from the English-based union, and from which, in turn, the Electrical Trades' Union (Ireland) very soon branched off to become an independent union in its own right. The private electrical contractors, who appeared to have been the principal object of the demand, provided conditions of work which were far from satisfactory and much in contrast with those provided by the ESB. Derek O'Sullivan[6] says:

> I started my apprenticeship in 1960, the beginning of the boom period, but I was always being told about the hard times of the previous decade. With the shortage of work in contracting, employers could pick whom they wanted and treat them as they wanted. The boat to England was the only alternative, if workers did not like the treatment. There were stories of people being paid less than the trade union rate, of non-union labour being used, of men having to queue up to apply for a vacancy. As the boom continued, the attitude of many of the

[6]Op. cit., pp. 11, 12.

lads was to 'screw' the employers for as much as they could, as after the boom they would start 'screwing' the workers again.

On 21 August time ran out and pickets were placed, not only on the private contract shops, but on the power installations of the ESB as well. There was uproar. The Minister for Industry and Commerce immediately became involved and met the parties for prolonged discussions. A meeting which began on 23 August continued right throughout the night, and from it emerged an offer which the union undertook to put to ballot, but they refused to remove the pickets. All the other eighteen unions in the ESB instructed the workers to pass these pickets, stating that electricians only were involved, but many of the manual workers refused to do so. They seemed to be of the view that they should not return to work until some arrangement was made for them as well. In the meantime, so alarmed had the government become, that both the Dáil and the Senate were recalled and the Electricity (Temporary Provisions) Bill was introduced, the object being to establish a tribunal which, in special circumstances, would arbitrate in a manner which would compel the parties to accept the result. This had a devastating effect on the trade unions. Before such provisions could be implemented, Leo Crawford, who had intervened in the dispute on behalf of the Irish Congress of Trade Unions, brought about a settlement. There is little doubt that the threat of legislation helped, although, in all probability, it was impractical. Perhaps Lemass never intended it to be more than a catalyst to secure agreement. In any event, by 1 September 1961 when the measure came before the Dáil again, the crisis had passed, and Lemass, roundly dismissing the very thought of compulsory arbitration, introduced a number of amendments which removed all the teeth from the bill, and left only the obligation to establish a commission of inquiry. In this form it was enacted for a brief period, and on 11 September, the day before it lapsed, the commission to inquire into industrial relations in the ESB was established in the manner provided.

The settlement gave an increase of twenty-eight shillings a week, a very large amount at the time, and twice that of the emerging eight round pattern of fourteen shillings, the amount that had been recommended by the Labour Court. This in fact influenced greatly the subsequent course of the eighth round. But because of their observance of the pickets, the other manual workers in the ESB insisted on a like increase which in fact was granted them. In one stroke, then, the differential between skilled and unskilled was put in question, a very substantial increase was won by the unskilled worker, although he had in no way initiated the dispute, and the astonishing vulnerability of the ESB was made only too obvious to all. There was a further phenomenon associated with the dispute. The workers' representative on the ESB tribunals was elected from among the employees, not appointed by the unions, and through this means, the dispute threw up, among the manual employees of the Board, a demagogic leader in the person of Joe Christle, who organised a number of mass meetings, and whose success was indicative (if nothing else) of the absence of adequate representative institutions for the employees.

And what of the ETU (I) which mounted the strike in the first instance? They would claim now that they did not cynically involve the ESB for the havoc this would create: for the first time, operations electricians had submitted a claim at the same time as the contracts men, and therefore the cushion of the down-town rate did not apply; secondly, the ESB representative on the national joint industrial committee was the leader in resisting the claim for an improvement in the down-town rate, which was the key point in the dispute, and, thirdly, both the operations and the contracts electricians saw in all this a development of the deliberate policy of the Board to discriminate between clerical and manual employees.

But the leaders of the trade union movement were shocked at the irresponsibility of the ETU (I) and helpless in the face of the overwhelming taboo of the picket, even where unions instructed their members to ignore it. Leo Crawford[7], when he addressed the following ICTU annual conference in Galway, said: "I am trying to convey to you the futility we feel when we do not know what steps to take when these problems arise; whether we should involve 2,000 workers for the sake of 100 workers, or whether we should take a firm stand, and when we do take such a stand, can we be assured that the rank and file members of the unions will take the direction given them." Larkin[8] at the same conference said:

> The reason we have this problem with regard to picketing is because in the Republic, picketing is at its most effective position. It is not uncommon for official pickets to be passed in the United Kingdom ... It is a long time since that happened in the Republic ... We do not ... go on strike every time we serve a claim. We negotiate, manoeuvre, we use tactics and strategy, but we are always able to fall back on the right to strike, if that is necessary. Equally we should have the same understanding with regard to picketing. Some people in this country seem to think that automatically when we go on strike, a picket must be put on. This is not correct.

[7]Irish Congress of Trade Unions, *Fourth Annual Report* 1962, p. 252.
[8]ibid., p. 253.

As diplomatically as he could, he brought the ETU (I) to task:

> The craft unions have got tremendous power and great economic power, but they can only use that power as long as there is a general trade union movement to hold the ring for them, and see that they are not interfered with unduly by the employers or by the Government. When it comes to the point of even the strongest craft union having to fight completely on its own, then they can find, as it has been found before, that they are not strong enough.

But the dispute had further disturbing consequences within the trade union movement. All the unions, apart from the ETU (I), decided that they would not pay dispute pay to members who observed the pickets and stayed out of work, since they did so contrary to their union's instructions; but the workers greatly resented this. The Amalgamated Transport, fearing that it might lose more members within the ESB, paid the benefit, and the Workers Union of Ireland made a grant to each worker which amounted to much the same thing, but the Irish Transport and General Workers Union, under John Conroy, remained inflexible. However, the payment of dispute pay by the others had created a serious problem, because it seemed to convey a tacit approval of what the men had done, and it may have helped to establish the notion that the worker's job, like the foot-soldier's, was to observe the order of the picket, leaving it to others to ensure that the pickets were justly placed. Even when workers did this in flat contradiction of their own union's instructions, there was an ambivalence in the minds of many officials, a recognition of the solidarity involved (although it was misplaced), and a fear of losing the effectiveness of such a force. In a word, there was a view, widespread but only partly formed, that it was not the observance of the picket that was wrong, but rather the placing of it. There was some recognition of this dilemma in Larkin's speech to the annual conference of Congress.

As a consequence of the stand made by the Irish Transport, approximately fifty unskilled and semi-skilled ESB workers in the Galway area, members of the Irish Transport, applied to and were accepted into membership of the ETU (I), contrary to the rules of Congress. The matter was brought before the Congress disputes committee who required the ETU (I) to mend their hand; they refused point blank to do so. They were suspended from membership of the Irish Congress of Trade Unions at the Galway conference in 1962 and remained suspended for some years afterwards. There was some opposition to the suspension from the AEU, but when Larkin, in particular, put his weight behind the proposal, it was carried by a very large majority. Here the trade union leadership showed no ambivalence whatever. "Any union is free to remain alone," said Larkin,

> to be a lone wolf, and hunt alone, but if it does, it cannot expect the rest of us to catch its prey, and hold it down while it feeds upon it. We are going to look after ourselves in the meantime. No union, whether it is the Electrical Trade Union or the biggest union in Congress, is powerful enough today to hunt on its own. The Electrical Trades Union should recognise that fact.[9]

Despite the fact that the dispute did not seem to spring initially from among employees of the Board, the commission of inquiry, established under the 1961 act, was curiously concerned with the ESB only, and not even with the reasons for the dispute but rather ". . . the procedure of the Electricity Supply Board for the determination of remuneration . . . and for the settlement of disputes."[10] However, it found that right at the centre of its enquiry was the problem of industrial relations in the ESB, despite the level of sophistication which at one time was a source of such satisfaction. It was established in November 1961, and reported a year later. Crawford (who with myself were the members nominated by Congress) was convinced that the difficulty lay in the involvement of the ESB in the National Joint Industrial Committee for the electrical contracting industry. He wanted to see them excluded altogether from these negotiations and committed in advance to following whatever was agreed; in this way, he hoped that the ESB could not be involved in any further dispute. There were a number of objections to this. It meant that clerical workers' pay, and others', would be determined by the Board's internal value system, while the electricians would be influenced by quite different norms; this had already been shown to be a dangerous arrangement when men were employed by the same authority. It meant that the major employer of electricians in the country would have little say in their pay levels; and finally it seemed to canonise the practice of following the down-town rate and the washing of hands that this implied. The commission, however, rather reluctantly followed Crawford's view because it seemed to them that this would reduce the danger of major industrial disputes in the ESB, and the ESB later adopted their recommendation and withdrew from the national joint industrial committee.

There were some other matters. The commission felt that there was co nfusion with regard to wage and salary structures and other conditions

[9]ibid., p. 288.
[10]*Gleeson Report,* op. cit., p. 1.

of service, and recommended that a comprehensive national agreement should be negotiated. There seemed to be a general opinion that the personnel department had not adequate authority in negotiation, and they urged that this should be remedied. They recommended that, in the interests of good order, claims for manual workers should be submitted through the Congress trade union group, and, in order to help in overcoming the divisions between salary and wage earner, they recommended that there should be one tribunal, not two. It is doubtful if the report of the commission had any particular effect. The two tribunals continued in existence and a great number of other things besides, and it may well be that the commission was seen by many rather as a formal consequence of the dispute than a real attempt to establish a better system, although the chairman of the ESB (who in practice was its chief executive) was a member. There was impatience too on the part of some members of the ESB management; they felt the exercise was quite beside the point, since the dispute did not spring from these difficulties in the first place.

But now the clerical grades in the ESB swept ahead again. We have already seen[11] that they secured seven per cent. in 1963, succeeded in getting the full twelve per cent. under the ninth round national agreement, and now their tribunal awarded them, in 1965, a further ten per cent., so that men, who, on maxima of £895 in 1960 had looked longingly towards £1,000 a year, now found themselves a short five years later with salaries very close to £1,400. This had the most serious implications for the government, quite apart from the internal problems of the ESB. All the other grades in the state and semi-state employments, who had painfully pulled themselves up near the old ESB figure, would very likely succeed in doing the same thing all over again, with inordinate cost to the state itself, because once the increase reached the civil service clerical grade, it would rush upwards through the differentials, and then run rapidly throughout the teaching profession, the police force and the army. Far from giving a status increase merely to ESB clerks, the tribunal appeared to have created a never-ending spiral. True, they had given an increase to their clerks on the grounds that their work was of higher value than that of a civil service clerical officer. but other employments were sure to follow, eventually pulling the civil service grades with them, and providing, thereby, sure grounds for a further claim by the ESB clerks—for the fact was that the various tribunals and arbitration bodies for salaried employees were quite independent of one another, and felt in no way obliged to follow a common value system. But more than all that, it was April 1965, the national agreement had well over a year to

[11]p. 85.

run, and a cascade of claims throughout other clerical employments would bid fair to wreck the agreement in the clerical field, just as the building dispute looked as if it might do so in the industrial field.

In the face of all this, and in the face of mounting restlessness among the wage earners, the government decided to sort the matter out by way of a tribunal of inquiry into the rates of pay for clerical grades in the public service, with the object of having one scale of salary that would settle the matter once and for all. The tribunal reported[12] in May 1966, finding unanimously that, by and large, all the clerical grades in the public service, including the ESB clerks, did much the same kind of work; and then a majority of the tribunal went on to recommend, as they had been asked, ". . . an absolute level of pay for the recruitment/clerical grades in the public sector," which was substantially below that already being paid in the ESB. It had in fact no other basis than that it was the scale in existence at the time in a large number of the other clerical employments. It infuriated the associations and unions concerned, but the line was in fact held, although the report itself was quickly dismissed as being of little account, and even the Labour Court (two of whose members were on the five-man tribunal) were reluctant to give it any particular status.

The report was important, however, since it attempted to deal with the comparability question: the tendency in Ireland to build an edifice of relativities so that if one employment moves there is virtually a total shift. In the case of the wage earner, the electricians dominated these shifts as the lead group for much of the decade,[13] and the salaried employments were dominated by the ESB clerk (highlighting once again the extraordinary significance of the ESB as an employment). The edifice of comparabilities itself was never seriously questioned (we shall discuss this phenomenon in a later chapter), and consequently it was within these unquestioned constraints that the tribunal attempted to find a means by which automatic escalation could be avoided, the continuous ever-mounting curve which came from differently perceived relativities. They spoke of the lack of order in adjusting clerical pay—". . . a serious force making for instability in the economy"[14]—but they were in fact concerned not with order—the whole edifice was very orderly and predictable—but with control, and particularly with control of the lead group who, manifestly, were the ESB clerks. But the clerks could claim that all they had got had been negotiated in an orderly way without dispute, and

[12]*Quinn Report.*
[13]C. Mulvey and J. Trevithick, 'Wage Inflation and Wage Leadership in Ireland 1954–1969' in A. A. Tait and J. A. Bristow (eds.), *Ireland: Some Problems of a Developing Economy* (Gill and Macmillan, Dublin, 1972).
[14]*Quinn Report,* p. 12.

this could be said also of all the other clerical grades. The tribunal therefore turned to the various councils, tribunals and arbitration boards. They first considered some common value system which all these could follow. At the time, many held a rather simplistic view of the possibilities of job evaluation, seeing in it a system of objective criteria, manifestly logical, which, if accepted, would resolve our problems. The tribunal sought the assistance of the British Civil Service Pay Research Unit, who did a quick survey of key clerical jobs. It was this that caused the tribunal to conclude that the work of the recruitment clerical grades in the public sector was broadly comparable; however the important point was that in regard to job evaluation itself:

> . . . such systems are designed primarily to assist in the determination of internal relativities, and depend upon subjectively determined codes of values, which have no relevance outside the organisation for which they are designed. We are satisfied that there are no absolute standards which could be reliably applied.[15]

While job evaluation has continued to be of great importance within certain employments, its limits were recognised more clearly from this point onwards.

Since there was no solution in a common system of job values, the tribunal, responding to the government's original thinking, swung the other way, and in their final recommendation tried, as we have seen, to drive through the edifice the shaft of a single scale for all the recruitment grades; but this was far too crude a solution. In a minority report, I recommended a vast procedural arrangement by which the common scale (which as a member of the tribunal I accepted in principle) could be negotiated by all the unions and all the employers concerned; but of course the answer did not lie here at all, but in the breaking up of the whole edifice by removing the relativity struts and sinking each grade, as much as possible, in the uniqueness of its own employment.

The tribunal was most concerned at the impact all this activity was making on the manual workers:

> In the immediate post-war period, there was a general tendency for rates in lower-paid employments to increase more rapidly than those in the higher paid because of the application of flat rate increases and tapering percentage additions during wage rounds. In recent years, however, this process of improvement in the earnings of manual

[15]ibid., pp. 22-3.

workers relative to clerical employees has been reversed. The social implications involved in this widening gap between clerical and manual workers' remuneration lie outside the consideration of this tribunal. But the growing disparity is directly relevant in other ways, apart from the aspect of social justice . . . An improvement in the relative position of one section of the community can only be achieved by a diversion to that section of a larger than average share of the increases in the national product. Such disparity is bound to create dissatisfaction among groups who find themselves left behind in the process.[16]

But even before the report was published, there was growing trouble in the ESB because of the increase for the clerks. The draughtsmen were first in the field in an effort to try to retain equality; they were in dispute in February 1966. The government promptly requested that all future ESB claims should be referred, not to their tribunals, but to the Labour Court, announcing their intention of disestablishing the tribunals (which required legislation), and in this way hobbling the initiative of the ESB employees. The ETU (I) had, for some considerable period, a claim before the Board for the grading of electricians in the same way as clerks. They were now under very great pressure, particularly from one of the informal groups that characterised ESB affairs, the Electricians' Association, who declared their intention to strike, but the ETU (I) took a firm line with them, and managed to relieve pressure by negotiating a system of proficiency payments in addition to normal rates, without prejudice to their claim for grading.

Now, however, the ESB fitters (largely organised by the AEU) became the critical group in the dispute that followed, because not only were other grades moving ahead, but the fitters themselves had not even kept abreast with the down-town rate. "In the mechanical fitters' strike of 1966," said the Fogarty Report,[17]

> the ESB does not seem to have appreciated the extent of its fitters' grievance arising out of the discrepancy between actual earnings in the ESB and those offered by good employers outside, as apart, that is, from downtown rates of pay, by reference to which fitters' pay in the ESB was established.

The fitters demanded the same scale as the clerks and, although the Board was prepared to make concessions, they resisted this. By the end of May

[16] *Quinn Report,* p. 13.
[17] *Fogarty Final Report,* p. 16.

there was a full-blown dispute with the Board. For a considerable period, although the fitters were on official strike, there was no picketing, or very little. Eventually, however, pickets were placed on all the ESB installations. The whole country was thrown into a panic. The union leadership, equally disturbed, managed to secure a withdrawal of the pickets after three days, as the lights everywhere flickered and power died away. The government, in the meantime, had introduced the Electricity (Special Provisions) Act 1966, which made it an offence for ESB employees to go on strike in certain circumstances. By this time, however, the strikes had been resolved, although the act remained on the statute book, to be revived at any time by a decision of both houses of parliament. The fitters secured a good settlement—a substantial increase and a scale system of payment, but on this occasion, there was nothing for the semiskilled and unskilled, —very much in contrast with their success in 1961—and this was to provide the seeds of future industrial strife.

There seemed to be a slowing-down on the part of the unions at this point, particularly in regard to the semiskilled and unskilled employees of the Board. The ETU (I) made some further advances for electricians during 1967 re-establishing differentials; and of course there was much concern among all the unions that the Electricity (Special Provisions) Act should be repealed. Congress very promptly in August 1966 had met the newly-appointed Minister for Labour, Dr Hillery; they thought that the act was hastily drafted, and that to legislate that men should work against their will was both woefully impractical and highly provocative. The Minister benignly claimed that he wished merely to avoid strikes in the ESB, and a joint working party settled down to examine the problem; but the act was not repealed and in 1968 would be called into operation. The unions also began negotiating a comprehensive agreement with the Board, but time dragged on, increases were common throughout industry, and the unskilled and semiskilled ESB workers were becoming more and more aggrieved. This period marks the rise of the Day Workers Association, an unofficial group of semiskilled and unskilled workers employed in the vulnerable generating stations, and often consisting of the unskilled workers who had continued in employment when the initial building of the stations had been completed. A previous group in 1963, the Linesmen's Association, had been pathfinders in this type of ginger group and joined the Amalgamated Transport eventually as a body, retaining their identity within the union—as the Day Workers were to do as well. At this point, however, the Day Workers Association was quite unofficial. Although negotiations were taking place on a comprehensive agreement, the members of the association, in frustration and despair, withdrew their labour, and mounted pickets.

This was most embarrassing for Congress, particularly as they hoped for a withdrawal of the offending legislation as part of the agreement then under negotiation. On the day before the strike was due to commence, they issued a statement during which they said:

> It may appear to many workers that an unofficial strike will strengthen the negotiating position of the unions in respect of present claims. In fact it will have exactly the opposite effect. The unofficial action taken to bring about a strike in the ESB in effect is a repudiation of the unions who are engaged in negotiation on the claim. The effect of the threatened unofficial strike action can only be to weaken the trade union side, and inhibit their ability to negotiate a satisfactory settlement.[18]

Congress pointed out that the Labour Court was to hear the case on 1 April, that is to say, the following week. The workers, however, went ahead with their strike, and Congress, nonplussed at this unofficial action, had to try to mediate between the government and the unofficial strikers, in order to get the dispute back on the rails.

Merrigan of the Amalgamated Transport[19] was later to claim:

> Absolute and continuing procrastination on the part of the Board of the ESB has created a situation where the initiative is passed officially from the unions into the hands of the unofficial organisations in the ESB, because, let us be quite clear about it, the unions officially are loth to take on the Government and the Board of the ESB in the presence of this Act on the Statute Book.

But the Fogarty Report[20] takes a harsher view of the unions' performance, saying that these workers' claim for special recognition was left lying for many months and it dismissed the argument (perhaps unwisely) that the unions were trying to deal with the claim as part of a general settlement; it appeared to take the view that the claim should have been given a run for its money despite the wider plans for a comprehensive agreement. But, in particular, it pointed to the complacent unions and the hostile membership and it quoted one member as saying: "We are not dissatisfied with the unions; we are bloody well disgusted."

The strike commenced on Tuesday, 26 March. The ESB asked industry to conserve power, and a number of firms actually closed down. The

---
[18]Irish Congress of Trade Unions, *Tenth Annual Report* 1968, p. 93.
[19]ibid., p. 297.
[20]*Fogarty Final Report,* pp. 16, 17.

government made an order under the Electricity (Special Provisions) Act, activating its provisions, and a number of workers on picket duty were brought before the courts. Fines were imposed for illegal picketing, and when the men stated that they were not prepared to pay the fines, they were committed to prison. Again there was a full-blown power crisis, which, in the words of Congress[21] resulted ". . . in a growing paralysis of the national power and light sources, the throwing of hundreds of thousands of workers out of employment, and the jailing of workers..."

Here then the power of the picket was demonstrated: the strike was unofficial and the pickets absolutely unauthorised, but they were widely supported, and the effect on power supplies was devastating. There were two perilous aspects to it: in the first place, because the strike was unofficial, it was extremely difficult to get under control; but the second aspect was even more alarming, because the jailing of the men gave the dispute wider implications. Congress, in fact, feared that there might be a general movement of workers springing from this, a general revolt, a *contestation*, such as was experienced in France some months later, although in retrospect the fear appears to have been exaggerated. They stressed, therefore, that the crisis was not a political one involving a challenge to the government or the democratic organs of the state; it was a crisis of industrial relations and should be treated as such. They rejected penal legislation but they emphasised that legislation was not the main issue.

> The first and primary duty of all is to get normal working restored in the ESB, the country's power and light resources safeguarded, and the thousands of disemployed workers back to their jobs. Lest it be suggested that the natural sympathy invoked by the jailing of workers arising out of an industrial dispute be reflected by official action by trade unions to add to the number of workers already thrown idle by the crisis, it should be realised that any additions to the total now out of work will not contribute in the slightest to the ending of the fines and imprisonment, and still less to ending the stoppage of work in the ESB.[22]

The object of Congress was to secure a return to work, speedy negotiations on the issues involved, and a commission of inquiry into the ESB in order to root out the cause of the continuous unrest. As a first and immediate step, they asked that no more men should be imprisoned and

[21] Irish Congress of Trade Unions, *Tenth Annual Report* 1968, pp. 93, 94.
[22] ibid., p. 94.

those already imprisoned should be released. But when they met the Minister for Labour, this last request—because of the independence of the Courts and the respect which they demanded—ran the discussions into deadlock. The ESB themselves resolved the problem by paying the fines and thereby securing the release of the imprisoned men. Just after midnight on Saturday, 30 March, both the unions and also the unofficial leadership—which was known as the National Strike Committee—recommended a return to work, which was accepted; and on the following Monday, the group of unions proceeded with the presentation of the case before the Labour Court, with, as it turned out, considerable success.

It was against that background that the Minister for Labour, on the 11 April, appointed a committee of enquiry into industrial relations in the ESB under the chairmanship of Professor Michael P. Fogarty, then director of the Economic and Social Research Institute.

II

In a very short time, indeed by early July, the Fogarty Committee issued its first report.[23] This may have been a preliminary run over the field but it was a very comprehensive statement of the thinking of the committee, based on what they described as a mass of evidence. The object was to publish the proposals widely, discuss them with the parties directly concerned, press for their implementation, and thereafter issue a final report. It was a very interesting variation of the idea which was unsuccessfully attempted by Tavistock in the case of the Dublin busmen. While the dynamic for change in the case of the busmen was the prospect of eventual publication, the public themselves were unaware that they would be involved as monitors of change; here, however, the public were involved right from the outset, with the promise of a later report on how the parties responded, giving much more point to the prospect of public review than the Tavistock proposal did. No doubt the committee also wished to demonstrate that this was not just a whitewashing job, as many of the ESB workers believed. By March 1969, the committee issued its final report,[24] a much more comprehensive document, vastly more impatient than the first, and inevitably, after further extensive discussions and inquiries, containing a number of significant changes; but the thrust of the committee's thinking remained the same. These two reports, the Interim and the Final report, but in particular the latter, are by far the most important documents we have on industrial relations in Ireland,

[23]*Interim Report of the Committee on Industrial Relations in the Electricity Supply Board* (Stationery Office, Dublin, 1968).
[24]*Final Report of the Committee on Industrial Relations in the Electricity Supply Board* (Stationery Office, Dublin, 1969).

since inevitably the questions they raise have an import far wider than the ESB. Furthermore, not only was the chairman, Professor Fogarty, of considerable standing, but the three-man committee included P. D. McCarthy, who was the chief adviser to the Minister for Labour on industrial relations, and a major influence on government policy.

Apart from introductory material, both reports fall readily into four divisions: the ESB tribunals and the Labour Court, employee representation, management changes, and pay determination. There were also some follow-up suggestions. The order in which these proposals were taken changed significantly, as we shall see, in the Final Report, and in this matter it is the Final Report that we follow. But before dealing with these four topics, it is necessary to recognise how impatient and hard-nosed the committee had become in its Final Report:

> There is a tendency on the side of both the unions and the ESB to blame everyone but themselves for anything that may have gone wrong and to give the impression that they are waiting for Godot (usually resembling the Government) to solve their problems for them . . . We had hoped to get them out of their defensive corners into a serious consideration of the ways in which each party's efforts had hitherto fallen short and what more each could do to improve its own contribution towards the results which the country expects; not simply waiting for and blaming others. We do not think that their reactions to our Interim Report show in these respects enough either of sincere repentance or of a firm purpose of amendment, and now, therefore, feel it necessary to speak more plainly to them than we at first wished.[25]

The Interim Report, with a nod to history and changing times, recommended that there should be only one voluntary tribunal instead of the two statutory ones, with their concepts of class division; in this, they followed the Gleeson Report. But the Final Report went further, recommending the abolition of the domestic tribunals altogether, and giving the parties recourse to the Labour Court in the ordinary way. The reasons for the change are not very convincing and some union officials were hostile to what they considered to be the influence of government thinking on the committee, for the fact was that the Labour Court was considered to be unsympathetic to the ambitions of the ESB grades, particularly to the salaried groups. The unions were not opposed to change as such, merely to the Labour Court, and although they subsequently campaigned for the retention of the statutory tribunals, they

[25] *Final Report,* op. cit., p. 18.

in fact were glad to agree to a voluntary tribunal (an industrial council) in 1971. If the truth were told, they much preferred it to the statutory tribunals for two reasons: firstly, of the two employee representatives, one would be nominated by the unions, thereby giving them a voice in the selection of the independent chairman; and secondly, the other employee representative, although elected, would have to be a member of the staff or a union official. This effectively excluded such persons as Christle, whose successful demagoguery we have already noted, and who later attempted, with no success, himself to call a strike in favour of the *status quo*. The Labour Court had always some ill-defined appellate role and this continued.

The second topic is employee representation. The committee saw a most inadequate trade union structure: patchy, astonishingly lacking in coordination, complacent and resistant to change, acting with some effectiveness perhaps at national level, but very sketchy at station and district level. The gentle nudging of the first report had no effect. "With the exception of a move in one union to provide itself with one additional staff member, the response to these suggestions has so far as we know been equivalent to nil."[26] And in their Final Report, they remarked that inefficiency and fragmentation was perceived as strongly by the rank and file members as by the ESB, so much so that

> ... one union representative claimed to us that there seemed to be a conspiracy between the rank and file (whether or not organised into unofficial associations) and the ESB to denigrate the unions and their full-time officers. We have found no signs of such a conspiracy, but plenty of signs that the unions do indeed have a long way to go to win the full confidence whether of those with whom they negotiate or of the members they represent.[27]

The answer, however, did not lie primarily in legislation, and they recommended the repeal of the Electricity (Special Provisions) Act of 1966. When arrangements had been freely concluded, a case might be made for giving them the force of law. "But the actual arrangements to be made, and in particular any that might in future be given legal force, should come out of free agreements between the parties themselves, not be imposed by compulsion from outside."[28] They were also aware of the character of a trade union, of the growing demand for participation, on the one hand, and on the other, the impossibility of strait-jacketing

[26] ibid., p. 18.
[27] ibid., p. 28.
[28] ibid., p. 39.

members in union officialdom. The answer, therefore, lay in that kind of major structural reform which would capture the willing support of the majority of the employees of the Board. Here then was a considerable change of emphasis from external legislation to internal trade union reform (prompted, and perhaps on occasion bargained for, by the employer). And the fact that P. D. McCarthy of the Department of Labour was a party to all this, marked a significant development in official thinking.

Before considering their far-reaching proposals for reform, let us remark on one assumption underlying all the committee's thinking: the essential rightness of the ordinary members. It is evident in their impatience with the unions for not processing a claim, when perhaps the reason was that the union believed that its wider policies should prevail; but, in particular, it is evident in the assumption that when members are impatient and angry with officials, it is always the officials that are at fault. In a period of vehemence and upheaval, such as the sixties, men and women often panic into anger, no matter how much information and explanation may be available, and it is as well to recognise this and to hold on to the halyard until the surge washes over. Approval by members should be the settled position in a democracy, not necessarily the condition of affairs at every particular moment; otherwise, democracy as a state itself becomes impossible. Let us be clear, however: all this in no way lessens the criticisms of the unions put forward by the committee, nor does it diminish in any way their explicit proposals for reform.

The committee recommended that each category of the ESB employees should be represented by one "most representative" union or association, and, in all, there should be no more than four groups of unions or associations engaged in negotiation. At local level, where things were most unsatisfactory, they proposed that in each station or district there should be established not only joint union committees but, following the German model, works committees as well. The two would be linked by the identity of their personnel, and in this way the dread of both Irish and British unions of the continental dragon of employer-ridden works committees could be avoided. They then recommended a national advisory council with ten representatives nominated by the national trade union groups, but with up to sixty representatives elected by the works committees at district and station level; and here indeed was the point in the whole restructuring, since its effect would be the absorbing of the trade union representation, even the overwhelming of it; but it would not be bypassed. Furthermore, not only would the national advisory council nominate representatives to an internal conciliation committee, but it would also nominate worker representatives to be members of the board of the ESB, and, in this way, the committee raised the whole question of worker participation in the management of industry.

The proposals on industrial democracy in the First Report were more exciting and self-confident. They were placed right at the beginning, but in the discussions that followed, they fell very much into a supplementary position. They began by contemplating a supervisory board and an executive board on the German model; they ended as an extension of the existing board, under whom there would be a managing director with an executive team. But the substance of the idea undoubtedly remained, probably because of the powerful advocacy of Fogarty himself. The trade unions could not very well resist it (indeed in principle it was warmly welcomed); and neither could the ESB, as a publicly owned undertaking; but there was at the time, and there still is, a marked lack of enthusiasm for its practical implementation, and many believe that while the proposal itself had virtue, it was irrelevant to the problems in the ESB. As for management, they seemed to live in a mist of mutual distrust.

> One of the puzzling features of this inquiry has been to get at the real reasons behind the honestly felt, but not always clearly explained distrust of the ESB's present higher management which we have found at lower and middle levels of the ESB's own management as well as on the union's side.[29]

This, however, is puzzling only if it is exceptional and there is much to indicate that it was a marked characteristic of much of Irish society, and existed between trade union officials and their members as well—even when the unions were more efficiently structured than was the case in the ESB. There were many domestic matters to be put right: the need for long term planning, the discouraging of the Board from engaging in day-to-day administration and the appointing of a managing director; and the committee wished to see personal leadership strengthened, the status of the personnel department raised, and some means provided by which the industrial relations temperature could be taken from time to time. In their follow-up proposals, they recommended a development unit for forward planning in personnel matters and in industrial relations, and also a system of outside audits of its industrial relations every three to five years—a social audit as it were, to parallel the financial one—the substance of the report being available to the unions and the government as well as to the ESB. But in the course of the report the committee gave

[29] ibid., p. 58.

a fascinating insight into a negative and authoritarian system of management which, in Irish circumstances, is by no means unique.

In their First Report, they did what they later described as some coat-trailing and conveyed the impression that middle and senior management were friendly and technically competent but weak; and in a somewhat avuncular way, they urged middle management to speak up before their superiors, since failure to do so could be a form of disloyalty. Middle management was stung to reply and from this it appeared that the ESB discouraged regular meetings between managers, even experienced ones of long service. And the committee quoted from a statement made to them by the district managers themselves: "Not alone is there no positive encouragement, but there is a long standing rule that no more than two district managers can meet for consultation without the Board's specific approval."[30] The manager as a result felt himself physically and socially isolated. But if horizontal communication was forbidden, vertical communication was impossibly inadequate:

> We have met frequently a feeling at middle level in the ESB that a proposal disappears up the line into a cloud of unknowing and re-merges, if at all, with a memorandum saying that an impersonal entity known as the Board, has turned it down.[31]

But could it all have been so grotesquely wrong? Let us pause here and recognise another possibility; that the system was conceived for more stable times when a manager had importance within the society, essentially because of the steadiness of the structure, because of the rule of law—not because of his personal relationship with a group of men in Dublin who were the Board; and it was only when the whirl of events defeated the clarity of the rule, that the men in Dublin became important; and the manager who once had a dignity and a freedom within the rule, now tended to find himself a client, a dependant on others. It is difficult to judge to what extent this was the case in the ESB, but we shall find it with bank managers, and especially with school managers, in a later chapter.

Finally, there is pay determination. Pay determination in the ESB is significant because, to many, it was the great trend-setter, spinning inflationary cycles into the economy, particularly in the clerical field, and encompassing within its system the tensions between the clerical and the manual workers that pushed up the latter's rates as well, not only in the ESB but right throughout the economy. It was because of this trend-

[30] ibid., p. 68.
[31] ibid., p. 69.

setting, that the government tried to damp back ESB ambitions in the matter of pay, and decided as well to disestablish its domestic tribunals; it was one of the reasons why the Gleeson Commission urged that the craftsmen should follow the down-town rate; it was the reason why the Quinn Tribunal urged one salary scale arbitrarily determined for all public service clerical grades; it was the reason why the FUE suggested to Fogarty a central board of conciliation and arbitration to determine pay right across the range of state-sponsored industry.

But this kind of trend-setting is only possible in a system which gives great dominance to the notion of comparabilities. We have already noted,[32] not only its dominance, but that during the sixties the system itself was never seriously questioned by government, by employers or by the trade unions, although the ESB occasionally expressed resentment at being cast in the lead role. All the attempts to overcome the problem were in terms of the comparability concept; they did not challenge it. But an outside observer, Professor Albert A. Blum,[33] was much struck by it as late as 1971:

> Comparability is a technique which has its place in any labour movement. Most unions use this tactic as a factor in their settlements, but, than is typical elsewhere, the Irish labour movement focuses on it as the key to wage settlements. Other factors, such as cost of living, productivity, profits and all the host of other criteria that would normally go into determining what would be a fair wage demand, or at least a rationalisation for a wage demand, are rarely expressed in collective bargaining. This is partly the result of how small Ireland is, and the fact that most Irish workers may know what other Irish workers are earning elsewhere. It is also the result of lack of research staff in the Irish labour movement, which makes the kind of sophisticated arguments necessary to support such terms as productivity increases, and cost of living increases, difficult to develop. Comparability is an easy argument to make.... Indeed it seems to be that the over-emphasis on wages and collective bargaining in Ireland, and the over-emphasis on comparability has weakened the labour movement's ability to deal with other issues that are important in the industrial relations sphere.

Actually the solution does not lie, as Blum suggests, with other criteria as much as with job evaluation and job redesign, but the substance of the point is well made.

[32] p. 110 above.
[33] Albert A. Blum, 'Strikes, Salaries and the Search for Solutions' in *Liberty Magazine,* Dublin, 1971, and *British Journal of Industrial Relations,* March 1972.

It is because the construct of comparabilities was so tightly gripped together that the ESB movements had such significance, but the Fogarty Committee does not discuss this problem at any great length, principally because they do not appear to regard the ESB as a trend-setter at all. They made this point in the Interim Report where they claim the authority of the FUE, emphasising the point once again in the Final Report:[34]

> We repeat the point made in our Interim Report, which we based notably on material supplied by the Federated Union of Employers, that the ESB and the unions with which it negotiates have not as a matter of fact been conspicuous in setting headlines. Some of the cases in which they are widely believed to have done so suggest, when examined closely, lessons rather different from those often drawn from them.

This is quite astonishing in the light of all that had taken place; and the points the committee used to support their view are singularly unconvincing: it is no answer, for example, to say that the ESB tribunal, not the Board itself, awarded the increase. But the difficulty probably lay in trying to evaluate such matters. One cannot take necessarily the order of time in the settlements; the ESB clerks, for example, were the key trend-setters in 1959, although the assurance clerks settled before them. Some wage settlements seem, by way of common consent, to have great significance; a judgment that such is the case must be almost always a subjective one; and, consequently, the anxieties of all parties with regard to settlements in the ESB provide our surest guide. But in other parts of the Final Report the committee appears to be taking a different view. For example, in a later paragraph,[35] they balance the cost of an expensive wage headline, set for the whole country by the ESB, against the cost of a strike; and I am personally satisfied that, despite their disavowals, they were greatly influenced by the trend-setting characteristics of the ESB when they recommended that the domestic tribunals should be abolished and claims referred to the Labour Court. Nonetheless, even if the comparability issue is not pointed up, the committee's discussion on wage determination is of the first importance, and in the course of it, they find their way through to a solution of the comparability issue as well.

There had been in the past much lecturing by the government to the ESB on its responsibility in fostering a proper policy regarding incomes, which the ESB in turn used to resist wage and salary claims. But the

[34] *Final Report*, p. 85.
[35] ibid., p. 90.

committee was of the view that while the ESB must of course take policy into account, it had no greater obligation in regard to it than anyone else. It was in this context that the committee denied that the ESB was a trend-setter, and of course it is clear that, at that point, such a view was necessary to the logic of its position. But the fact was that the ESB was not the same as everyone else, and the solution lay in making it so, that is to say in the breaking up of its role as a trend-setter, not in denying that it existed.

Nor in a business so technologically advanced and innovatory as the ESB was it proper that it should tie itself to a down-town rate; and the committee was particularly caustic at the idea of adopting some mechanically determined salary scale or wage rate and attempting, as a result, to dodge the whole bargaining process. And what of a large public service negotiating unit which was recommended by the FUE and indeed which I had recommended myself at an earlier stage? "In our Interim Report," said the committee,[36]

> we rejected a proposal for a grand national consolidated negotiation fixing pay and conditions right across the board of the semi-State enterprises and the State itself. We stand by this, for that proposal as it first reached us (it has since been modified) was consistent neither with management efficiency nor with good industrial relations.

For wage rates and conditions are primarily the responsibility of the employer himself, not somebody else's, and the solution therefore lay, in the view of the committee, in getting matters right internally in the ESB first: clearing up, particularly in the manual grades, the chaos of relativities, breaking down the barriers between wage and salary grades in the ESB, and engaging in an expert programme of job evaluation. And if the clerical workers were recruited for higher work, as was claimed, then their jobs should be redesigned. This then was the key: a programme of job clarification, job evaluation and eventually job redesign, the last inevitable, as the plus rates demanded for more flexible working became inordinately expensive. But all this was the key as well to the comparability issue which depended on the ability of others to make a clear, unquestioned comparison between themselves and the appropriate ESB grades. A programme of job redesign, aimed at meeting the internal needs of the organisation itself, defeats the comparability argument, because the relationship with others becomes obscured.

[36]ibid., p. 87.

And what of the bogey of strikes and pickets? The committee found the observance of pickets by such vast numbers both mysterious and alarming. (Its mystery, of course, is somewhat lessened when one remembers that the unskilled grades who observed the electricians' pickets in 1961 did very well, and their disappointment in not advancing in 1966 was the root cause of the mass movement which led to the unofficial breakdown of 1968). The committee thought that a peace clause could be introduced for a stated period, but they abandoned in their Final Report a rather dangerous suggestion that it might have a money value. The national wage agreements of 1970 and 1972 show an interesting development in regard to such peace pledges. But in any event – and this was the committee's really significant contribution – they were quite hardheaded regarding the alternative: one should accept that in the ordinary business of industrial relations, strikes could well occur in the ESB as everywhere else, and if one ran immediately to the law, not only was this solution ineffective but the position could arguably be worse. Neither should it be necessary to buy off the dispute with a high settlement:

We reject the thesis, which we suspect is too widely spread in the ESB, that electricity supply must be maintained at all costs. In certain circumstances the cost of maintaining it could be far higher than the cost of an interruption.

This view was to be of the greatest importance. In the past, the panic-stricken speed at which the government intervened, either in ministerial conciliation or by legislation, led workers to believe that a dispute in the ESB would be mercifully short and remarkably fruitful; everything up to then supported this view, and contributed greatly to the ESB's difficulties.

III

The committee had every right to hope for some general response to the many perceptive and highly important concepts it had put forward in the matter of industrial relations in Ireland; the public, however, even the experienced and concerned public, remained inert. The government, for its part, probably through the influence of P. D. McCarthy, acted from that time onwards in conformity with the ideas in the report, changing the emphasis in their legislative programme, and in particular, refusing point-blank to intervene in the perilous breakdown of 1972. But the reports were directed in particular to the management and board of the ESB and to the unions with members employed there; and here there was a considerable contrast in the response, the board launching on a far-reaching programme of reform, but the unions demonstrating a considerable reluctance and even the kind of sullen hostility one feels when one is despairingly confronted with somebody who is vastly articulate and forceful but not always right.[37]

The committee appreciated, of course, that the unions are conservative bodies, difficult to change, but it was obviously somewhat shocked at the trade union structure in the ESB, the jabbing away at the centre, the lack of involvement outside Dublin, the sketchy, inadequate and unsupported way the group operated. Its programme of reform was shrewd and far-sighted and deserved to succeed. It proposed the strengthening of the unions, it proposed the strengthening of the group, but it proposed as well such a development of the democratic system of representation through works committees, trade union committees and the rest that the unions would be enlivened and greatly enriched, whether they wished it or not. The committee had hopes that the Irish Congress of Trade Unions would take the initiative in getting reform under way, but that body initially was blandly non-committal, conscious no doubt of the reluctance of the unions.

Eventually, in 1971, the president of Congress at the time, Maurice Cosgrave[38] (who was to show great personal initiative in many matters), invited the ESB unions to come together under his chairmanship with the object, at the very least, of getting agreement on the appointment of a wholetime secretary to the negotiating group. The suggestion was that such a secretary should serve only the officials and never the members, but even this careful recognition of union impregnability ran into heavy weather, particularly with the Amalgamated Transport and General Workers Union. This union had responded to the committee's proposals by offering group membership to the unofficial Day Workers Association, who joined on a ballot just as the linesmen did at an earlier stage, and the Amalgamated Transport in the circumstances saw no reason why it should not negotiate directly with the Board in respect of a category of which they had the overwhelming membership, solving the group problem, as far as the Day Workers were concerned, by making it irrelevant. Furthermore, they saw this development as the pattern for the future, and consequently had little enthusiasm for strengthening the group. Naturally the group did not take kindly to this, but to some outside observers it represented at least one solution, particularly when the Amalgamated Transport managed to shrug off the overwhelming dominance of Dublin members on their executive, a problem which

---

[37]The evaluation which follows, written in 1972, does not take events beyond that point, nor for the purposes of the argument is it necessary to do so.

[38]Maurice Cosgrave in 1973 was appointed deputy chairman of the Labour Court.

continued to dog the electrical and engineering craft unions. Discussions in such circumstances were protracted and testy, and it might have been wiser if Congress had take a deep breath and plunged for discussion on the far more radical issue of a broadly based national advisory council and board representatives. It would at least have shifted the debate out of an area which had become dankly domestic.

The difficulties, however, should not be underestimated. Some officials considered that the Fogarty Committee was plain wrong about communication, claiming that they visited the generating stations regularly and knew their local representatives well; to them, complaining about communication was a classic response given by all trade union members no matter how well served, and its significance should not be exaggerated. Most officials, however, would be prepared to concede that there was a great deal of truth in the Fogarty analysis; but the fact of the matter was that they saw the committee's proposals – and even the ICTU suggestion – as a threat to the existence of the unions. Almost all the unions were vulnerable to a loss of members to other unions or to new groupings. The idea of a full-time secretary to the group – who would deal directly with the employees – was therefore resisted, since the unions would be displaced; and even if they were not, it would not be at all clear why members should continue to pay them contributions. *A fortiori*, the committee's proposal of a parliament with a minority position for the unions was regarded with much hostility. "Unions," remarked one official, "will destroy what they can't control." "But", he added, no doubt thinking of the unofficial associations, "the vacuum will be filled."

And the vacuum, indeed, could be filled readily enough because of the significance in all this of the local union representative, the local shop steward, on whose personal loyalty depended very frequently the existence of a particular union in a particular station. The employees tended to follow, not the union, but their local representative (who was seen, not so much as a leader, as an advocate and adviser); and the Fogarty Committee remarked on how such a representative, disciplined by one union, could reappear with all his members in another. His considerable influence could well be a consequence of what Tavistock identified as the privatisation of the workers; and as far as the ESB was concerned, the Fogarty Committee noted also not merely a demand for more participation and better service, but "....what appears to us to be a decline in general union solidarity, leading to greater readiness by sections and groups to pursue their own interests irrespective of general union policy. Slowness on the unions' part," they continued, to develop the policies and structures needed in these new conditions has contributed not only to the growth of unofficial associations but to the danger that the potential of these associations will be diverted from constructive to destructive purposes.[39]

But the unions' approach was to attempt to secure and retain the loyalty and support of the local representative, and in this the Amalgamated Transport had some success. There are a number of union officials who hold that a union can operate only on the basis of deliberately cultivated support, that a passive membership is mildly hostile, and that once claims are handled in a reasonable way, the cultivation of the personal support of local representatives is more significant in union strength than improved communications and sophisticated services; in other words, a local representative whose attitude to the union is one of support and trust, is of much more significance in the paying of contributions (and particularly in their increase) than the promise of weekly bulletins and the most perceptive of statistics. But the only way in which this support could be secured on a permanent and healthy basis was by some structure such as that suggested by the committee; officials who try to attract restless members on a personal basis are tempted to display a greater militancy than is either appropriate or safe. Such a development may not have been unconnected with the shift workers' strike in 1972. All in all, therefore, the unions drifted away from the committee's reports, since from the outset they clearly had no intention of giving effect to its proposals for trade union reorganisation.

In contrast to this, the ESB management pushed ahead with a comprehensive policy of reform. The key change was the appointment of a director of personnel with adequate staff and prestige along the lines indicated by the Fogarty Committee. (Interestingly, the men staffing the new personnel department seem on the whole to be promoted from within, not persons brought in from outside the Board.) Within a short few years, by late 1971 when the management confronted the unions with their programme for reform, the whole approach to personnel matters had undergone a considerable change. They expected more disputes before the rush of problems of the sixties worked themselves out, but their strategies were clearer and their morale was high. They could now joke about 'the disease of comparative deprivation,' by which they meant that workers are satisfied until they see another group do better – a principle, however, which reflected their commitment to a continuous system of job evaluation; and there was no dodging of responsibility in

[39]Op. cit., p. 31.

the 'law' which ran: "The climate of industrial relations in a firm is conditioned by the quality and style of management more than by any other factor." And finally they had 'Finnan's law': "A group will optimise the conditions of employment available to them to the benefit of the group," which leads them to expect that a shift worker, for example, is more likely to go sick on night duty than on day duty, because his replacement gets double time, a bonus which he may well share. What all this reveals of course is a hard-headed recognition of the realities of an industry employing 11,000 people. It is in marked contrast to the approach of the management in the past, which was not unlike that of a Hebrew prophet, groaning over his people.

They began to work towards a comprehensive agreement with the unions, to be introduced in April 1973, which reflected much of the Fogarty thinking. They set as an objective the idea of a single status, a common structure of basic conditions for all staff, eliminating the differences between wage and salary earners; they proposed a system of continuous job evaluation in which they sought to relate pay to the job done, not to criteria which sprang from structure or status, and they in turn sought as a *quid pro quo* the abandoning of restrictive practices, demarcation limits and other impediments to productivity, which, as we saw earlier, quickly enlarged the idea from one of job evaluation for pay purposes into the business of job redesign. And they sought as well a joint commitment to the maintenance of electricity supply at all times. All this was presented in an imaginative way to the unions – and to the employees generally. While they sought by agreement the improvement of trade union procedures, they set out in the meantime to do their utmost to involve all those employed by the Board, as far as they could do so, in the proposals for change. They suggested to the unions a joint working party to visit all the local stations and districts in order to talk to the workers about the way things were handled and about their expectations. They hoped that if there was revealed a large groundswell of opinion in favour of reform, then the reluctance to change might be overcome.

But what was particularly marked was their changed attitude towards strikes, an attitude so clearly articulated by the Fogarty Committee. They accepted fully that, in the past, management tended to panic in the face of a threat of strike, and highly excited government intervention made matters worse. The unions, and more particularly the unofficial groupings, achieved success by threats of stoppages; they probably never faced up fully to the consequence of their actions since everything encouraged them to believe that someone would pull them back from the brink; that indeed in order to win, one should go headlong for the brink, relying on someone else to rescue one in time. In the view of the ESB management, the only way to overcome brinkmanship of this kind was to allow the worst to happen; if they were not prepared to contemplate the complete shutdown of their business, then they were not in bargaining but in blackmail. The effects of this change of policy were demonstrated in the disputes that followed.

We must bear in mind that in 1969 Ireland experienced in the maintenance dispute a strike which appeared to be cynical, self-seeking, widely destructive and overwhelmingly successful in that the employers capitulated completely. While the dispute shocked some people into a commitment for better procedures for the future, it also had the very contrary effect, encouraging certain groups within the trade union movement to emulate the maintenance workers at their worst; and inevitably some of this crept into the wide, fruitful employments of the ESB. There were two threatening groups in 1971 and 1972, apart from a moment of anxiety in the case of the professional engineers, some of whom were now represented by the Draughtsmen's and Allied Technicians' Association. The first of these groups was a small union of electricians, the Irish Electrical Technicians Association, which, although registered and with a negotiating licence, was in fact a remnant of the tedious and difficult amalgamation between the Irish Engineering, Industrial and Electrical Trade Union, and the National Engineering Union, a small minority who were so powerfully aggrieved that the amalgamation had taken place, that they challenged in the courts the whole creaky and antiquated procedure, the matter being eventually decided in favour of the amalgamating unions in the Supreme Court. Their dispute with the Board was essentially for the purpose of recognition, which the ESB quite properly refused to give them, holding to its prior agreements with the other unions. A number of crises occurred during which IETA placed pickets; they were observed to an extent; but the group of unions and Congress were unshakeable in their hostility, and although it was initially alarming, the threat petered out as support fell away.

A more dangerous threat arose, however, from an unofficial group known as the Shift Workers Association, made up of key workers – semi-skilled – in the generating stations, who, like the maintenance men, found themselves personally to be at a control point over the supply of electricity and who – without the aid of pickets – could by their own act of withdrawal disrupt the service. These men were originally recruited from the Day Workers, that is to say, the unskilled workers in the generating stations, and their work typically was that of boiler operators, bunker men and turbine attendants; although they sprang from what were described as unskilled grades, much of the work in the generating stations was of a reasonably skilful kind, rather in contrast to the more pick-and-shovel work of the unskilled grades in Dublin city. This contrast between the less skilled in Dublin and the higher skilled elsewhere added to the impatience which the men felt with the heavily Dublin-centred trade union administration. Unlike the Day Workers Association, however, which was a general grass-roots movement, the Shift Workers Association appears to have been a ginger group led from the top, perfectly content to cause a storm of pressure within the unions rather than form a separate organisation. Their approach was the calculated one of men who recognised the strength of their position and had decided to milk it; it was greatly in contrast to the broad general support given to the Day Workers movement, and in that respect it was easier to deal with.

The dispute concerned a reduction in the working week, and negotiations had been protracted. A recommendation by the ESB industrial council in March 1971 was rejected by the unions on a ballot, although firmly held to by the Board, and the Shift Workers Association quite independently declared that they would take strike action on 21 April 1971 in support of the claim. Although the whole thing was unofficial and the association had no standing, Maurice Cosgrave, the president of Congress, wisely took the initiative in calling a meeting between all the parties, at which the shift workers' representatives were also present in their capacity as representatives of the other recognised unions. A revised offer was made by the ESB which was accepted by all the parties concerned, a feature of which was a lump sum payment for a transitional period. The actual amount remained to be determined, but it was agreed that the industrial council's word on the matter would be final. But of course it was not, because when the amount became known, the Shift Workers Association declared that it was entirely inadequate; they therefore proposed to continue to work the longer hours, stating that if they were not paid overtime for these, they would be in dispute with the Board. In any event, the recommendation was rejected by ballot of all the members; the offer was further augmented by the Board, and in that form it was accepted by ballot in mid-October. But the shift workers were still aggrieved, and while accepting the new arrangement from 15 October (the date of the ballot), they now claimed overtime for the period from 1 October (the date of implementation of the new arrangement) until 15 October. The official trade unions would have nothing to do with this claim; neither of course would the Board; and the shift workers promptly threatened to strike and disrupt all electricity supplies. Here then was a tangle, a public service vulnerable to attack, a group of men bent on realising their ambitions, a trade union movement frustrated and helpless in its own lack of order, and an issue of great triviality, which threatened the power supplies of the whole nation, pointing up more than any other single factor the whole helpless muddle which the dispute had become.

The Minister for Labour was in a dilemma in view of the strictures on intervention by the Fogarty reports on the one hand, and the apparent helplessness of the unions on the other; yet because the threat was a very real one, he had to take some action. He decided to ask the Labour Court to investigate and report, and this they did by early December. The issue had now resolved itself into whether or not there had been a binding agreement between the unions and the ESB in April. The Shift Workers Association claimed that there had not, for some reasons connected with procedure; the unions most vigorously claimed that there had been, and said that it was of vital importance that agreements made in good faith should be observed. It is doubtful if this was the key question in the dispute, but at least it was one that could be dealt with; and the Labour Court did so by dumping the whole problem in the lap of Congress, on the grounds that they, by means of their appeals board, should decide whether or not a binding agreement had been reached in April and whether a claim for overtime should now be made. Perhaps it was the only thing that the Labour Court could do in the circumstances; and it may have been wise to identify the only group that could ultimately resolve the problem – the trade union movement itself. The appeals board, however, was hardly the appropriate means; the shift workers were unlikely to accept an unfavourable decision, and at best the board could only attempt conciliation.

In the meantime, the Shift Workers Association had broadened their claim to that of a new grading structure, quite apart from the general negotiations that were taking place, and since this could not be dealt with separately, they notified the ESB on 28 March 1972 that they intended to take strike action on 12 April. The final stage had been reached; the men were heading for the brink; they anticipated total disruption for a short period and then capitulation, and, in the view of some, carefully decided on the date of the strike so that they would have the additional payments arising from the long Easter weekend to tide them over. The government held firm, refusing to intervene; the ESB itself began to prepare for a major period of disruption, involving the public in its plans and giving the impression of being in control of the situation.

When the strike occurred on 12 April, it looked both highly dangerous and highly effective, and Congress issued a statement aimed at trying to isolate the unofficial strikers as much as possible:

> In the interests of the trade union movement and its members throughout the country who are suffering hardship and loss of employ-

ment as a result of the unofficial action of the members of the Shift Workers Association, the Irish Congress of Trade Unions calls on all workers in the employment of the ESB to cooperate in securing that the maximum possible amount of electricity is made available, and full output resumed as soon as possible.

However, this was not of great assistance, because even if the others passed the pickets and went to work, the vital work of the shiftworkers would remain undone, and consequently there would be disruption of power. The only solution was not merely for others to pass the shift workers' pickets but actually to do their work, normally the unforgiveable crime in industrial disputes.

On the morning of 13 April, the group and Congress representatives met at Congress headquarters. The purpose was merely to review the position, but one of their number, a member of DATA, told them that the Poolbeg station was closing down and that this would result in the collapse of the whole system. It is not clear that this in fact would have been the consequence, but the meeting was satisfied that they were confronted with a national crisis of the most serious kind, and there was an immediate decision that the engineers should be permitted to do the work of the striking shift workers. The discussion that followed was not on the question of principle but on the method by which it would be accomplished and the manner in which it would be communicated to the members. The DATA representatives insisted on behalf of their engineer members that they should be instructed to take over the shift workers' duties by the trade union movement, and that, far from being hindered, they should be supported in this by the members of the other unions. DATA, in the Irish scene, was a militant and rather radical union, and if engineers had not been members of such a union, if they had all been merely members of a professional association outside the trade union movement (as they had been for many years), it is not at all certain that such a decision could have been made. The instruction was given to the DATA members, and a further statement was issued by Congress and the group of unions:

> A meeting of ESB unions and Congress was held at Congress Headquarters this morning. In view of the imminent danger of a total breakdown of the electricity system and the grave emergency now facing the nation, the meeting unanimously agreed that all ESB workers must now take all steps necessary to secure the immediate restoration of power. Wherever shift workers are not at work prior to 4.00 p.m. other workers must be prepared to undertake the work

which the absent shift workers would have undertaken. The meeting also decided that the fullest support should be given to those ESB workers who have gone to their work and carried out loyally the instructions of their trade unions.

There was confusion for some time; but always there was some power which the ESB distributed on a planned basis. Gradually, however, matters righted themselves, until power was fully restored, and the shift workers, angrily stating that they would sever all connexions with the official unions and would establish a union of their own, eventually returned to work.

It is tempting to think that perhaps this last dispute marks the close of the long cycle, encompassing all the stresses and tensions which stemmed from the clerical workers in 1958 through the disputes of the electricians and the fitters, and ending in the demands for equality by the skilled and unskilled. Nineteen seventy-two found a government far wiser in what it should do about such disputes; it found a management far more progressive and confident, and it found a trade union movement, which, while still inchoate, was at least more assured in its principles. But the shift workers' dispute had no great general support, and it is not at all clear how things would have turned out if the same hardline approach were adopted in the case of a general movement of Day Workers.

How then can we evaluate all that took place? We must face the fact that neither the ESB management of the time nor the trade unions were in Irish conditions very unusual; indeed they represented fairly the general position, and when all things are considered, the ESB probably had no worse a strike record than any other; the difficulty was that their strikes took place in a climate of high drama. Furthermore, the problems which the ESB faced during the period were very great. The tensions within the ESB have been only too clear, between clerical and craft, and craft and unskilled, tensions made all the keener by the new attitudes of society generally, impatient with old snobberies; and we have seen too that because of its very vulnerability, the ESB may have been selected as the arena within which many of these tensions were worked out. But the ESB employees were restless because of other difficulties, difficulties of a kind only partially explicable in industrial relations terms, if at all. There were of course the difficulties encountered by everyone in the vast changes of the sixties, the wider educational opportunities, the challenging of set ideas, the new dimensions opened by television by which men created new relationships and new images of themselves in their society, and above all the greater expectations which expressed themselves so readily in claims for higher incomes. And all this had a special impact on the ESB, although the effect was more complex than at first appears.

As we have seen, the growth rate in the ESB created expectations among the employees; if productivity in the ESB were higher than anywhere else, then the men expected to be paid more than anyone else. But, on the other hand, although the ESB itself was developing rapidly in Irish conditions, it was no longer unique. Before the war, it was the only industry of its kind in Ireland; and immediately after the war there was the vast rural electrification programme to continue its special position. But since the nineteen fifties, there was such development industrially that employees of the ESB could no longer feel a special sense of privilege. Although their income expectations were high, there was, distressingly, a feeling of falling status at the same time. This was reinforced in a number of ways. The power stations in the midlands, for example, where the men were particularly militant, were the first turf-burning generating stations, and had been the showpieces of Europe; they had now become relatively insignificant when compared to Poolbeg. It was reinforced by the fact that frequently, while qualifications were high, the job demand was low. The shift workers, for example, carried considerable responsibility for ten or fifteen minutes when taking on and off the load, but the rest of the shift made little demand on the men's abilities. In a wider context, the clerical employees came to the ESB on the basis of a competitive examination designed to recruit only those who could go to the highest level of management. The actual work asked of them was often below their capacity, and while it might have been tolerable if the job carried special prestige, the evaporation of the unique character of the Board and the rising incomes of the manual workers, all contributed to a feeling of being cheated, and a feeling of anger and frustration as a result.

However, all this merely touches on points already amply demonstrated in the disputes we have examined; and while these difficulties were indeed substantial, they were not helped by the approach of either management or of the trade unions at the time.

I believe all this shows clearly too the immense difficulty in securing trade union change; and, in all probability, it demonstrates that if changes are to be secured, then they must be attempted little by little in modest and scarcely felt experiments, although the prospect is a most daunting one; and we must eschew the grand design, even when, as in worker participation, the proposal has the wholehearted support in principle of the trade union movement.

Finally, the ESB disputes manifest in a very explicit way almost all the characteristics of industrial relations in Ireland, characteristics well-scrutinised and reported on, and, consequently, they are of the greatest importance in seeking an understanding of the Irish industrial scene.

IV

The dispute in Bord na Mona, to which we now turn, was also the subject of a special investigation. The NIEC had suggested that such inquiries should be carried out by a team but, as we have seen, the minister decided to ask only one person to conduct the inquiry, assisted by two assessors, one from the trade union side and one from the management side. Mr Charles Mulvey, a young economist from Trinity College, was appointed in June 1968 and he reported the following September. Although the report was very critical of trade unions and management, nonetheless both parties agreed to its publication,[40] and in this we are fortunate.

Bord na Mona is concerned with the production of turf, which is the word commonly used in Ireland for peat. In 1934, the Turf Development Board was formed by the government under the direction of Dr C. S. Andrews, who later became chairman of CIE, and who was prominent in the busmen's dispute. The Board took over a private venture in Co. Offaly and acquired two additional bogs. By 1940, they had also acquired a briquette factory. During the war, because of the difficulty in importing coal, turf became a basic fuel; and immediately after the war, it was decided to develop the saving of turf into a major industry. Bord na Mona was established for this purpose, and while its initial capital was provided by the state, it was expected to pay its way without subsidy[41] or tariff protection. This constraint was to play a significant part in the disputes that we shall examine here.

Bord na Mona operates fourteen bogs and three briquette factories. It became national policy to rely on turf as much as possible, and, consequently, apart from its domestic market, the Board supplied hospitals and factories, and the turf-fired generating stations erected by the Electricity Supply Board. This last has significance for our study, since local workers employed by Bord na Mona were in direct contact with workers employed by the Electricity Supply Board in their generating stations, and the difference in their wages contributed to the unrest among the Bord na Mona workers.

In 1964, an unofficial strike of the unskilled and semiskilled workers had revealed seriously inadequate trade union organisation, with perhaps only thirty per cent. of the workers in membership. Their organisation was undeniably difficult; they were scattered throughout the bogs, and at that time they appeared to drift from one union to another, probably because the number of temporary workers was very large. The four unions concerned were the Irish Transport, the Amalgamated Transport,

---

[40] *Report of Inquiry into Strikes in Bord na Mona* (Stationery Office, Dublin, 1968).
[41] Its relationship with the ESB actually resulted in a form of subsidy, which, however, does not affect the substance of the position.

the Workers Union of Ireland and the Federation of Rural Workers. The unions suggested that union membership should be made a condition of employment and that there should be a check off system for the payment of union contributions. The Board rather crossly pointed out that it had itself recommended that the workers should vote for one union to negotiate for them, and that the unions should agree to abide by this. Although the other unions agreed, the Irish Transport demurred, and eventually a modification of the system was agreed where each of the twenty-two works declared for a particular union as the majority union so that, while all four unions continued to represent the men, there was only one negotiating union in each of the twenty-two work places. In return for this, Bord na Mona required membership of one of the unions as a condition of employment and agreed to a check off system for contributions. This was the agreement of 1965.

While the problem of recruitment was overcome, the problem of communication was not. The labour force was essentially rural in character, with little tradition of trade union organisation; more than that, the number of unskilled workers varied enormously between winter and summer, the July figure in 1967 standing at about 2,300 and the November figure standing at only 1,300. Despite these difficulties, the trade unions appeared to have a well-developed system of negotiation. There were works' conciliation councils, originally established in 1946 under the auspices of the Labour Court; there was a head office conciliation council; and the unions themselves were organised in a group at national level for negotiating purposes. Furthermore, the 1965 agreement also contained three points which normally would be expected to indicate mature industrial relations. It was agreed that unofficial strikes or stoppages of work would not be recognised or declared official *post factum;* it was agreed that no strike would take place until all procedural steps had been taken, including reference to the Labour Court; and thirdly, it was agreed that, in any event, there would be a lapse of four weeks—to be known as the 'reappraisal period'—between the issue of a Labour Court recommendation and the serving of a strike notice on the same issue. Even in the operation of the trade union group, the usual criticisms were less appropriate, since the group's secretary, Mr Patrick Murphy, was president of the Federation of Rural Workers, the union which represented approximately half of the unskilled and semiskilled workers. Since so many of his members were involved, servicing the group to him was a question of more paper rather than more time. Indeed there seems to have been almost an air of complacency. Mulvey[42] says:

[42]Op. cit., p. 12.

In general, these procedures have been effective, and industrial relations in the Board have been good throughout the years since 1946. The vast majority of disputes are resolved peacefully in the works conciliation councils and only a fraction require to be dealt with at Head Office level. The number of issues which have been incapable of resolution at Head Office level and have required Labour Court investigation are fewer than 30 and with few exceptions the recommendation has resolved the dispute. In the 22 years of the Board's existence only one official strike involving semi- and unskilled workers has occurred.

Yet despite this, Mulvey, in his report, is extremely critical of the trade unions both in regard to their performance and their structures. His criticism of the Board, although not quite as condemnatory, is equally sharp. He believed that in the Board there was an inadequate recognition of the importance of industrial relations, and there was the adopting of a narrow technical approach, probably because of the engineering environment. He also found the management structure wholly inadequate to the demands of industrial relations. His conclusion is:

> The two strikes under consideration in the Report occurred largely as a result of the failure of both sides to recognise the fundamental nature of the issue in dispute and to relate their negotiating behaviour to the realities of the situation at the workplace. The failure of both sides to recognise the fundamental nature of the issue in dispute is primarily a consequence of poor communications and understanding between the Group and its members and the Board and its employees.[43]

The unofficial strikes which began in November 1967, and which spread gradually but relentlessly throughout all the workings, arose from two apparently unrelated causes: a dispute with regard to Saturday working, and a dispute on overtime rates for balers in the briquette factories. The underlying cause, however, was a blinding resentment about wage rates, based once again on the question of comparabilities, which had emerged so often as the dogged theme of the disputes of the sixties. In October 1966, an agreement was reached between the Federated Union of Employers and various trade unions covering all tradesmen employed in a maintenance capacity in concerns associated with the FUE, that is to say, in effect, tradesmen employed in industry generally. It was an agreement much influenced by the prevailing views on comparabilities

[43]ibid., p. 58.

and gave rise to a new experiment in national bargaining, which, when it collapsed, caused immense damage industrially and nationally. This was the maintenance dispute, and its implications we shall examine in the next chapter. The October 1966 agreement gave increases right throughout industry, and although Bord na Mona was not affiliated to the FUE, it was impossible to avoid a similar increase for the maintenance craftsmen employed by the Board; and this was conceded also in October 1966. The increase made a considerable impact on the Board, since it affected so many; in industry generally only a small proportion of the skilled workers are on maintenance work as a rule, and consequently only a small number in each firm were affected by the agreement. In the case of Bord na Mona, however, all the skilled workers, apart from electricians, were on maintenance work, and therefore got a substantial increase. Despite this, the increases were given with alacrity.

The reason was that the Board had committed itself to following the downtown rate; it saw itself as a wage follower rather than a wage leader despite the great size of its employment, and its management made this a point of enormous and inflexible principle. But the very same principle had the effect of driving the differential the other way in the case of the semiskilled and unskilled workers, because the Board related them to local, rural wage earners, and refused point-blank to give them any increase at all because of the absence of wage movements among these occupations. Matters were made worse when in June 1967, after a lengthy dispute, the clerical employees of the Board had their pay increased, under the influence of the ESB settlements.

But the ESB rates had a more direct effect because the local semiskilled and unskilled workers of the ESB received, not the rural rate, but a rate which was related to the skilled rate. Here was a sharp difference of policy between the ESB and Bord na Mona, and tensions increased when the man who delivered the fuel found that the man who received it was paid at a higher rate, not because of any difference in the work but because of a different approach to wage structures. As if all this were not enough, a very rainy summer had also kept incomes low, since most semiskilled and unskilled workers were paid either piece rates or time rates plus a production bonus, and, consequently, earnings varied directly with weather conditions. Indeed like the plagues of Egypt, this was the seventh rainy summer, one after the other, so that dissatisfaction was accumulating over a substantial period of time.

But the Board itself had also suffered because of the rainy summers. An act of parliament was introduced in June 1968 waiving both interest on previous government loans and the repayment of advances for a period, in order to let the Board get on its feet once more. The Board, therefore, was seriously embarrassed financially at the time; but any arguments along these lines bewildered the men still more when they saw substantial claims conceded both to the skilled workers and to the salaried grades.

During the winter of 1966-67, the semiskilled and unskilled workers became increasingly dissatisfied; it was the practice during the winter for them to be given indoor work, and they were therefore in close contact with the maintenance men just at the time when the differential between them began to widen. In such a climate of unrest, men feel aggrieved about many matters, not merely one, and a variety of claims were pushed up to the unions from their branches. From these, seven points were submitted by way of claim by the group in March, and they covered not only wages and a wage structure, but holidays, shift rates, bonus earnings, hours of work and superannuation. The Board was prepared to yield a little on all points except wages, but, as might be expected, their offer, when it was put to ballot vote, was rejected by an overwhelming majority. It was in these circumstances that the claims were referred to the Labour Court for a full hearing.

We can see here the determination of the Board not to yield on their principles of comparability, even when it led to great tensions. The unions' position, however, was particularly interesting. They, as well, clearly accepted the principle of comparability; their quarrel with the Board was that such comparabilities should be based on internal relativities, not external ones; that is to say that the unskilled workers should have their wage rates related to the Board's maintenance men, not to rural employments generally. They also recognised the inflexibility of the Board on these issues. Their strategy, therefore, was to negotiate the wage rate over time, since it appeared impossible to secure it immediately, and in the meantime to make fruitful the pressure of the members by picking up as many other benefits as possible. It was probably for this reason that they gave prominence to matters in addition to the wages claim when they must have known that the men would have been far better satisfied with a straightforward fight on wages, and a postponement of the other claims. Mulvey appears to be critical about the unions' reluctance to mount a strike on the wages issue at that time. If they wished to reflect the feelings of their members, they should certainly have done so; but there are many who would say that the attitude of the unions was a sensible and responsible one, and they would claim themselves that if the rush of disputes had not occurred, their strategy would have paid off handsomely. As it was, it led to accusations of dilatoriness and inadequacy. It was not until June that the Labour Court issued its report and found for the Board; and now began a series of ballots which, to Mulvey, manifested a serious lack of leadership. In the course of the dispute, there must have been eight such ballots in all, each ballot taking a number of weeks to accomplish.

First the finding of the Labour Court was put to ballot and was rejected; then there was a ballot on whether or not strike notice should be served. A majority of the men voted in favour, but the poll was a low one, 53 per cent., and those in favour of strike action amounted to less than 40 per cent. of those entitled to vote. The unions believed that they had not a sufficient mandate, although one would have to examine the ballot very closely indeed to conclude that this was not so. However, in a manner which most people would regard as very responsible, they reopened negotiations on the wage claim under the Labour Court. In the difficult discussions that followed, they got improvements in shift rates, working hours and service pay; but there was a proviso to the effect that they would not pursue the basic wage claim for the present. These further proposals were put to ballot vote, and they were accepted by a very small majority, approximately half the members voting.

Any such settlement is bound to leave a great deal of resentment behind it. Sometimes one recognises the existence of a strike situation, a general climate of industrial unrest, which may need only a small dispute to send it flaring into a major confrontation. This appears to have been the case with the general workers of the Board in the autumn of 1967. The unions recognised it, at least in part, and hoped to let it die down by working away – perilously but continuously – at the various claims. The Board, on the other hand, seems to have believed that once agreement had been reached, the matter was at an end. They were taken completely by surprise by the outburst of unofficial action in November.

Arising from the reduction in hours of work, there was a problem regarding Saturday work during the winter. The unions claimed that it should be eliminated; the Board was willing to reduce it. The details need not delay us, but the onset of winter itself imposed a deadline on the negotiations. A conciliation officer of the Labour Court recommended a compromise; the unions took the proposal and began to consult with their members. The Board, after consideration, decided to reject the proposal. On 13 November, the Board conveyed its rejection to the Labour Court (which, they claim, was all they were expected to do) and sent a copy to the secretary of the group, who received it the following day. On 13 November as well, the Board had a meeting of works' managers in Athlone; a copy of the working plans for the winter, including Saturday work, was circulated, and the works' managers got consent to use the circulars as notices in their works. These notices were posted on the following day, 14 November, the same day on which the secretary of the trade union group was notified, and indeed while the trade unions were still in consultation with their members on the proposals of the conciliation officer. The posting of these notices seemed to have been a genuine mistake at the time, but it was a mistake for which the Board was not prepared to shed any tears, claiming brusquely that the works' managers had to have clear authority, by that time, on Saturday working in any event. The Board appears to have believed that the unions were delaying with intent, because, while the negotiations were proceeding, no Saturday work was taking place, and they feared that they would ultimately be faced with a *fait accompli*. Consequently, when the management and the group met on another matter on the following day, 15 November, and when the unions, angry at what they regarded as a breach of faith, asked the Board to withdraw the notice and continue negotiations, they bluntly refused to do so. It is still their view that in the event it would have made no difference, since unofficial action was under way; yet unofficial action did not begin until the following day, and it spread quite slowly throughout all the works of the Board.

By an extraordinary coincidence, a dispute broke out on the same day in the briquette factories, on an entirely unrelated matter. This concerned overtime rates for balers and, when negotiations failed, the men at one of the briquette factories refused to work. By the following day, pickets were placed on the three factories, and, simultaneously, the unofficial stoppages began in the other works of the Board. As Mulvey points out, the separate issues involved became quickly obscured in the general discontent manifested by the mass of unofficial strikers. On Thursday, 16 November, the number of men involved was not more than 300, but by Monday, 20 November, as widespread picketing took place, some 2,000 men became involved; by midweek, nearly 3,000 in all were out.

Although Mulvey in his report gives a good deal of attention to the balers' strike, it is unlikely that, by itself, it would have caused such a widespread stoppage even in the factories, since the balers had not general support. The critical dispute was the one on Saturday working; if a confrontation could have been avoided on this issue (and confrontation it really was), then the industry might well have survived into better times without undergoing such an upheaval.

Hurried conciliation conferences took place at the Labour Court, but the Board refused to withdraw the notice on Saturday working. More than that, on the following Monday when the unofficial stoppage became general, they refused to negotiate further until the men returned to work. This too was a key point in their approach to industrial relations – an absolute insistence on agreements once they are concluded – and even though Mulvey in his report has charged them with inflexibility, they are entirely adamant still that their approach was the correct one. The unions, in the meantime, as is frequently the case, were being harassed by their own members who began picketing the various union head offices. It was clear from the placards carried by the strikers that wages were at the very root of the unrest. The group tried again to get the Board to withdraw the contentious notice. The Board refused, and, clearly in an effort to gain control of the situation, the trade union group decided, at the end of this very eventful week, to ask the men to resume work on the understanding that if they did so, the unions would officially serve seven days strike notice on the Board immediately. The trade union officials then went from mass meeting to mass meeting, persuading the men to return to work in order that the position should be regularised. They achieved a full resumption by the end of the following week, and on 1 December an official strike notice was served on the board to expire on 11 December. Now the Board accused the unions of a breach of faith, because they regarded what had taken place as a *post factum* declaration by the union that an unofficial strike was official. They have never wavered from their position on this, although it is difficult to see what alternative the unions had. In Mulvey's report, the question is examined on the basis of niceties of interpretation of the 1967 settlement; there seems little appreciation of the efforts made by the trade unions at least to get the men back to work, and so avoid the hardship, psychological as well as physical, of an unofficial, extended, and uncontrolled stoppage.

Again the Labour Court held a conciliation conference, on 6 December. There were now three claims, the balers' claim, the Saturday working, and a straightforward claim for a wage increase. On the first two issues, proposals were quickly worked out and within three days were put by the unions to a consultative conference of their members in Tullamore, and were accepted. Strike notice therefore was suspended, so that negotiations could continue on wages.

The Board was prepared to give some increases in the wage rate, but they also wanted to effect a comprehensive domestic agreement covering many matters but aimed essentially at ensuring that during the currency of the agreement no further claims on any of these subjects would be made by the group. The key point, however, was the wage increase and, during the negotiations at the Labour Court, impatient workers demonstrated outside the building. By early January, the proposals for a comprehensive agreement and for an increase in the wage rate were put to ballot and were overwhelmingly rejected, the result becoming available towards the end of January. The Board refused to improve the offer, strike notice was given, and on 8 February the official strike of semiskilled and unskilled workers began which involved 3,000 workers and also

400 skilled men who refused to pass the pickets. The conciliation officers of the Labour Court continued to try to find a settlement, and eventually, on 4 March, an improved wage offer was made which again was put to ballot, this time, however, under the auspices of the Irish Congress of Trade Unions. The result was announced on 9 March, the proposal being rejected by only 20 votes. The strike dragged on. The Board refused to increase the offer any further, and because of this impasse, the group decided to submit to a ballot of their members a recommendation that work be resumed on 21 March on the understanding that the dispute would be investigated by the Labour Court within one week of the resumption of work. It is necessary to note here that, while the conciliation service of the Labour Court is carried on in private, a full Labour Court hearing (which was now proposed) meant essentially a public hearing during which a formal examination of the case would be made and a recommendation issued.

The proposal to return to work was accepted by a majority, and a full resumption of work took place on 21 March. The Labour Court immediately began to examine the case in public, and recommended a further increase in the wage rate, which was accepted by the Board, and which was once again put to the ballot vote of the members. On 16 April, it was announced that a majority had voted for acceptance.

Mulvey, in his evaluation, is, as we have already noted, very critical indeed of what he regards as the complacent and leisurely manner in which the Board and the trade union group conducted the negotiations on the issue of Saturday working. "I consider the Board and the Group in failing to meet much more quickly and frequently in the period immediately following the submission of this claim to have been negligent of the serious and urgent nature of this dispute."[44] His view was that this reduced the time available for effective third-party intervention, by which he meant the Labour Court. He accepted that the trade unions were hoping to gain a tactical advantage by dragging out the negotiations, but, in his view, they seriously underestimated the risk of an unofficial strike. When the notice of Saturday working was issued, the risk was greatly increased by the circumstances of the notice which caused the workers to feel that they had been misled by their representatives. But even if the question of the issue of the notice had not arisen, he believed that the risk of an unofficial strike was substantial. In regard to the Board, he thought it very strange indeed that they did not refer the matter immediately to the Labour Court. It appears to me, however, that their style of bargaining would lead one to expect instead the creation of a confrontation similar to that which occurred.

[44] ibid., p. 32.

With regard to the balers, Mulvey takes the view that the unions were negligent of the interests of their members in the briquette factories: "...the unions responded painfully slowly to events on the factory floor and therefore represented the claims of their members in the briquette factories quite inadequately."[45] He also castigates the Board in that, although it was not obliged to make good the shortcomings of the trade unions, nevertheless it had it in its power to avert the unofficial strike by postponing the implementation of the shift system which caused difficulty for the balers, pending settlement of the dispute. This he regards as quite extraordinary since all that was required was a postponement of one week, and he attributes it to the inflexible attitude shown by the Board when confronted with the threat of unofficial action. There was no great point involved since the matter in dispute was soon conceded in any event. However, we have already made the point that, in all probability, Mulvey makes too much of the balers' dispute.

But Mulvey is correct in stating that the wage issue was really the key one.

> Despite the concessions on other issues which were obtained in this agreement, and notwithstanding its acceptance by trade union members in a ballot vote, it is evident that during the months of October and November, 1967, there existed a feeling of deep frustration amongst many of the men over the failure to secure a wage increase. It is against this background of discontent that the disputes which led to the unofficial strike originated and developed.[46]

It is because of this that he accuses both sides of a notable lack of urgency. Let us consider how Mulvey saw each of the bargaining partners.

With regard to the Board, Mulvey examines its view of itself as a wage follower, and its inflexible adherence to what it perceived as its principles. The consequence of this we have already examined. Because of this policy, and because of the contrasting policy of the other great rural employer, the ESB, deep tensions were inevitable. The increase in the wage rate which was eventually conceded did not mark any departure from the inflexible position of the Board, so much so that Mulvey anticipated that on almost every occasion that a wage claim on behalf of non-skilled workers would be submitted in the future, there would be a fundamental conflict of view similar to that which occurred in 1967-68, and which in his view could only lead to further serious and prolonged strikes. These strikes have not in fact occurred. There may be

[45]ibid., p. 37.
[46]ibid., p. 39.

a number of reasons for this: summer weather improved from there on and, consequently, earnings were higher; because of the various national wage developments, actual increases in money came faster; and apart from all that, the men had experienced serious loss of income during the strikes. The fact is as well that the men did not understand the situation with the same clarity that Mulvey did, and once incomes went up, the principles became obscured. However, the basic dilemma still remains to be resolved.

Mulvey also argues, more philosophically, that a certain machine-like approach to management produced much of the Board's inflexibility.

> The remarkable development of Bord na Mona since it was established in 1946 has depended almost entirely on the innovation of engineering techniques appropriate to Irish conditions. It is not surprising therefore that the management personnel of the Board has always been dominated by engineers. I suspect that this situation has, in a rather fundamental way, caused the board's approach to industrial relations to be characterised by a narrow technical consciousness... that the predominance of the engineering mentality in the management structure of the board has encouraged the general acceptance of a technical frame of reference in almost all aspects of management, including industrial relations.[47]

But the picture which emerges of the Board is of a body which is far too involved in the day-to-day affairs of the organisation, meeting as it did fortnightly, and indeed more frequently when there was a crisis. There was a good deal of confusion regarding responsibility for industrial relations between head office and works' managers, negotiating authority was inadequate and there were unnecessary delays and poor communication. In those circumstances, Mulvey recommended, on the one hand, flexibility in regard to internal relativities, and, on the other, the establishing of a proper personnel department with clearly-defined functions and clear relationships with the works' managers. He was much influenced by the Interim Report of the Committee of Industrial Relations in the ESB[48] which had just been issued. "This would suggest," he says,

> that there is a need to re-examine the whole question of industrial relations management in the semi-State bodies. Quite apart from questions of structures and procedures there seems to be a clear need to define the role of semi-State bodies in the field of industrial relations

[47]ibid., p. 53.
[48]Op. cit.

vis-à-vis the private sector. My own view is that the semi-State bodies could become an example to the rest of industry in matters of industrial relations if sufficient resources and encouragement were given to permit them to innovate in this field. One immediately thinks of industrial democracy in this regard....I have been struck by the quite explicit manner in which many of the Board's employees have expressed to me a desire to become more closely involved in the control of the Board's affairs. There appears to be a clear demand for the introduction of democratic procedures in the formulation and implementation of policy in Bord na Mona...[I] suggest the Board consider the matter in view of the foregoing remarks.[49]

One gains the impression that while the proposal may technically have been considered by the Board, it was never really taken seriously. Somehow the whole idea appears to be so unlikely to many Irish managers as almost to damage the credibility of those who recommend it.[50]

And when we turn to the trade unions, we see that they too must regard the idea of worker participation as somewhat unlikely in practice, however much they might support the theory. Although the Board does not number among its members even one trade unionist, there appears to be no pressure for this kind of development. Let us however consider, as we did in the case of the Board, how Mulvey saw the trade unions at the time of this dispute. Firstly, he saw an unnecessary and irrational multiplicity of trade unions, and he identified in particular two weaknesses which sprang from this, an inability to make any selection between claims, and an unnecessary reliance on ballots:

> A ballot is at best a very limited method of conveying information from the trade union rank and file to head office level and, unless its limitations are clearly recognised, is capable of conveying misleading information.[51]

The means used to overcome the problem of a multiplicity of unions is the group system of negotiation, but from Mulvey's point of view it might be as well if it never existed. He saw in it a lack of effective communication and a lack of authority to negotiate. He was particularly critical of the fact that unions did not employ full-time personnel. For all practical purposes, the group existed only to engage in head office

[49]Op. cit., p. 64.
[50]Very recently, EEC proposals and the initiative of the FUE in sponsoring debate on them may have improved matters somewhat.
[51]Op. cit., p. 49.

negotiation; they were out of touch, they did not possess a real mandate, and at local level the system of organisation was "fragmented and irrational and so tends to undermine the ability of the Group to coordinate the policies and activities of its affiliates."[52] Therefore, he would rather not see a group there at all: "Hence, in so far as the Group arrangement in Bord na Mona serves to obscure the real need of reform in the trade union structure, it may be a positive obstacle in the way of progress."[53] If all this is so, it must be seen in a wider and more important context, for the fact is that the Bord na Mona group is one of the better organised groups within the trade union movement.

But in all this there is something more to be said for the trade unions than appears in the report. We have already noted the assumption that the function of a trade union is merely to reflect the desires of its members in much the same manner and with much the same vehemence as the members themselves would; but the task of a trade union is much more complex than this and we must respect a trade union official who tries to take a larger view: who sees his task as lowering the temperature for a period until he is in a better position to bargain. In any event, he is usually anxious to make his gains without undue hardship to the men. There is a harsher view that if men want strike they should be given it on the grounds that they have consciously chosen the way of risk and hardship; but this is only partially true. Group movements, such as occurred in Bord na Mona, are often blundering and unnecessarily hurtful.

However understandable the union's policy was, it may not have been the right one to follow just at that time in Bord na Mona, and Mulvey may have been right in that. One is struck by the remarkable similarities between this dispute and that of the Dublin busmen; again one can detect three quite distinct positions. The men were distressed at their low incomes and very angry at what they considered to be a policy of wage discrimination, which nothing but a substantial wage increase would resolve. The unions saw it all as the science of the possible; when they found it impossible to gain immediately what the men required, they raised alternative objectives for which they won reluctant support by ballot, and while indeed they made gains, they also caused a deeper frustration because it could not be properly articulated. In any event, they were in the shadowy business of tactics and timing; but they confronted a management who saw it all as a straightforward bargain. Agreements were made to be observed in every particular and, when they found what they considered to be tedious prevarication and even

---

[52]Op. cit., p. 50.
[53]ibid., p. 52.

bad faith, they decided to proceed by confrontation, because this in fact was the mood, if not the direct purpose, of the notice on Saturday working. All in all, although it ended disastrously, there was a lot of good sense in the trade union approach. There is, however, the deeper question of the democratic propriety of substituting one set of more attainable objectives for another. Probably the normal consensus of democracy permits a certain amount of this, but when the consensus is exceeded, as it was with the Dublin busmen and the Bord na Mona workers, there is the devil's own uproar as a result.

No great changes have come as a result of the Mulvey report. Bord na Mona have appointed a director of personnel, and have provided some supporting staff. The group of unions now holds annual conferences of the unskilled and semiskilled members of the various trade unions; while they can make only recommendations to the various union executives, nonetheless, the recommendations are in practice followed. These steps appear to have improved procedures somewhat, but they are not intended to do more than that. Both sides seem to have regarded the disputes in 1967 and 1968 as unfortunate episodes in an industrial situation which, while not being particularly good, is reasonably stable and which cannot be improved on to any great extent.

Nevertheless, the report was a very useful one. It would have been far wiser if more than one person were engaged in it, in order that a balanced view could be given. Recommendations from such a report may be ephemeral, but criticisms are not; they have a heavy finality about them. Yet if they are to be useful, they must be blunt; it remains only that they should be balanced.

CHAPTER FIVE

The Maintenance Dispute

I

ALTHOUGH we were not aware of it at the time, in 1967 we had reached the high point in the decade – a decade which began with a feeling of great promise and in which, up to then, there continued to be a strong underlying optimism, despite the plague of difficulties. From there on, the clouds began to gather. Seán Lemass, recognising that a general election must soon be held and conscious of his failing strength, had retired from the office of Taoiseach, and as a result, much of the initiative and thrust gradually went out of Irish government. In 1967, however, the impetus he had given to the administration was still there. He had been succeeded by Mr Jack Lynch, a compromise choice, who, while he showed a great commitment to peace in the dark years that followed, nonetheless was much more a chairman than a leader, and a somewhat negative chairman at that. But his pleasant reliability had considerable popular appeal, and in the general election of 1969 the government party swept home with a joyous majority and settled down, as they thought, to reap the fruits of a growing prosperity. But already events in the North were building up day by incredible day and, in July, Derry erupted, and soon after, Belfast.

In early 1969, industry generally and the trade union movement in particular were shattered by the most devastating and cruel strike which we had yet experienced. This became known as the maintenance dispute, and concerned the maintenance craftworkers employed generally throughout Irish industry. It built up to the autumn of 1968, broke out into nation-wide strikes and picketing towards the end of January 1969 and continued until March. Not only were there pickets placed by the striking unions, but there were 'counter-pickets' placed by other unions in protest at being put out of work, and industry was thrown into chaos. The fact that men would not pass pickets was used by the striking unions as their principal weapon, judiciously placing pickets where thousands of workers would be affected, but where they themselves, because of their small relative numbers, would not suffer greatly. It was seen by many as an act of outrageous cynicism, and the dispute was the subject of two published reports, one by the Irish Congress of Trade Unions itself, and one commissioned by the government and carried out by Con Murphy. The maintenance dispute will be the subject of this chapter.

One union that was deeply affected by the dispute was the Marine Port and General Workers Union, the union of which the president of Congress, Jimmy Dunne, was general secretary. Right throughout the maintenance dispute, he was vigorous and explicit in his condemnation of what was taking place, and at the annual conference of the ICTU in Bundoran in County Donegal in July 1969 he spoke with great bitterness of the effect of the dispute on his own union.[1]

> I've come through a year in which I've seen my own Union smashed to the ground and bereft of everything except its fighting spirit. Smashed in a way that no employer or combination of employers could achieve in the 37 years of militant and up-hill trade unionism that is the history of my Union. I would be a liar and a hypocrite if I came to this rostrum and left aside my feelings of hurt at the senseless and almost completely unnecessary damage done, not alone to my own Union, but to other of our affiliated Organisations. To be broke, to be smashed, this can be a proud fate and boast of a Trade Union but only when such has been suffered in a just cause and in an unavoidable conflict or involvement.

Throughout his year of office, Jimmy Dunne had an extraordinary impact on the Irish public quite outside the trade union movement. He was a Dublin man, he represented a tough union of dockers and general workers, but he had a compelling commonsense, unusual insight and great sincerity. He was elected to the Senate later in 1969 without his campaigning for it, and when he died prematurely in 1972 after quite a lengthy illness, his funeral was extraordinary in the vast numbers of persons who attended it and the widespread feeling of loss.

In the bitterly cold February of 1969, when the wretched maintenance dispute was at its height and the trade union movement in disarray, the

[1] Irish Congress of Trade Unions, *Eleventh Annual Report* 1969, pp. 327–8.

two men who had given it much of its stability and purpose died within a week of one another. John Conroy died on 13 February and Jim Larkin on 18 February. They were buried quite near one another in Deans Grange cemetery. While John Conroy had expected in any event to retire soon, Jim Larkin, although in his early sixties, seemed until his fatal illness to have many years of vigorous life before him. It was a dismal spring.

In other ways, too, the trade union movement was changing. Dominick Murphy, a past president, was appointed to the Labour Court, and Jack Macgougan was appointed general secretary of the National Union of Tailors and Garment Workers, of which he had been Irish officer, and consequently moved to the London head office. On the other hand, the voice of the public service unions was growing stronger. The Association of Secondary Teachers, Ireland, had now affiliated to Congress to join the primary teachers and the vocational teachers; and two key civil service unions became members, the Civil Service Alliance and the Civil Service Executive and Higher Officers Association. The Irish Local Government Officials Union had affiliated some years before, and these unions together gave considerable drive to the public services committee of Congress.[2] In 1969 as well, a prominent civil service trade union official, Maurice Cosgrave of the Post Office Workers Union, was elected vice-president of Congress, and he later became a powerful influence in bringing to the trade union movement the public tradition of patient and skilful bargaining that was to contribute so much to the national wage settlements of 1970 and 1972.

But in this period of general disenchantment, there was much soul-searching and recrimination on the one hand, and little structural reform on the other; and a special delegate conference of Congress to consider the structure of the trade union movement made little progress. Nor was there much evidence during the year of any serious desire to improve group negotiations and procedures. A good example was CIE where the management offered to help in financing the administrative costs of the shopworkers group by a check-off system and a grant; but the group blandly replied that they had appointed a new secretary who would be able to devote sufficient time to its affairs and that this eliminated the need for the appointment of administrative staff for the group. Yet, not so very long before, individual shopworkers in CIE had appealed to the appeals board of Congress complaining of lack of service by the unions in circumstances where the group administration was clearly at fault. In the public field, the Industrial Relations Act became law, but the Trade Union Bill lapsed with the dissolution of parliament prior to the 1969

[2]Harold O'Sullivan, general secretary of the ILGOU, became the vigorous chairman of the public services committee and a prominent member of the Congress executive.

general election. Under the Industrial Relations Act, rights commissioners were appointed for the first time.

But the trade union movement had also looked to wider horizons. Congress had campaigned vigorously against a proposal by the government to abolish the system of proportional representation in voting; the proposal had been defeated and Congress felt pleased at their performance. The trade unions were also associated (although with some reserve) with a rather grotesque productivity campaign carried out by the Irish National Productivity Committee and bearing the name MOVE as its *nom de guerre*.

A topic of overwhelming importance at the 1969 annual conference of Congress was the question of an incomes policy. In the spring of 1969, immediately after the maintenance dispute, the government became deeply concerned that the increase given to the maintenance men might spread rapidly throughout industry generally. They therefore urged very strongly on Congress the acceptance of the principle of a prices and incomes policy, referring in particular to the report of the National Industrial Economic Council, number 11, which pointed out the commonsense of such a policy.

Congress replied that the great majority of the eleventh round agreements did not terminate until the beginning of 1970, and in their view, any general strategy of constraint was unnecessary. The fact, however, was that those in the trade union movement who were hostile to the idea of a prices and incomes policy had become more and more dominant, not only because of the way things were developing in this country but also because of the influence of the British-based unions; and indeed, when the annual conference opened in Bundoran in July, it appeared that any support for such a policy was in shreds. But the delegates took quite a different view. A resolution from the Cork Trades Council, broadly in support of a prices and incomes policy, carried the day triumphantly in the face of a proposal from some of the British-based unions condemning such an idea outright. The Irish trade union movement, despite the mauling it had given itself during the maintenance dispute, still wished to be positive and constructive, still wished to cooperate as a partner in economic and social development.

II

The maintenance dispute had its genesis in a number of earlier disputes but, in particular, in the building dispute of 1964. When the working hours of craftsmen in the construction industry were reduced in 1964, the building craft unions attempted to get a similar reduction for their members employed in maintenance work in industry generally. Inevitably, the claim ran into vigorous opposition from the FUE; and in July 1965, it was rejected by the Labour Court. But pressure built up from the unions, imperilling at one time the national wage discussions then under way. In May 1966, the Labour Court was quite explicit that the building trade settlement should not be extended to the maintenance men; their pay and conditions should be settled in relation to the pay and conditions of the other workers in the same industry. In the meantime, pressure was building up as well among the maintenance engineers and electricians, a much more populous group. Rates of pay here were negotiated between the Dublin Engineering Employers Association and the unions concerned, and many firms who employed maintenance engineering workers had little part in the negotiations, being merely notified by the FUE of the change in the rate. A large firm, therefore, found itself confronted with a complex problem of different rates and different conditions for its maintenance workers. In these circumstances, the FUE responded to the pressure of the unions on the question of hours, and when the tenth round negotiations were concluded in June 1966, they invited all craft unions with members employed in maintenance work to a conference, for the purpose of working out an overall agreement covering all maintenance craftsmen. The concept was a most difficult one. On the one hand, there was a large number of employers, whose only link with one another was that they employed some maintenance workers, and on the other hand, the workers themselves, spread as they were throughout the whole of industry, formed no geographic community; on the contrary, as far as skills were concerned, they formed a number of quite distinct and to some extent mutually hostile communities, as was very evident in the case of the engineering workers on the one hand and the building craftsmen on the other.

The agreement was concluded in October 1966. It provided the necessary flexibility regarding hours, but where before firms followed the downtown rate of pay, the new agreement provided for a single national rate for all maintenance craftsmen throughout the whole of industry. This was quite an extraordinary example of centralised bargaining, and since it is the key to all that followed, it is necessary to examine some of the deeper reasons that lay behind it. The initiative for such an agreement came from the FUE, not from the unions, and it was much influenced by their desire for such strong centralised bargains. We have already noted this in the fruitless discussions between the FUE and Congress on a wage settlement during 1965 and the earlier part of 1966; there was an enormously strong, even emotional commitment on the part of the FUE to the idea of a national agreement tightly drawn, explicit in every respect, for a period certain, and costed precisely, which, it was believed, would permit firms to plan more readily with regard to their costings.

This was the substance of the FUE approach at the time; industrial relations were seen impatiently as a straightforward bargain with the trade union representatives, who were expected to be in a position to conclude a detailed agreement and who were expected as well to be able to enforce such an agreement, once concluded, on all their members without exception. The idea seemed to spring from a misunderstanding of industrial relations in some continental countries, but may have sprung as well from the inadequacy of perception of some of the senior managers in Irish industry; it must be remembered, of course, that the rather unglamorous work of the FUE did not always attract the entrepreneurs of Irish industry. In retrospect, it appears that the support for this kind of centralised bargaining was by no means unanimous in the FUE, but it was overwhelmingly dominant at the time; it had contributed to the collapse of the tenth round talks but remained nonetheless to facilitate the idea of a national maintenance bargain. Con Murphy[3] in his report says that the FUE also saw the maintenance agreement as a first step in preparing the country's industrial relations system for entry into the European Economic Community, and furthermore, they believed that they were laying the foundations of subsequent progress towards an industrial type union. These are rather windy ideas but they identify well enough the curious sense of mission, a sense of men engaged in a significant adventure which some of the employer leaders appeared to have had, and which made the later collapse so poignant.

This initiative of the FUE had the effect of calling into being a single negotiating unit on the trade union side – the national group of maintenance craft unions. This was the body that concluded the 1966 agreement, and although they had headed notepaper with the names of their officers and an official address, they did not draw up any rules of procedure nor did they enter into any formal relationship with Congress or with any other negotiating group. In fact, they did not meet again until 11 September 1968 – and then for the purpose of considering a wage increase, since the 1966 agreement was coming to a close.

There were eighteen unions in all. Two of these were engineering unions, the AEF[4] and the NEETU; and in fact they represented the great

[3]Con Murphy, *Dispute between FUE and Maintenance Craft Unions: Report of Inquiry* (Stationery Office, Dublin, 1969, Prl. 798).
[4]This was the large British-based union which passed through a number of name changes about this time because of amalgamation. It was originally the Amalgamated Engineering Union (AEU), became in 1968 Amalgamated Union of Engineering and Foundry Workers (AEF), and eventually in 1970 Amalgamated Union of Engineering Workers (AUEW).

majority of maintenance craftsmen. There were fifteen other unions in the group, ten of them being building unions, but, apart from the ASW, they had few members involved in maintenance work, and it appears that some of them had none at all. Finally, there was the ETU(I) which, because of its special position, had an ambiguous relationship to the group and to the negotiations. While the AEF, NEETU and the ETU(I) represented the vast majority of maintenance craftsmen, they were nonetheless only three unions out of eighteen, and the group appeared to operate, in so far as any procedure was clear, on the basis of one union one vote. But there were deeper conflicts of interest which made such a procedure even more unreal, as we shall see later.

When the unions met on 11 September 1968 to consider a wage claim, the rates had become a bit of a tangle. The actual basic wage for forty hours was a little over 7s. 9d. an hour, but, during the currency of the agreement, hours had been reduced in many cases and the effective minimum was 8s. 3d. an hour. However, there was great casualness in the unions' approach. The AEF suggested ten shillings an hour, and the ASW fifteen shillings; in the event, they decided on 11 shillings which later in the negotiations was reduced to ten. But it was not at all clear whether this was to apply to the 7s. 9d. or to the 8s. 3d., although some representatives said that existing differentials should be preserved. One way or the other, the increase they sought was a substantial one, and reflected, in the case of the dominant engineering group, a growing sense of grievance that their skill was being discounted, since production workers in industry, who were often on incentive payments, sometimes earned as much if not more than the maintenance men who tended their machines. This recognition of skill was of great importance to both the engineering workers and the electricians, and the fact was that they had little time for a national wage rate which treated them the same as painters and plasterers, whatever about carpenters and joiners; but there was no way in which they could give this expression in the current wage demand, and their reaction was to regard themselves as the essential group, letting the others tag along if they wished to gain from it. There was a further conflict of interest within the group: a claim based on the hourly rate was essential for the engineering workers, while a weekly rate would have suited the building unions better. Although the reasons for this are complex and need not delay us, they were clearly perceived by the people concerned.

While the FUE, therefore, were attempting to build up a strong unified employer movement capable of negotiating and enforcing a national agreement, the unions as a group had little coherence and had indeed confused objectives, which their claim concealed rather than revealed.

This then was the background when negotiations opened between the FUE and the group of unions in September 1968 with the object of negotiating a further national agreement for maintenance workers in Irish industry. The collapse of the negotiations and the dispute that followed are, as we have said, the subject of a report by the Irish Congress of Trade Unions[5] and also a report by Con Murphy[6] commissioned by the Minister for Labour. A confidential report was also prepared by the FUE for its members.

In view of the fact that the previous agreement was to run out on 31 December, negotiations had begun very late; but even so, there was little urgency. Two meetings took place in October and two in November, where the details of an agreement were discussed but without a price tag. (As we have seen, the FUE adopted a similar strategy in the tenth round discussions a year earlier). Eventually, some understanding was reached on these matters, and on 9 December the FUE made an offer; it was for an increase of $10\frac{1}{2}$d an hour in three phases and it was so far distant from the claim as to cause a hostile reaction from the unions, who now believed that the FUE did not intend to negotiate realistically but merely wished to push the claim to the Labour Court.

Up to now, the unions had pointed to electricians and fitters in the ESB and in Aer Lingus, but in November an agreement was reached for contracts electricians in industry. It was a substantial settlement for 9s. 9d. an hour on a phased basis and, since contracts electricians were members of two of the unions concerned, a settlement for an amount less than this became extremely unlikely. The battle lines were now drawn.

A national wage movement, to become known as the eleventh round, was throwing up a figure of about £2 a week; the government had appealed for restraint within this figure, and the FUE, fortified by this and fearful of the impact of a major increase on wage rates generally, decided to hold the line at all costs. It is clear now that they underestimated the strength of feeling in the engineering unions and perhaps in the ETU(I) who were, under no circumstances, prepared to settle for a sum substantially less than that secured in the electrical contracting industry.

Once the course was set, there was a deadly inevitability about it, a frightening slide into chaos, partly because the FUE on the one hand and the unions on the other saw the dispute so differently. To the FUE it was now a straightforward confrontation – almost between light and darkness – in which a number of basic principles had to be defended, while the trade unions, with uncertain and divided leadership and

[5]Irish Congress of Trade Unions, *Eleventh Annual Report* 1969, p. 257 ff.
[6]Op. cit.

objectives of considerable ambiguity, were now in the grip of forces, some of monumental selfishness, over which they had little or no control. It is not surprising then, that before the dispute ended, there were casualties in the leadership on both sides.

By 31 December, the FUE had offered an increase of £2 a week, that is to say the eleventh round settlement, and when this was rejected, they referred the dispute to the Labour Court for a full public hearing, confident of the justice of their position. The hearing took place on 13 January but the unions refused to attend; a week later, the Court announced that it was unable to make a recommendation. Con Murphy, for the purposes of his report, asked the Labour Court to make some comment on this aspect of the dispute, but for reasons of public interest, they would not do so. It is clear, however, that the unions saw in the Labour Court a body which followed precedent already established, but which did not itself attempt to formulate new departures; and consequently they feared that they would be recommended merely an eleventh round settlement. But the fact remains that neither at this time, nor at any other, did the unions attempt any public justification of their position.

On 9 January, without waiting for the Court hearing, the group secretary informed Congress of the group's intention to serve seven days' strike notice to terminate on 24 January 1969; copies of the letter were sent to the FUE and to the Labour Court. There were two difficulties about this strike notice. The first concerned a breach of agreed procedure. The 1966 agreement explicitly laid down that no strike action should take place until all normal procedure had been exhausted, including a Labour Court hearing. Con Murphy[7] is quite caustic about this aspect of it:

> When asked at the Inquiry why they had not observed the grievance procedure......some union representatives observed that because the Agreement had expired on 31 December 1968 it was no longer in force; this is so, but it was stretching strict interpretation of the agreement to the limit.

This matter, however, was not given much prominence either by the FUE or in the report of Congress (probably the best report of the three and certainly the harshest on the performance of the unions). The fact is that in a crisis, these matters, so significant in other countries, are often in Ireland regarded as mere technicalities.[8]

---

[7]Op. cit., p. 15.
[8]The developing practices under the national agreements may have improved matters somewhat.

The second difficulty was much more serious from the trade union point of view. The object in giving notice to Congress of intention to strike was to provide an opportunity for other unions to be consulted who might be affected by the strike, and a year earlier a standard form had been devised by Congress for the purpose. But while the group gave notice to Congress, they did not indicate the names of the firms on whom they proposed to serve notice; and when Congress pressed for the information, they were told merely that the firms concerned were members of the FUE. On 21 January, the chairman of the group gave an officer of Congress a list of the firms, which later turned out to be incomplete and inaccurate. The unions who might be affected by the dispute, therefore, were not consulted at all by the group. Congress was infuriated by this cavalier treatment. It is doubtful if ever before there had been such a total disregard for its policies. Only six months before, at the 1968 annual conference, it had been formally agreed that good trade union practice required consultation with other unions affected by a dispute prior to a stoppage of work, and in their report on the maintenance dispute[9], Congress condemned the lack of consultation in terms so vehement and explicit as to be almost unparalleled:

> The terms of this motion were completely flouted by the group and the unions involved. There was no consultation whatever with other unions. Indeed these unions were not even afforded the courtesy of being informed as to the employments involved. This failure is the more reprehensible in so far as the number of members of unions in the group involved in the dispute was but a small fraction of the number of other workers affected. Accurate figures will presumably have been compiled by the Murphy Inquiry set up by the Minister for Labour. It would seem that only about 1,700 members of Group unions were involved as against many times that number of other union members (perhaps up to fifteen times as many). Many of the difficulties and much of the confusion that subsequently arose would have been avoided and the dispute adequately prosecuted at the same time, if there had been proper consultation between all the unions affected. In the circumstances the anger of the general unions at being so precipitated into a dispute that was to cost them enormous sums of money (apart from any other consideration) can be understood.

But Congress believed that there was something more sinister behind what they described as the inexcusable and grossly neglectful failure of

[9]Op. cit., p. 264.

the unions to supply an accurate list of the firms who were to be put in dispute:

> To put it bluntly, there was a strong impression abroad that the Group (or unions in the Group) selected the firms to be picketed on a basis that would involve few firms employing any large number of members of these unions. Certainly the failure of the group to indicate the basis for the selection of the firms lent support to the assumption made at the time that circumstances unconnected with the pursuit of the Group's claim determined the inclusion of certain firms and the exclusion of others. The general unions in particular had a well justified grievance on this score and the almost casual attitude adopted on the picketing of firms rightly gave rise to considerable criticism.[10]

At an early stage, then, the other unions saw all this as a cynical intention on the part of the unions in the group to use the picket in such a way as to cause maximum disruption to others and the minimum inconvenience to oneself.

For their part, the FUE saw the strike notice and the manner of its being served, not as a dispute with certain employers, but as a straightforward attack on the FUE itself; firstly, their requests for information lay unanswered, and then it appeared that among the firms selected by the unions were those firms whose representatives were on the FUE maintenance committee—and very prominently so. Con Murphy points out that the group were not equipped to deal with a dispute which involved one hundred and ninety-three different employers; in fact, it appears that the unions had no records at all, and that one source was the attendance list which was circulated at one of the conciliation conferences. In the event, however, some employers who were not members of the FUE received strike notice while others within the FUE did not. Despite all this, it is clear that there was a strategy adopted by the group of unions which was cynical and discriminatory, and it emerges clearly enough from the welter of ineptitude and confusion.

Congress, now very alarmed, made a bid for more time, and two days before the deadline, 23 January, the executive council, in a confidential letter to the eighteen unions, pointed out that tens of thousands of workers were likely to be affected, yet there had been no consultation. They asked that no pickets would be placed for at least one week during which time ". . . steps should be taken to consult with these unions and bring the position into line with Congress policy, in the event of a stoppage of work proceeding."[11]

[10]Op.cit., p. 263.
[11]ibid., p. 277.

The relationship at this time between the group and the executive council of Congress was a complex one. The chairman of the group of unions was Jim Cox of the ASW, who was a member of the executive council of Congress and was later to become president.[12] Cox, as we shall see, resigned when the group split and Brian Leonard of AGEMOU (the automobile union) succeeded him as chairman; he, at that time, was also a member of the executive council of Congress, although exceptionally so. When we turn to the engineering unions, we find that the Irish officer of the AEF, Jim Morrow, was vice-president of Congress and would take up office as president at the close of the very conference at which his union was condemned. Although he himself took part in some of the negotiations, his leadership appears to have been rejected. He was a formidable official but at that time he was nearing retiring age; apart from that, he was based in Belfast. Tim Keane was the principal officer in the Republic, but there were voices more dominant than his, because in the AEF tradition a district committee had considerable autonomy and they, and their secretary Frank Callaghan, were the driving force in the maintenance dispute. The other engineering union was the Irish-based NEETU, and its general secretary, Jack Cassidy, was vice-chairman of the group, and had been for many years a member of the executive council of Congress, although he was not currently so. Once again, however, the vehemence among some of his own people quite overwhelmed whatever guidance he was in a position to give. If all these men could have exercised the influence which their offices implied, then it is certain that the bitterness, the injustice and the damage to thousands and thousands of people would not have occurred. But in fact their influence was much diminished and they had no alternative but to hold on and do the best they could, caught in a tempest of events which they could do little to control.

The appeal of the executive committee of Congress appeared to have little effect. During these last critical days before the strike took place, conciliation talks continued in the Labour Court under the chief conciliation officer, Dermot McDermott. The strike began officially at finishing time on Friday 24 January and pickets were placed on some firms that evening. Discussions continued in the Labour Court all Friday, until 2.30 a.m. on Saturday morning when they broke up without any result.

Jimmy Dunne, the president of Congress, immediately asked that the parties should come together again under the chairmanship of McDermott, which they did on Sunday afternoon, and they remained in session all night. At 6.30 a.m. on the following Monday morning, it appeared that agreement had been reached. The employers undertook to recommend

[12]He died in office in April 1972.

the terms for acceptance to their members, and as for the trade unions, ". . . the maintenance group of unions and the Electrical Trade Union have decided that the strike should be discontinued immediately pending reference to the executive of the unions with recommendation from the Group and the ETU that the proposals that emerged be accepted."[13] The text of the agreement was read out twice by Dermot McDermott with both parties present and indeed the word "immediately", a key word in the circumstances, was inserted at the suggestion of Brian Leonard of AGEMOU with no dissent from the trade union side. But all this concealed substantial disagreement among the unions.

At an earlier side conference, Jack Cassidy of NEETU had read a statement to the group as follows:

> Agreed that AEU and NEETU would instruct the members to lift the pickets but that their members would not return to work pending the proposals being referred back to their respective Executive Committees for a decision. This based on the grounds that we did not have a mandate from union to lift pickets without reference back to Executive Committees. This decision would be conveyed to Group and Court.[14]

The trade union representatives were therefore aware that the two engineering unions could not discontinue the strike immediately, and even the agreement to lift the pickets was somewhat ambiguous. Although this was so, no mention of it was made at all when McDermott read out the agreed statement, nor even when Leonard suggested that the word "immediately" be inserted. Jim Cox, the chairman of the group, explained to the Murphy Inquiry that the decision to discontinue the strike and to recommend settlement terms was by a majority vote of the unions present, and that this was the accepted procedure. This was all very well, but the two engineering unions (and the ETU (I) outside the group) had the vast majority of maintenance men, and some of the unions who made up the majority had probably no members involved in the dispute at all. Both the Murphy Inquiry and the Congress Report were critical of the engineering union representatives for remaining silent at this crucial point when McDermott read out the agreed proposals. Indeed, they were at fault; but at the same time the group spokesmen should have done more than set out the formal majority position. I cannot but believe that something of these deep-seated divisions must have been known to McDermott as well; and this may have been why he read the proposed agreement twice

[13]*Murphy Report*, p. 19.
[14]*Murphy Report*, p. 19.

with considerable deliberation. Perhaps after two marathon sessions, those taking part hoped against hope that an agreement known to be fragile would nevertheless stand up. But the FUE representatives seem to have been quite unaware of these divisions, and when the arrangement collapsed, as it did almost immediately, they were extremely angry. They claimed that NEETU and the AEF reneged on the agreement within thirty minutes of leaving the court premises. Certainly some picketing began almost immediately, the plants affected being in the vicinity of the Labour Court; and among these was Jacobs, whose personnel director, Arthur Rice, was chairman of the FUE negotiating team. But the position was confused. According to a radio news bulletin at 8 a.m., the AEF and the NEETU, while they were continuing the strike, had asked their members not to picket. But picketing continued in some firms. As a result, tempers flared and attitudes hardened.

Picketing continued on Monday and Tuesday, affecting some thirty firms in all. But the engineering unions would not, or could not, say whether these pickets were official or not. Eventually on Wednesday, the AEF and NEETU held what they described as a joint executive meeting and instructed all members in FUE firms to withdraw their labour, but decided that pickets would continue to be withheld until 5 February.

By the end of the week, the two engineering unions had ceased to work with the group, and of course the ETU (I) had never been a member at all. Because of the effective disintegration of the group and because of the attitude of the engineering unions, Jim Cox resigned as chairman of the group on Wednesday 29 January and he was succeeded by Brian Leonard, as acting chairman. The FUE also made it clear that they would not enter into separate negotiations with the two engineering unions who, in their opinion, were bringing the whole system of collective negotiation into disrepute, and they called on all employers of maintenance craftsmen to discontinue the employment of members of the AEF and the NEETU.[15]

But the engineering unions swept on. On 2 February, there was a joint meeting of members of the AEF and the NEETU (reportedly about 900) and this meeting reaffirmed the decision to picket on 5 February. Talks continued in the Labour Court and they gave rise to one of the most astonishing episodes in the whole affair. It was now discovered that the unions themselves were by no means in agreement with regard to their claim, and on the very eve of the pickets, on 4 February, Congress called a meeting of the eighteen unions to try to work out a claim on which all were agreed. The president of Congress, Jimmy Dunne, again appealed to

[15]Only one firm, Cement Ltd., responded.

the eighteen unions to suspend picketing pending the formulation and processing of a common claim; and the executive council of Congress, called together urgently for the purpose, endorsed the president's appeal. Although the others agreed, the two engineering unions and the ETU (I) failed to respond.

On the following day, 5 February, the strike was on in earnest; pickets were placed, thousands of workers were thrown out of employment, and in Congress head office, the eighteen unions were still in discussion on what the claim actually was. It took eight hours in all before a common claim was formulated. It became clear now that the suspension of picketing would not by itself prevent large scale dismissals of workers, and the president of Congress the following day asked the unions to suspend the strike for the month of February so that negotiations could take place. Once again the three unions refused.

Although the Irish Transport and General Workers Union formally supported the strike, nevertheless Irish Transport members in Limerick began a retaliatory picket and this became a feature of the strike. The power of a picket—irrespective of its object—to stop a job was sufficiently great to make this a real tactic. Soon after, the president's own union, the Marine Port and General Workers Union, also decided to mount retaliatory pickets which they called protest groups. And so the strike went on during the whole month of February. By this time, a strike committee formed by the AEF and NEETU became the effective authority in the dispute. Con Murphy[16] says:

> It appeared from evidence submitted that the authority of senior officers in the engineering and electrical unions was usurped by officials and persons of less responsibility and that the actual power did pass to the strike committee particularly towards the end of the dispute.

Negotiations, however, continued as best they could with growing dissension, and they were reflected in the mounting and lifting of the retaliatory pickets. But even if an offer were made, there was no agreed procedure by which a ballot could take place; in fact, agreement was not reached by the unions on a balloting procedure until 18 February, that is to say when the strike was already in full swing for almost two weeks. In the event, the fifteen unions left in the group decided to ballot on the basis of one union one vote; the NEETU and the AEF decided to ballot on an aggregate basis, and the ETU (I) decided that they would carry out an independent ballot. When proposals were made on 19 February, the joint executive of the NEETU and the AEF decided to put them to

[16]Op. cit., p. 26.

ballot without any recommendation. This must be taken, in the climate of the time, to be a favourable enough response; but the strike committee which included members of the ETU (I), recommended rejection and, indeed, they were rejected by 586 votes to 271 with approximately 100 abstentions; the ETU (I) also reported rejection without giving details. This shows how dominant the strike committee was; but it also shows the very small number actually involved in bringing about this industrial catastrophe.

At the height of the strike, over 31,000 persons were out of work. Of these, less than 3,000 were members of the unions directly involved in the dispute. The AEF had 581 members on strike, the ETU (I) 127, and NEETU 483 (a further 534 were affected indirectly). The ASW had 157 out on strike, and the National Union of Vehicle Builders 21 directly involved, although in the case of this union an additional 500 were indirectly affected. These numbers were indeed small and caused little financial burden to the unions concerned, with the exception perhaps of the NEETU which had come through a difficult and contentious period of amalgamation. But what of the other unions, who were in no way involved in the dispute, who had not been consulted about it, and whose members were nevertheless thrown out of work? Here the position was very different: the Amalgamated Transport, for example, had over 5,700 members out of work, the Bakers' union nearly 2,000, the Marine Port and General Workers Union nearly 1,300, the Workers Union of Ireland 4,500, and the Irish Transport and General Workers Union nearly 16,000 members. By this time, the strike pattern, while extensive, had a certain arbitrariness about it. Labour was withdrawn from 143 of the 193 firms who were parties to the maintenance agreement; the remainder were unaffected. On the other hand, ten firms were closed who were not parties at all to the 1966 agreement. Other firms were affected because of pickets on common entrances, and to complicate matters further, the large and strategic Cement Ltd., on the advice of the FUE, dismissed craftsmen covered by the maintenance agreement and became involved in the dispute, thereby affecting cement supplies throughout the country.

Negotiations continued in the Labour Court, but they were immensely difficult. On three separate occasions the parties shook hands, believing that agreement had been reached, only to find it rejected later. All negotiating authority on the trade union side appeared to have collapsed. Rarely was there such evidence of division: executive committee against strike committee, amalgamated against national, building against engineering, and, within the same union, representative against representative, and frequently the trade union side broke down into separate groups meeting in separate rooms. But also, in the long desperate late night sessions in the Labour Court, the employers occasionally heard, grotesquely, the sound of singing from the trade union room. Nor was there much contact between the union representatives and the members; indeed it is difficult to see how there could have been. The trade union side had fallen into a squalid domestic wrangle which was resolved ultimately only by the complete capitulation of the employers.

All this was difficult for the FUE to grasp. They had gone into the dispute under the impression that they were dealing with a group whose every move was planned and who were working in accordance with a clear strategy, albeit the strategy was the destruction of the FUE. They had not bargained for this kind of confusion and continued to act as if they were dealing with fully competent negotiators on the other side. In fact, their approach was in almost ludicrous contrast to that of the unions. Probably because of the large number of employers and their diversity, they adopted procedures which, while they kept everybody informed, made them heavy and slow in negotiations. The negotiating side proceeded on the basis of unanimity, an almost impossible task in the circumstances; they did so not because of rule but because of an anxiety to meet every dissenting voice. Furthermore, right throughout the dispute, there were weekly meetings between the negotiating team and the 160 employers, where reports were made and affirmation given. Ultimately, some private initiatives were made to bring the key people on both sides together, but to no avail.

Towards the end of February, the employers began to crack. Individual firms began to make settlements with the unions and, to make matters worse, in doing so they approached not the official leadership but the strike committee, initiating, in the words of Con Murphy[17] ". . . a dangerous process in industrial disputes in conferring a *de facto* negotiating authority on a strike committee which it did not properly possess." Whatever about negotiating authority, they possessed such real power as existed, and this was demonstrated in the fate of the proposals of 27 February. McDermott of the Labour Court considered that they were practically certain of acceptance; the executives of both the AEF and NEETU unanimously recommended them; but the strike committee was not prepared to put its weight behind them. There was a joint meeting of the members of the AEF and the NEETU in the Metropolitan Hall in Dublin which the press described as ". . . tempestuous, stormy, rowdy, noisy almost throughout," and when the proposals were later put to ballot, they were rejected by a three to one majority.

By 5 March, fifteen firms had settled with the engineering unions. The

[17]ibid., p. 27.

FUE found themselves with their backs to the wall and appealed to the Taoiseach to intervene; he refused to do so. But now firms that were actually represented on the FUE maintenance committee began to settle privately with the strike committee; one of these was the firm of the chairman of the committee, Arthur Rice. The settlement apparently was made without his knowledge; he resigned from the chair. The FUE representatives were now authorised to return to the negotiating table with freedom to make the best settlement they could; Dr C. A. Cusack led the deputation which met the unions in the Labour Court on 7 March, while at the same time a general meeting of the employers awaited their report in the Gresham Hotel. They now recognised that all they could hope for was a common agreement, whatever the cost, so that the disorder of individual settlements would be avoided. The unions insisted on 1.3d. as a first step and 6d. later within the context of an eighteen-month agreement (they also accepted a commission of inquiry into the dispute). By an overwhelming majority, the employers at the meeting in the Gresham Hotel decided to concede the claim. Normal working resumed in the majority of the FUE firms on 10 March. The Marine Port and General Workers Union, however, continued the strike in eight firms for a period, in protest at the manner in which their members had been abused.

The second-string leadership in the engineering unions, those that dominated the strike committee and became the effective authority, no doubt regarded all this as a victory. They had achieved a wage settlement of around twenty per cent., one of the largest amounts ever given by Irish industry. The official trade union leadership was discredited; the moral authority of Congress suffered grievously; the FUE was in disarray. Albert A. Blum,[18] in the evaluation of the dispute which he made in 1972, puts down a good deal of the difficulty to lack of experience: "It is also important to note that this was only the second time that these negotiations had taken place in that form. This change in format helped to explain the many strange and somewhat unethical practices of those involved . . ." It would be consoling if this were actually the case; but the fact is that the top trade union leadership did not lack experience; rather did they lack the grip, drive and effectiveness which the situation demanded. And the second-string leadership that came to dominate the dispute in its later stages, seemed in many respects to be not so much inexperienced as blatantly self-centred.

While one cannot excuse this self-centredness, one can understand it, and indeed note its occurrence in similar circumstances in other disputes. It is a dangerous matter when a group of people with a common economic

[18]Op.cit.

interest find themselves frustrated over a period of time—and not only in their objectives but by what they believe to be inadequate leadership; they not only occasionally break through to grasp command of events but they manifest often a considerable selfishness and irresponsibility, almost in defiance of their own leadership and indeed of everyone else. While top leaders must as a rule moderate themselves in a climate of mutual responsibility, men who have continuously experienced constraint from without, show little personal discipline or moderation when they break through into command. Despite all this, however, there was still the sheer cynicism of many of the decisions that were made, the contempt for the trade union movement, the disregard of the suffering imposed on thousands of people, the indifference to the devastating effects which the strike would have on the economy; these things cannot be excused either on the grounds of inexperience or frustration.

Professor Blum is right, however, in seeing the origins of the dispute in the 1966 agreement. Con Murphy, in his conclusions, puts it in better perspective:[19]

> The FUE in requesting and promoting the 1966 maintenance agreement increased the vulnerability of its members by mustering so much of the country's industrial resources, including so much of its labour force, into a single highly sensitive target for a small but powerful group of employees. Although many people proclaim the defects of the 1966 Agreement, none of them has advanced a more viable alternative. Individual house agreements would certainly reduce the risk of so widespread a dispute occurring again but they would multiply the danger of leapfrogging action (without solving any of the real problems).

Murphy, in raising the question of an alternative, puts his finger on the major problem. Of course, in the case of the 1966 maintenance agreement, it could in truth be said that it probably was not necessary; the embarrassing problem of hours could have been overcome by some form of local bargaining. But the question remains as a general one, quite apart from this dispute; and the argument wavers between the extremes of centralised bargaining on the one hand and local leap-frog bargains on the other, a very real peril to the whole economy in view of the overriding importance given to comparabilities in negotiation. Once again, the same theme becomes dominant.

To Murphy, the dispute demonstrated the irrational state of the trade unions:

[19]*Murphy Report*, p. 34.

It seems to me that the principal obligation, so far as trade unions are concerned, rests with Congress which should institute an inquiry of its own into the present state of trade union organisation in Ireland and place proposals for radical improvements before its affiliated unions and organisations.[20]

Congress should be given more authority, there should be a massive programme of trade union education, and Congress should monitor major negotiations and have some early warning system. In quite a number of respects, the recommendations are similar to those in the ESB reports; but before the Murphy report was published, the public became aware of the extremely critical report prepared by the executive council of Congress on the dispute. Although it was confidential, it reached the press before the annual conference and was given wide coverage. The executive council, in placing the report before the conference for approval, were in fact asking the delegates to endorse a very explicit condemnation of the unions involved. There was some fear that the unofficial publication of the report sometime earlier would cause a backlash among the members; since the report at no time dealt with the position of the employers but confined itself to the performance of the unions, it could be attacked as offending against all the traditions of trade union leadership. But feeling was still very strong four months after the dispute, and while some defiant and emotional speeches were made in defence of the engineering unions, the report was adopted overwhelmingly. But this was as far as Congress decided to go. No other disciplinary action was taken.

III

This dispute marks a watershed in Irish industrial relations; there was of course some growth in cynicism (we have seen it in the case of the shift workers), but there were also long, hardheaded efforts on the part of both Congress and the FUE to make some sense of the whole tangled mess of wages and salaries, which led to the very sophisticated national agreements in 1970 and 1972. The effects of the dispute on the economy were devastating, as we have seen, but for our purposes we can detect, arising from this period, four quite distinct developments, which were greatly influenced by the dispute and the agreements associated with it. These are the restructuring of the trade union movement, the power of the picket, the rise of the fixed term agreement and the efforts to control inflationary pressures by means of national agreements and price surveillance.

Initially, at any rate, the dispute appeared to revive interest in trade union structures. Con Murphy, in his report, had urged Congress to

[20]ibid., p. 37.

institute an inquiry of its own into the present state of trade union organisation in Ireland for the purpose of making radical improvements both in regard to structure and also in regard to picketing and other dispute procedures. The Murphy Report had not been published when Congress met in Bundoran in July 1969, but reorganisation was in the air, not only because of the maintenance dispute but also because of the more fundamental problems of communication and tension within the trade union movement, problems which arose because of what Jimmy Dunne described as the two-tier responsibility, one tier of responsibility being concerned with direct negotiations on wages and conditions, and the other with broad national problems of a social and economic character. In such circumstances, some unions might have wished to witch-hunt the Congress administration, but in fact the conference itself turned to emphasise the two topics identified by Murphy, reorganisation and picketing. For the purposes of this account, we shall treat of them separately, although they were both dealt with to a substantial extent by the same committees and conferences.

Congress began by appointing a committee on organisation and structure, and this body had meetings with various trade unions and with the Congress industrial committees and groups. There followed in February 1970 a special conference in Dun Laoghaire. On any showing, the position was very unsatisfactory. The trade union groups, for example, who were often the key bodies in disputes, had, on the whole, no clear method of arriving at decisions, and furthermore appeared to be inadequately serviced; this, as we have seen, had already created many difficulties. But the unions showed little interest in changing the structure, perhaps for reasons of self-interest, but also perhaps from a feeling of helplessness. In such circumstances, the recommendations which the executive council placed before the 1970 annual conference were blandly pious and non-committal:

> The observations of the Conference delegates as well as the observations of the preliminary meeting with the groups showed the need for Congress to assist in the development of group working by continued meetings of this character, which the representatives concerned regarded as being helpful, and these continued meetings should include on their agenda the evolution of improved basic group constitution as well as affording the opportunity of an exchange of views on group practice and on methods of securing its further evolution. It is suggested that the Executive Council should make a commitment to arrange for further group meetings on a quarterly basis.[21]

[21]Irish Congress of Trade Unions, *Twelfth Annual Report* 1970, p. 59.

In view of the damage that was done during the maintenance dispute because of the confusion in group procedures, this was hardly good enough, but it was as far as the unions were prepared to go.

Another possibility for restructure lay in the Congress industrial committees. They had been established during the heyday of economic planning but, in practice, only two showed signs of vigour: the construction industrial committee (because it dealt with one type of employer, and was engaged in straightforward negotiation) and the public services industrial committee (because, in practice, it provided a necessary forum, since the Irish Conference of Professional and Service Associations had declined and become irrelevant). There was no longer any real hope of associating all the unions in eleven or so strong comprehensive industrial committees; but the idea could not altogether be abandoned. What then could Congress do except engage in some evangelism, promise some secretarial support and recognise that more money would be required? There was also a suggestion that the ILO might help in sending an expert to advise.

The third possibility was the old radical one of amalgamation or perhaps federation, and a great deal of time was spent on it at the Dun Laoghaire conference. The last public report of the committee on trade union organisation had recommended that the future structure of the trade union movement should be on an industrial basis, and this had been adopted as policy and circulated to the unions. However, the Dun Laoghaire report[22] observed: "The extent of the response and the nature of the observations received were not consistent with a general feeling of either urgency or enthusiasm to take practical steps to implement the report." And the committee[23] reported sadly to the 1970 annual conference:

> The Committee considers that at the present time little new can be added to the review considered by the Conference, except that the proposed examination of Trade Union Structure by an I.L.O. official might contribute towards further progress.

Jimmy Morrow,[24] who was president at the 1970 annual conference, put explicitly what everybody knew to be true:

> At the same time, let us admit unions only merge because their members decide it is in their best interests to do so. This perhaps is a self-evident fact. But it is worth stating every now and then. It

[22] ibid., p. 162.
[23] ibid., p. 61.
[24] ibid., p. 245.

reminds people that unions do not merge in somebody else's interest, neither do they create new structures, just for the sake of it, or because it makes everything look neat and tidy.

He said this with some sense of hope, however, since his own union, the AEU, was busily changing its initials to AEF and then to AUEW because of recent amalgamations; this note of hope found little echo in the Republic of Ireland. In the aftermath of the maintenance dispute, it appeared that a small union had nothing whatever to gain from amalgamation when it could act quite independently and at the same time bring all other unions out in support of its dispute, whether they liked it or not, by merely placing a picket.

In 1971, and again in 1972, the executive council reported frankly that they had got so absorbed in other matters that they were not able to arrange any meetings of the committee on structure, and even the visit of the ILO consultant was deferred. But there was one significant change brought about by legislation. The Trade Union Act 1971 made it very much more difficult for a union to secure a negotiating licence; in the future it would have to deposit £5,000, certify 500 members and suffer a time-lag, after application, of eighteen months. There was some discussion with the Department of Labour on simplifying the tangle of law associated with amalgamation, but the matter was brought no further.

As for the engineering unions themselves, there appears to be little change either in their structure or in the character of their leadership, and no great pressure from Congress to bring it about. It seems that Congress had now, after the maintenance dispute, recognised that general restructuring was almost a hopeless task, and that therefore one should try to avoid conflict by systems of national bargaining and agreed rules on strikes and pickets; in other words, if one could not improve a particular area, one hoped to neutralise it to some extent. This then was one of the reasons why the emphasis changed so sharply to strike procedures, and in particular to the negotiation of sophisticated national agreements. This was not necessarily a conscious strategy; things are rarely as clear as that; but it emerged strongly nonetheless.

Let us then turn to the question of picketing. This was the only area where the Dun Laoghaire conference and the Congress committee made very explicit and rather far-reaching proposals. Obviously something had to be done. The maintenance strike had demonstrated the astonishing power of the picket in Irish industrial disputes, even to the point of tit-for-tat pickets, a phenomenon that had reality only where workers blindly stopped when a picket was mounted, without inquiring whether it was proper or improper, official or unofficial. It was also peculiar to the

Republic; they had no such experience in Northern Ireland, and Jimmy Morrow emphasised this uniqueness in his presidential address:

> I say in the Republic, because in Northern Ireland we can claim that trade union pickets can be used and have been used with effectiveness on the one hand and discretion on the other. The two are not contradictory. Insofar as the proposals coming before the conference this year represent an effort to bring about in the Republic a somewhat similar situation, I think that we from Northern Ireland must look upon them with understanding and appreciation of the differences in context, even if the fairly elaborate organisational aspects of these proposals would not be necessary in the different circumstances apparently obtaining in the North.[25]

Morrow, of course, may have been influenced by a desire to avoid the introduction of such "elaborate organisational aspects" to the North; but Denis Larkin, who had reservations about the Congress proposals, was no less explicit about the uniquely southern character of the phenomenon:

> Of course you don't have the same system in the North as we have here; you don't have the same system in Britain, with all the thousands and thousands of militant trade unionists; you don't have a situation as soon as a single individual decides that he's going to have a strike—takes a piece of stick and puts a paper on it, and walks in front of an industry and everybody stops. That doesn't happen in Britain, it doesn't happen on the Continent, it doesn't happen in the North of Ireland. It happens here because we have a particular commitment to being militant in this regard.[26]

Yet it is important to recognise that this practice was by no means universal. It seemed to be confined not only to certain types of employment, but to pickets placed by certain categories of worker. Clerical and professional workers, for example, could not hope to command the same kind of instant loyalty from other workers in the same firm. Denis Larkin himself referred, without specifying details, to recent occasions where official pickets placed by his own union were passed by members of other unions. But where it did operate, it operated powerfully and comprehensively.

The proposal of the executive council regarding picketing was quite a

[25]Irish Congress of Trade Unions, *Twelfth Annual Report* 1970, p. 248.
[26]ibid., p. 341.

modest one. They drew a distinction between a picket which was placed in order to secure a stoppage of work by all trade unionists employed in the firm—that is to say an all-out strike—and a picket the object of which was essentially to inform the public and which affected only the members directly concerned. In the latter case, the unions were in no way prevented from mounting pickets at their discretion; but where they required an all-out strike, where they required that all trade unionists should observe their pickets, then the picket notice must be issued not by the union but by Congress. This, if it were observed, would put Congress into a strategic position, because it would not issue the picket notice until the other unions had been consulted and their reasonable objections met. The proposal was persuasively presented to the 1970 conference by Maurice Cosgrave, the incoming president. There was a good deal of opposition to it. Some could not see how any such idea could possibly work in the trade union movement, and their point of view was ably captured by Betty Sinclair, which the Belfast humour sharpens rather than conceals. She described a recent conversation she had with Ruaidhri Roberts, at a time when the North was torn with civil disturbance:

> I was in Dublin on May 9 and 10 and was very happy to be part of a delegation from Belfast, guests of the Dublin Council of Trade Unions. And that evening I met Brother Roberts, the General Secretary of our Congress, and I said 'Ruaidhri, the Executive Council haven't got one motion on the agenda of Congress about what is happening in our country.' 'Oh, Betty,' he said, 'we have a motion.' I said 'You haven't, Ruaidhri.' He says, 'We have, Betty.' I said 'What is the motion?' He said 'It's on picketing.' Well I said it was like Billy crossing the Boyne, it was a pious hope of immortal memory.[27]

Others felt that this particular proposal would not work because it was far too cumbersome. This was the view taken by a delegate from the Workers Union of Ireland; indeed he was of the opinion that the proposal was irrelevant: "The problem concerning pickets is not that members would know which picket to pass and which picket not to pass. The problem is that members will not pass any picket irrespective of whether it is official or otherwise."[28] Nonetheless, the conference obviously wanted to make some headway, however uncertain, in this highly difficult area, and the proposal was adopted by 173 votes to 123.

The whole idea of discipline in the conduct of strikes got a powerful boost in the national agreement on wages and salaries which was concluded

[27] ibid., p. 340.
[28] ibid., p. 332.

between Congress and representatives of virtually all employers at the end of 1970. In a later section, we shall take up its more general implications; here we are concerned with its bid to secure industrial peace. It did so by limiting the areas where conflict could occur. The agreement provided for specific increases for a specified term; a claim in excess of this was contrary to the agreement and so were all other matters, holidays, overtime, sick pay and all the rest. Broadly, there were two exceptions to all this; the first was the claims that were still in the pipeline from the last or twelfth round; and secondly, there were the claims aimed at removing "genuine anomalies in pay", a phrase which was to prove a rich field for the clerical workers. Very explicit procedures were insisted on here; and furthermore, the Employer-Labour Conference established itself as an interpretation committee to ride herd on the problems of implementation. It was in this context that the parties agreed that

> . . . employer organisations and trade unions collectively or individually shall not encourage, support or assist any of the parties involved in a strike or lock-out or other form of industrial action intended to contravene the processing or settlement of such claims in the manner described above.[29]

Congress, furthermore, were determined on making this work, and when they issued copies of the new national agreement to the unions towards the end of December 1970, they also issued the following statement:

> Both the obligations accepted under the enclosed Agreement and the obligations accepted by affiliated unions when they adopted the "All-Out Strike" proposal at the Annual Delegate Conference in July 1970 can be endangered if any support is given to unofficial strikes. My Executive Council desire me to request affiliated unions to take all necessary steps to advise their members that under no circumstances will strike pay be given to any of their members who directly, or indirectly, become involved in unofficial strikes, or refuse to work in observance of unofficial pickets.[30]

Here then were the two struts to the edifice: the areas of dispute would be sharply limited by the national agreement, and the conduct of disputes would be controlled by the all-out picket notice. Of course strikes were by no means excluded, and a number occurred where Congress authorised

[29]Irish Congress of Trade Unions, *Thirteenth Annual Report* 1971, p. 197.
[30]ibid., p. 112.

an all-out strike notice, but the area in which they could occur was much reduced.

Inevitably, the whole arrangement was challenged and the challenge came, not surprisingly, from two engineering unions, AGEMOU[31] and the AUEW. The dispute concerned mechanics in CIE, and the unions claimed an adjustment in holidays, a matter which was expressly excluded by the national agreement. In May, both unions determined on strike action, and the AUEW applied to Congress for an all-out picket notice. While consultations were taking place, AGEMOU, ignoring the whole procedure, mounted pickets selectively in support of their claim, and did so in a bus depot where in fact no member of theirs was employed, making nonsense of the Congress strike policy. Thus, the first strut in the edifice came under attack. But worse was to come; the AUEW, when a plenary session of the Employer-Labour Conference found against them, went ahead with their pickets, and the national agreement was threatened. Initially the NBU, the influential busmen's union, observed the pickets, and bus services were brought to a standstill, despite the appeals of the other unions. However, after a short time, the NBU became impatient with this piece of cynicism, made all the more distasteful by the arrogance of some of the engineering union officials, and decided to instruct their members to pass the pickets. The strike collapsed.

Congress followed this up with the threatened suspension of both unions, and, by the time the annual conference came in July, Charlie Hull from Belfast, the highly embarrassed principal officer of the AUEW in Ireland, had to make some rather tortured attempts to get his union back on the rails, demonstrating more than anything else the virtual independence of his Dublin district committee. We have already noted the collapse of the ESB shift workers in circumstances not too unlike those we consider here. But it is important that we recognise that the ordinary workers saw in these events a good deal of selfish cynicism on the part of a small number; it would be dangerous to assume that the system would survive a large group whose disaffection was widespread and real.

On the whole, Congress was by no means displeased with the way the all-out strike system worked, although, as was anticipated, the administration was difficult.

The arrangements place a heavy burden upon the Industrial Relations Committee of Congress, necessitating numerous meetings to consider these applications. In all but a very small number of cases the All-

[31]Automobile, General Engineering and Mechanical Operatives Union.

Out Strike application was approved and All-Out Strike notice issued. Up to the time of writing this report, however, in all but one case settlement was reached, or negotiations leading to settlement commenced prior to the expiry of the All-Out Strike notice.[32]

And as for the peace clause in the national agreement, there were quite a number who thought that the unions had not fully recognised its implications when they agreed to it in 1970; but when, in 1972, a similar clause was again put to the unions, it was accepted without much difficulty.

This courageous strategy, largely devised by Ruaidhri Roberts, has so far been effective, and deservedly so.[33] And yet there is little feeling of success about it all; if trade union leaders speak about it, they do so with a shrug of acceptance, conscious no doubt that they may be witnessing the disappearance not only of the wrongheaded use of the picket line, but also of that deep solidarity and loyalty which humanises much that is regrettable in industrial disputes.

We turn now to the question of the fixed term agreement. The idea appears to have arisen first in the maintenance agreement in 1966, that is to say, the agreement that produced the centralised bargaining that led directly to the collapse in 1969. The employers were anxious to get some return for the large increase of the time, and they won an undertaking from the unions that there would be no further claims for a period of twenty-six months; furthermore, the increase was not given all at once, but in two stages, or phases, as they came to be called. Thus the idea of a fixed term with phased increases was intended as a protection for employers. Bord na Mona adopted the same idea, and gradually it began to spread throughout industry, constituting throughout 1967 and 1968 the eleventh round. And now we note the second major characteristic of the period: the fact that agreements operated not from a common or near-common date, as they did in the past, but generally from the date on which they were negotiated. The eleventh round rolled slowly through 1967 and 1968; the idea of a common national date quite disappeared, and by 1969, we were confronted with a large number of agreements which terminated on widely different dates, the span being approximately eighteen months. This meant that some were pressing for a new or twelfth round settlement when others had hardly begun the eleventh round.

Initially these agreements, industry-based and sometimes quite comprehensive, were "... welcomed by many as being a new and improved

[32]Irish Congress of Trade Unions, *Thirteenth Annual Report* 1971, p. 43.
[33]The 1973 annual conference of Congress confirmed that strike pay should not be paid to workers who observed the pickets of other unions where they were not authorised as all-out strike pickets.

approach to wage negotiations and as providing a basis for stability."[34] And this was still the case when the 1969 maintenance agreement precipitated the opening of the very substantial twelfth round, and workers waited impatiently for their earlier agreements to terminate in order to come abreast of what the maintenance men had begun, becoming more and more conscious, in our comparability-ridden climate, of how agreement overlapped agreement and phase overlapped phase. There are many who would say that by holding workers to widely scattered terminal dates these agreements contributed a badly-needed stability in 1969 and 1970, but, in the view of the Labour Court, far from giving stability, the new arrangement built a dangerous momentum into wage movements, increasing both their size and their tempo. The arguments for this they set out in their 1969 report,[35] but their voice was lost in the clamour of the times. In the first place, they considered that the arrangement would inflate the size of settlements. Workers undertaking not to make a claim for a substantial period will seek a higher rate; those settling later in the round will seek compensation for the delay, and those settling earlier will try to make up for such lost ground on the next settlement. They also thought that the frustrations of a tight agreement would lead to higher claims on renewal. In the second place, they expected that the term would tend to be shortened without any reduction in the amounts claimed, as workers attempted to reduce the risks of the future.

. . . [In] short, workers try to obtain compensation for the past and insurance against the future by way of ever larger increases and/or shorter periods. The result of all this is that the size of wage increases continues to grow and the periods covered by agreements to shorten.

They contrasted this with what happened before fixed agreements became the practice: "Rounds of wage increases then generally lasted for two years, and workers who settled early in a round . . . [could] come back for an adjustment before the round expired . . . There was not the same urgency to initiate a new round."[36] This was very true. Wage negotiations in the past were occasional episodes, essentially open-ended; once they were accomplished, the parties relaxed. Now, however, wage adjustment was a matter of continuous activity in one form or another and the body politic was locked in a state of hypertension. Whether all this can be attributed to fixed term agreements is of course quite another matter.

But the plight of the ordinary workers was well described by the Labour

[34]Labour Court, *Twenty-Third Annual Report* 1969, p. 4.
[35]ibid., p. 4.
[36]ibid., p. 5.

Court.[37] They worried about rising prices; they would probably have been happy with less, but they had to remain in the race.

> As a result there is at the moment a panic rush to get big increases in wages and this is something that the general run of workers may not want. Having regard to all these factors, the Court feels that the parties concerned would be well advised to give urgent consideration to the necessity for and desirability of continuing the present practice of making fixed term agreements.

But all this was far easier said than done.

Let us turn finally to the efforts that were made to dominate the surging prices and incomes. We have seen how powerful was the impetus of the fixed term agreements; but the very magnitude of the 1969 maintenance agreement was itself most alarming. The full increase over eighteen months was £3.10.0, and this amount continued to increase in the various settlements as the round developed, so that by 1970, £4 a week was quite common. This, as the Labour Court[38] pointed out, represented an increase of 30 per cent. for many general workers. To make matters worse, the maintenance agreement ran only until June 1970 when the question of a further increase would arise. All this looked very perilous. However, a commission under Professor Basil Chubb[39] won breathing space by arranging a short-term agreement which gave the maintenance men £2 a week for six months, that is until the end of December 1970. This was gradually extended to other craftsmen.

The government had thought that a way through might be found by controlling prices and seeking thereby a voluntary restraint by the trade unions who they hoped would seek no more than seven per cent. or thirty shillings a week. This they discussed with Congress in late 1969 and early 1970, but Congress could see no prospect of a general agreement of that kind while the twelfth round (with its many different terminal dates) worked its way out; all they could offer was that the Employer-Labour Conference might find some solution in the context of a thirteenth round national agreement. However, both this and the short-term maintenance agreement meant that there was breathing space only until the end of the year 1970 when the avalanche would begin.

The pressure for some control of the situation now developed in the National Industrial Economic Council, the planning advisory body whose prestige was considerable and which included Congress representatives,

[37]ibid., p. 6.
[38]Labour Court, *Twenty-Fourth Annual Report* 1970, p. 2.
[39]Both an interim and a final report were issued, the latter reviewing the rates in some depth.

as well as employers, the state and independent persons. Its chairman, Dr T. K. Whitaker (who had done so much to initiate and guide economic planning), was most insistent that they should push ahead with a prices and incomes policy. Furthermore, although up to then the NIEC worked by consensus, both Whitaker and some of the independent members were growing very impatient with the tedious business of bringing the trade union movement along with them, particularly when the country was in such a plight, and they were pressing for the issue of a recommendation on prices and incomes, even if it had to be by a majority. Eventually, a report was issued to which all agreed, although it went somewhat further than the Congress representatives wished, particularly in regard to institutions. It visualised that the NIEC would issue guidelines, the Employer-Labour Conference would make them 'operationally useful', and an incomes and prices committee would decide what increases should be investigated. The arrangements for investigation were sloppy because the existing institutions were reluctant to change their character, but it was expected that in a short time the incomes and prices committee would become dominant. (We shall discuss this more fully in the final chapter).

All this was presented to the annual conference of Congress in July 1970 as part of the annual report of the executive council, and it emerged rather late in the debate that the adoption of the report would mean the acceptance of these institutional arrangements, subject of course to the approval by a special delegate conference of any guidelines which might be proposed. Reference back was moved by the Irish Transport, for the rather confused reason that they had not had time to decide their policy, despite the fact that the NIEC report had been published three months earlier. The reference back was carried. To make matters even more difficult, a motion from the Workers Union supporting a prices and incomes policy was defeated, a motion from the AUEFW offering implacable opposition was also defeated, and a motion which spoke merely of price surveillance and of an orderly and equitable growth in incomes was accepted. The whole question of a prices and incomes policy was in confusion and disarray, and the immediate plans of the NIEC were in ruins. In fact, the NIEC itself never recovered from this. It had become an embarrassment to many people in these rather negative times and it was too vulnerable to attempt the venture it did. Some time later, it was disestablished in order to make way for a more representative National Economic Council, which, because of points of disagreement, has never got off the ground.[40]

[40]The national coalition government, soon after taking office, announced their intention of establishing such a council.

Congress salvaged what it could, turning now to the Employer-Labour Conference which had been reconstituted in May with Basil Chubb as independent chairman. The expectations of the workers were however inordinately high. Despite the difficulties which we have set out here, ministers of state in their public statements were bland and confident (probably for other reasons altogether), and workers found it very difficult to accept the jeremiads of the officials. In these circumstances, the employer-labour talks came to nothing. Suddenly, however, the government became thoroughly alarmed; the end of the year was nearly upon them and many agreements were running out. On 16 October, they announced the immediate statutory control of all incomes, holding them to 6 per cent. or 36 shillings a week; they also proposed to control fees, dividends and rents, without however specifying a maximum; and since prices could not be immediately frozen, they proposed to strengthen and extend the limited machinery which existed. These statutory restrictions would run until the end of the year. The trade union movement was outraged; they saw this as wage control by law in all its nakedness. Only in wages and salaries were maxima specified; prices and other incomes could escape the net. The manner in which it was done, the cries of urgency, seemed to them all the more sinister since no major claim fell for renewal before the end of the year. The influential public service were doubly aggrieved. Their second phase increase under the twelfth round was due on 1 January and the government, fearing that it would generate too much pressure, had decided to repudiate the arrangement. Vehement statements were issued and a political action committee was formed. The government began to crumble. First they decided to honour their commitment to the civil servants and, then, after lengthy discussions with Congress representatives, they agreed to remove from the bill any mention of a wage limit (this being left to ministerial order), opening the way thereby to a resumption of discussions at the Employer-Labour Conference. The whole episode had introduced a new realism into the negotiations, a consciousness of the current economic perils, which, as Congress had pointed out, the government up to then had done little to popularise. The Employer-Labour Conference, however, had now to proceed without a chairman; before the government's move, Basil Chubb, their independent chairman, had felt obliged to make clear his own view of the impasse, and Congress refused to accept him for the purposes of the renewed discussions. (He was later to resume as chairman.) Despite all this, a national agreement was painfully hammered out, and when the text was placed before a special delegate conference of Congress on 11 December 1970, it was adopted.[41] The Prices and Incomes Bill was withdrawn by the government at the same time.

[41]Irish Congress of Trade Unions, *Thirteenth Annual Report* 1971, p. 193 ff.

In this build up towards the 1970 national agreement, we have seen up to now principally the activities of the government and Congress; but, as must be clear, the FUE and the other employer organisations displayed through it all a steady commitment to a negotiated settlement, and were prepared to go a considerable distance to achieve it. In view of all they had been through, they could have been forgiven for doing less.

It was a little miraculous that any agreement was reached at all. There were so many complexities to be met, so many tensions to be overcome in this highly ambitious attempt to achieve agreement on the wages and salaries of virtually every employee in the state. In the first place, nothing could be done about the terminal dates, and so it was decided that the new settlement would arise only when the current settlements ran out. Secondly, it was decided to make the agreement for eighteen months on the basis of two payments or phases, the first being for two pounds a week flat for all male workers, the second being on a percentage basis. This made it more acceptable to the general workers. Thirdly, it was decided to build in a cost of living escalator clause in the second phase which a number of us opposed at the time as being inflationary, but which in the event was probably essential for acceptability in view of rising prices. Virtually all other matters, apart from anomaly claims, were excluded, and the Employer-Labour Conference, in its interpretation role, held a firm grip on its implementation. These questions of interpretation were usually dealt with by a small committee of the conference and gradually there developed, quite uniquely, a judicial function in industrial affairs jointly exercised by the employers and Congress.

During the period of its operation, the agreement worked well. There were of course problems. Apart from those we have already described, there were two major sources of tension. The lengthy span of terminal dates caused those benefiting late in the round to feel somewhat cheated; and the public service unions made such profitable use of the anomaly clause as to establish an independent and additional salary movement. Yet despite this, when the agreement fell in in 1972, another along the same lines was negotiated by the Employer-Labour Conference. This was contrary to all precedent, and indeed the ICTU had a tense series of delegate conferences before consent was finally won. On this occasion, the emphasis turned to percentage increases at all stages; the agreement itself was somewhat more flexible, but little could be done about the span of terminal dates which pushed the increases in some cases into the quite distant future. In the meantime, a Prices Commission had been established, whose sharply independent reports have done much to give confidence to the trade union movement. The ideas developed and promulgated by the NIEC have therefore borne fruit, although not in the manner they expected. The habit of bargaining in this way is therefore growing, and a move during the 1973 annual conference of Congress—to oppose in principle any future national agreement—was defeated comfortably enough, the delegates deciding instead to examine the position in September.

But there is much as well to cause concern. The impetus identified by the Labour Court is still building up within the system, creating pressures of its own; and furthermore, the impact of comparabilities on wage rates has become more starkly effective. The agreements do give some flexibility, of course, but the urge to conformity is enormous; thus one wage settlement, however justified, can shift the income of the whole nation. A substantial measure of peace has been won, but at a very high cost. To this we shall return in the final chapter.

CHAPTER SIX

The Banks and the Teachers

I

AT the beginning of February 1970, all the offices of the clearing banks in the Republic of Ireland began working restricted hours because of an industrial dispute. By 1 May, they had closed completely and did not open again until mid-November; it was not until the middle of February 1971 that full banking hours were resumed and full services restored; that is to say, business was disrupted for a whole year and the banks were closed completely for over six months. It was the most prolonged and comprehensive stoppage in banking yet recorded for any country in the world.[1] The damage done to the commercial life of the country was very great, but curiously not as devastating as one might imagine. A sophisticated money system continued on the basis of cheques and trust, although, towards the end of the dispute, overseas traders were reluctant to go much further. There were some collapses when the day of accounting came and bank credit had indulgently soared, but, on the whole, things were not at all as bad as one might have expected; and later the Central Bank undertook an economic survey of the phenomenon of a modern money society doing without its banking services.[2]

Our concern here is with the dispute itself rather than with its economic effects. An inquiry was commissioned by the Minister for Labour. It was conducted by Professor Fogarty, then director of the Economic and Social Research Institute, who reported on 1 May 1971. It was a personal commission.[3] His report sets out the events, evaluates them and indicates

[1]Michael P. Fogarty, *Report of Bank Inquiry* (Stationery Office, Dublin, 1971), pp. 24, 25.
[2]*Survey of Economic Effects of Bank Dispute* 1970 (Central Bank of Ireland, Dublin, 1971).
[3]*Report of Bank Inquiry*, op. cit.

where future peace may lie, and is a model of its kind, although since he saw the inquiry essentially as a consultancy, his criticisms may be somewhat muted.

For many years, bank officials in Ireland were a privileged group of people, particularly in the towns that served the rural population. Fogarty remarks on this and on the fact that up to 1941 the bank officials were insulated against the effects of change in the cost of living and in income tax. But the privilege ran even deeper than Fogarty suggests. Not only was the bank official's income tax paid but his golf and tennis subscriptions were paid as well, and if he eventually became a manager, he received a large salary, insurance commissions, an impressive house, and a porter to keep his garden. But it was privilege which was buried in paternalism. A young man had to have a director's nomination before he could sit the entrance examination; his initial salary was deliberately low and had to be subsidised by his parents; he could not marry below a certain income without the banks' permission; his wife was permitted to trade only in certain shops; and in all this, the bank directors saw the officials as protégés as much as employees and expected them to be grateful. The directors, however, were remote from the official; his immediate relationship was with the bank manager who commanded, in such a system, considerable authority and prestige.

And yet there was unrest throughout the years, the 1970 dispute being a climax rather than an isolated event. Professor Fogarty brings us back to 1919 when there was a threat of strike action and later the making of the two key bargains, tax free salaries and cost of living support. But the officials themselves put the beginning of unrest at a much later date, in 1933 in fact, when a radical departure was made in salary scales. New entrants from then on were offered a lower salary, more in keeping with the cost of living of the period. At that depressed time, men were only too glad to take the jobs that were offered, but when things improved, those who entered after 1933 felt very aggrieved when they compared themselves to their colleagues; it was from these that much of the later militancy came.

In 1941, the banks at a price shed themselves of the 1921 commitment regarding income tax and (to an extent) cost of living, but while the war years suppressed salary movements, they did not suppress the growing restlessness which became vehement in 1948 and 1949, leading to the Christmas strike of 1950. At the same time, the bank officials' union, the Irish Bank Officials' Association, acquired a new and more militant leadership and appointed as their full-time official John Titterington, who, to outsiders at least, appeared irascibly, implacably, and stubbornly to dominate the whole scene from then on.

The story of the fifties was a story of the defence of privilege. The IBOA never joined the Irish Congress of Trade Unions but were prominent in the Irish Conference of Professional and Service Associations. Despite this connexion, they, as a matter of policy, tried to negotiate outside and against the pattern of the wage rounds; they vehemently declared their uniqueness, and while they greatly influenced the ICPSA, the logic of their position made them always a little remote from it. The other salaried groups both resented and admired them, and so successful was their policy, that to a great extent they were excluded from direct if not general comparability arguments because of their exceptional position. Inevitably, this was achieved only by a number of long and tortuous strikes.

The IBOA, and indeed the banks themselves, serve not merely the Republic but Northern Ireland as well, although in the North the Ulster Bank is dominant on the employers' side, while in the South it is the Bank of Ireland. IBOA initiatives, however, seemed to spring much more from the South. There were exceptions where the initiative was taken in the North, as in the case of the five-day week, or where the move was made in both areas at the same time, but, on the whole, the IBOA moved first in the Republic, which provided a far richer militant streak. There were of course difficulties in the North; in the forties, some officials challenged the compulsory wage orders of the time and were prosecuted; the religious divide did not help in creating a unified feeling, but all that apart, workers generally in Northern Ireland are (or perhaps were) more disposed than those in the South to accept the views of the establishment and therefore less likely to respond to a union's clarion call. This in itself is a fascinating topic where the same leadership has different followers and different foes, but it lies outside this study, as it lay outside the Fogarty report as well. In the discussion that follows, then, we shall concern ourselves essentially with affairs in the Republic.

The changes in banking in the sixties were immense, greater in a few short years than in the whole of the previous century.[4] Where before there were a number of small employment units doing a standardised routine business, there was suddenly a great reconstruction, the creation of two giant systems by a series of mergers and a radical development of banking business. At the same time, a coincidence of retiring ages brought in a flood of young people and, in changed circumstances, a number of young women as well. In all this, the bank manager, in particular, experienced a great shift in his position; where before, in an admittedly standardised situation, his word was virtually law, now, although his responsibility appeared larger, he was in fact more dependent on the

[4] ibid., p. 18.

strategies of head office, and was no longer the one who personalised the whole employment to the young official.

Yet in 1968, in the full flush of all these changes, the major pay negotiations went very well. A joint industrial council had been established under the chairmanship of Dermot McDermott of the Labour Court; there was talk of the dawn of a new era and both Mr Titterington and Mr Edward Gray of the banks were very pleased. Gray, who later died tragically in an air crash, was employed as secretary to the Banks Staff Relations Committee, to negotiate with the union and little else; all other personnel business was conducted by the banks themselves. When he resigned in 1968 to go elsewhere, his post was not filled for nearly a year, and his successor, Mr E. A. Grace, was confronted with a situation already coming to the boil. It appears that the banks at the time were very anxious to overcome the distressing staff relations of the past; indeed Grace felt that they were virtually intimidated by Titterington and the IBOA. Grace resigned in February 1970 on the eve of the strike, and Gray returned on loan as spokesman of the banks.

The agreement which the banks and the IBOA made in June 1968 was for a fixed term of two years. This is the point on which the later dispute turned, since it was understood that there could be no further increase until the end of June 1970, and pressures mounted in the meantime. There was however an escape clause: the Association could seek a revision ". . . in the event of extraordinary circumstances arising within the period."[5] Already by the end of 1968 there were murmurs of unrest because of the mini-budget of that autumn. The massive increase which the maintenance workers got early in 1969, however, gave the movement impetus, and by the end of 1969 the national discussions on price control and wage restraint convinced the IBOA that, if they did not move immediately, they might be fixed with a national pay pause. Mass meetings of members in January 1970 gave a wholehearted and militant mandate to the executive. The issue was quite clear: the banks said that there could be no movement until after June when the two-year agreement concluded; the association declared that exceptional circumstances had arisen and therefore a new agreement must be negotiated, and to that end they submitted a wide-ranging claim which was also deliberately imprecise. No headway was made at the joint industrial council, arbitration was agreed upon, but, despite this, the IBOA decided on immediate industrial action and in February the bank officials began to work restricted hours.

Nevertheless, the arbitration went ahead, the arbitrator being Professor Martin O'Donoghue, an economist with a very lively awareness

[5]ibid., p. 25.

of what was happening in the economy. We have seen that, in the aftermath of the maintenance dispute, Congress counselled calm, since the various term agreements had often a substantial period to run and the impact of the maintenance increase would be muffled; and although the Labour Court might have disliked term agreements, no one anticipated that the term agreements themselves would be set at naught and the maintenance increase pumped instantly throughout all employments. But this might well happen if the banks broke through and others followed. This must have been the arbitrator's dilemma, although its full implications may not have been realised by the IBOA who regarded themselves as exempt from all such considerations. O'Donoghue, not surprisingly, found against the IBOA, but, before he issued his finding, the IBOA indicated an interest in accepting a somewhat watered-down version (which in the event they later rejected), and as a result an arbitration process was turned into a piece of straightforward bargaining, with somewhat sour results.

Yet O'Donoghue's final formula deserved to succeed. After all, June was not far away and in effect he recommended immediate negotiations, the results of which would be implemented after June, when even retrospective payment would not be excluded.

On reflection, it is doubtful if this was an arbitrable matter at all, or if it were, whether any well-informed economist could arbitrate in a neutral manner. This aspect is not dealt with in the Fogarty Report, dwelling as it does rather on the defects of imprecision in the 1968 agreement which the arbitration was intended to resolve. But there was much more at stake than interpretation. The IBOA saw it as an early strategic move in a militant campaign, and O'Donoghue, recognising this, was prepared to help in getting negotiations moving, as long as the term agreement in some clear form remained.

Because of the restricted hours, the banks curtailed services from the beginning of March, and by the end of that month they cut salaries by twenty-five per cent. to correspond with the reduced working. The clearing house had fallen into a dreadful tangle and the banks transferred more staff there, which contravened the IBOA decision on restricted working. The IBOA instructed their members to reduce hours still further, the officials in the clearing house were suspended as a result, and three days later, on 30 April, the banks, faced with a total breakdown, closed their doors altogether.

This dispute dragged on through May and June. Meetings of the joint industrial council took place but there seemed to be an atmosphere of siege more than battle. Many officials had got jobs elsewhere for the period of the strike and, in addition, there was an expectation that any settlement would include provision for the payment of the salaries lost during the strike. This, on the face of it, seems astonishing, but the banks had done just that on a previous occasion, and although they tried to dispel any expectations in the current dispute, they were markedly unsuccessful. An offer which emerged in July was rejected, the JIC talks broke down, and the Minister for Labour referred the dispute to the Labour Court.

At this point, it appears that the salary offer itself was not the central problem: what was in issue now was payment for the period before June and payment of salaries lost during the dispute, and these were two very sticky principles of much greater significance than their money cost. The Labour Court had, however, no difficulty in resolving the first, recommending increases from dates substantially earlier than June, but they were sharply opposed to the idea of payment during the strike; even though they had conceded an earlier date, they considered that the banks were perfectly within their rights to have resisted the claim. In their view, strikes would be much prolonged and employers would be slower to concede ". . . if workers were to maintain that, because an employer, in the end, made a concession on a claim which he originally resisted, he was wrong in the first instance and that he should, therefore, pay the workers while they were out."[6] Because of this, the recommendation as a whole was rejected by the IBOA when it was made public at the end of July. The Minister for Labour instantly supported the Labour Court in their judgment on the issue of pay during strike, and the IBOA therefore turned, as they should have done in the first place, to bargaining on the means by which the back-log of work would be cleared in order to achieve much the same result in money terms. The wrangle continued on this until October, when eventually a proposal was accepted by ballot vote. While that part of the settlement was substantial, and while in immediate terms some officials received impressive increases, nevertheless, when Fogarty later compared the actual scale adjustments with other current settlements, he concluded that the remarkable thing about the terms was that they were so unremarkable.[7]

Was all this fuss then quite unnecessary, all the damage, the disruption and the stress? Certainly, on the face of it, there was nothing of great difficulty to be negotiated. When it came to crisis early in 1970, the issue appeared to be merely one of timing: whether the negotiations could open immediately or the following June. As June passed by, the point was made largely irrelevant, and, instead, a major confrontation developed on payment for the strike period; and so the dispute dragged on until October. Apparently, the salary claim was not itself the major issue.

[6]ibid., p. 172.
[7]ibid., p. 33.

Why then should the country have been crippled financially for so long? In attempting to gain some understanding of this, there are three lines we can pursue: firstly, whether some deep feelings of unrest and alienation were taking command of events and producing an intractable situation; the second, whether there was great ineptitude in the negotiations; and thirdly, whether, in fact, other policies were being pursued and other matters fought out within the cockpit of the claim. These matters are not mutually exclusive, but it is useful to see where the major emphasis falls.

We have seen in the case of the busmen, the Bord na Mona workers and the day workers in the ESB, how a wave of anger and frustration swept the leadership aside and drove everyone headlong into dispute. There are no grounds for believing that any such phenomenon occurred in the banks in 1970. True, we saw the curtailment of privilege (which we must take up again later in the discussion), we saw falling relative standards, and the sudden recruitment of many young men and women who suffered the traditionally low initial salary. Fogarty also notes the history of distrust over the years, the crude insensitivity to the effects of radical change, the conservative centrality of the IBOA, and, over the whole banking system, the inadequacies of communication and participation. Of course feeling was high because of these things, but there is no evidence that the leadership of the IBOA had in any way lost control. And Fogarty is careful to point out that the claims put forward by the Association were the real points at issue and did not merely stand surrogate for some inarticulate cry of stress. The Association itself is in no doubt that it was at all times in command of the situation, and far more explicitly than Fogarty's report indicates. The leadership discount completely the idea of a surging group of bank officials pushing them into action, and they point to the 1964 negotiations where feelings were equally high and where nevertheless they followed a policy of restraint. This view is confirmed by those close to the dispute but independent of it: the impression they had at the beginning of the dispute was of a restless but muddled membership; the IBOA leadership, on the other hand, was determined, ruthless, and unswerving. One could not suggest, of course, that the IBOA would have got away with a lax and laggardly approach to the problem; but what is clear is that they had a good deal of flexibility, they were not being pushed hard up against the event, and therefore they must have chosen, with some freedom, the path they followed.

Let us turn secondly to the question of ineptitude. Fogarty, whose report is rather over-gentle, is quite caustic about the sloppy drafting of the clause in the 1968 agreement which dealt with exceptional circumstances. We have met this point before in the 1964 national pay agreement.

It is somehow assumed that if terms are agreed they must always be precise, and implicitly that there is no place for the deliberately imprecise statement which tries to represent at least some degree of consensus. It may be in fact impossible to avoid such a term, and in the banks' case the alternatives would have been to tie the settlement to the official cost of living figure (which would have been unwise) or not to have any such term at all (which might have been the breaking-point.) If there was a blunder, it was in assuming that such a term was an arbitrable matter. There were three other features of the negotiations identified by Fogarty. Firstly, the IBOA asked for a substantial increase but would not indicate any precise amount, leaving the banks fumbling in much of the early negotiation; secondly, Fogarty considered that the IBOA escalated the claim sharply and unnecessarily at the early stages, and, thirdly, they invited a head-on collision on the issue of salary payment for the period of the strike, when the object could have been otherwise attained. But these, even the last, are largely dispute tactics, which, while in some respects deplorable, show no ineptitude whatever, nor indeed does Fogarty suggest that they do. On the other hand, the banks had no negotiating secretary for a whole year up to August 1969, that is to say during the period when the 1968 agreement was maturing, and while it is difficult to evaluate the impact of this on the growth of the dispute, it must demonstrate at least, that even at that stage, despite their statements of good intent, the banks had a very casual approach to industrial relations.

Let us turn then to our third question—whether other deeper matters were being fought out in this dispute, making the whole thing very much more intractable. Of course, the salary claim was the centre-piece and must not be lost sight of, but the two issues that really blocked settlement were the exceptional circumstances clause and the claim for payment of salary during the strike. Let us take the second question first.

Both sides displayed a kind of intransigence on this issue which to an outsider was almost lunatic; did it not appear that the IBOA, initially at any rate, were attempting to enforce their demand in the form of a moral penalty, and did not the banks, certainly after August, seem almost obtusely inflexible in what had now become a piece of horsetrading with no principle really involved? It becomes somewhat more explicable if one recognises the tradition of conflict which had grown up between the two sides. The banks had always kept the IBOA at a distance, rarely consulted with them, and confined their dealings with them to the limited area of bargaining. In the early years, the IBOA was seen as a troublesome, alien influence, never as part of the banking system, and when John Titterington was appointed first in 1948, he was treated with scant courtesy.

The IBOA and in particular Titterington, perhaps because of this, saw the banks also in terms of conflict; Titterington himself, a gifted man socially, never progressed to first-name terms with his opposite numbers. To the banks, he was Attila the Hun, to be fought or to be bought, but always striking terror, with his aggressive statements and displays of flaring temper. Even when the banks wished in later times to adopt a more conciliatory role, this was now hardly possible; the IBOA had become a militant command-type union, highly organised for conflict at the centre, massively supported by its membership, but with no representative or participative organs at local bank level—typically an embattled organisation with no participative role. So powerful was this idea of conflict, that moves by the banks to become more closely associated with the Federated Union of Employers would be regarded as a hostile act, the gathering to oneself of allies in the war, not an understandable move for a joint approach on certain national issues. This, in any event, is one of the reasons why the banks did not progress beyond a loose association with the FUE; and since the IBOA (perhaps for reasons of exclusivity) would not join the Irish Congress of Trade Unions, the moderating and sensible influence of other interests was not experienced, and the two stood naked to battle on a promontory of their own. This mythology of conflict convinced the bank officials generally that one gained nothing except by strikes and the threat of strikes, and all their long-term strategies were designed to that end. They saw in the banks a capacity to maintain their income even though their doors were closed, and they themselves built up a situation where, by and large, after disputes, members made up the money they had lost. In this way, officials on strike could get jobs elsewhere and sit the strike out, confident that they would get back in one form or another the salary they had lost. (In point of fact, although the closure in 1970 lasted six months and many of the staff—often young men and women—scattered to England and elsewhere, nevertheless almost everyone returned when the strike was over.) If the armoury was to be preserved for the future, then, it was essential that the officials should get back in some form the salaries they had lost, and the wringing of a penalty from the banks was not so much the point, despite the play made of this by the Labour Court and by the Fogarty Report. It is reasonable to conclude, as well, that the banks—and particularly Gray—saw the issue in much the same way as the IBOA did; they therefore tried to resist payment under any guise, causing the dispute to drag on from August until October. They too were concerned with the larger strategy, with the strength of the armoury on the other side.

The second issue, the one which precipitated the dispute in the first place, was the question of seeing the term out to the end, an issue which, in the event, became irrelevant in the course of the dispute. Of course, it was difficult for the IBOA to accept O'Donoghue's formula because the postponement of implementation would probably make immediate negotiation meaningless; but there was a deeper reason for the IBOA's rejection of the recommendation. Their policy of going-it-alone, which we have already noted, had brought them success down through the years; they believed that they had an edge on other salaried people—an edge which perhaps others deserved as well, but which they had actually won by their militancy and which they had no intention of losing now. They reacted violently, therefore, to the idea of being trapped by the national pay movements or being restricted by national considerations; they wholly distrusted arguments of that kind, fearing that they could lead only to a relative fall in their status, and this in turn made them hostile to any public explanation of the dispute. Ned Gray, on the other hand, had a profound feeling of national concern, which took the form of trying to make some personal contribution to good order in salary movements. He had been a powerful voice in the Quinn tribunal which tried to establish one clerical salary for the whole public service. Certainly, to him at least, the whole IBOA approach was irresponsible. The collision course was therefore set, and when the whole thing worked its way out, there was little one could say on the issue other than that it was a drawn game.

In December 1970 came the national agreement on wages and salaries, imposing new constraints, and sharpening the raw edge of disagreement on this issue. Fogarty, who reported in May 1971, recognised this, and gently tried to woo the bank officials to consider other approaches. He emphasised that the 1970 agreement had by no means produced exceptional scales, that the banks' scales were now broadly in line with everyone else's, that in the future other salaried people would not let the banks go their own way as in the past, and consequently that the bank officials should come in from the cold. But all this would hardly be possible in a climate of drawn battle, and so he urged a substantial improvement in participatory management and a new-look participative structure for the IBOA as well. We have found the same ideas put forward more crisply and confidently in the ESB reports, for the fact was that the next salary claim would begin to bite in a few short months (the current agreement terminated in December 1971) and, while Fogarty called for urgency, it seemed highly unlikely that any such radical changes could be effected in time.

To evaluate a dispute as contemporary as the banks' is difficult, since it throws its shadow well into the future, and in this case beyond the time of writing; because arising from these and subsequent events, a bill was enacted in early July 1973 (that is contemporaneous with the writing of this account) which, as we have seen, was designed to limit future bank settlements, and the way ahead is quite unclear.

There was, in view of what we have said, a certain inevitability about this. Yet very soon after the bank strike ended, some interesting changes in personnel took place which some saw as having considerable significance. Both sides appointed new chief negotiators. John Titterington had announced his retirement and his successor was in the wings, while in the case of the banks, they had some time before appointed John Gogarty as their negotiating secretary. The two newcomers had considerable experience in industrial relations, but all of it in England; and while the IBOA, and perhaps the banks, had probably searched as much for warrior-leaders as anything else, one could not expect the two newcomers to see it all in quite that way; and in the event, whether for that reason or another, both men have since moved to other pastures. John Titterington, returned from retirement, is once again leading for the IBOA, while the banks are in the process of appointing their representative. Yet in this period since the summer of 1971, the IBOA and the banks seem to have made common cause, both gradually drifting instead into a common confrontation with the government.

In the autumn of 1971, talks got under way between the parties on the question of a new agreement, and early in 1972 a settlement emerged which on the face of it departed so radically from the terms of the national agreement that an anxious Minister for Labour referred the matter for investigation to the Labour Court. This he did early in February, but the Labour Court did not issue its report until 20 March; they consulted at some length with the steering committee of the Employer-Labour Conference, who, it appears, were much more alarmed than they were. The Court found in the event that the banks' settlement contravened the national agreement in a very considerable way, but the banks, by this time yielding to pressure, had paid the increases. The Minister for Finance therefore demanded that the banks adjust the settlement to conform with the national agreement, but this was easier said than done.

The bank settlement did indeed appear to be alarming. In the first place, the agreement was for one year only, when the national agreement required an eighteen-month term. Secondly, junior officials, in exchange for a temporary allowance of £40 a year (which was abolished), had their salaries increased by £75 to £100, in addition to the £2 a week provided for in the national agreement, and those in senior positions, also in addition to £2 a week, received increases ranging up to £183 a year. Of course, the banks had faced a major difficulty. After the strike, overtime at inflated rates had continued for a very long time, and it was protracted further by the introduction of decimalisation early in 1971. Expectations were therefore high; yet as the banks pleaded before the Labour Court, relations now were much improved, and if additional increases had been given, they were in return for greater flexibility and were consequently permitted by the national agreement. And with regard to the term of one year, they submitted that in December 1972 they could proceed to negotiate a six-month settlement in accordance with the second phase of the national agreement. These agreements, as they are presented in the Labour Court's report, look quite bogus, and perhaps the productivity arguments were; but the fact seems to be that the settlement, although overgenerous, was not nearly as bad as it looked. The temporary allowance which had been extinguished, for example, was an average, and the amounts which had actually been paid to individuals were often three times as great; and much of the increase in the case of senior officials resulted from the shortening of a scale that was inordinately long. But Titterington, then on the brink of retirement, had made considerable play of the success of the negotiations, and the banks did not think it prudent to contradict him. Furthermore, the settlement in 1970 had been applied automatically to the officials in the North of Ireland, and the 1972 settlement contemplated the North of Ireland as well, making it difficult for both parties either to wait on a decision of the Republic's Labour Court or to attempt to adjust their settlement to it.

Indeed the inclusion of the Northern banks in the settlement caused both sides to play down the national agreement and any commitment they might have to it, despite the submissions they made privately to the Labour Court. In fact, the IBOA did not appear to have changed its policy in the least, but the stubbornness of Ned Gray in the national interest seemed to have largely disappeared from the banks' approach, and they now saw the national agreement not as a commanding commitment to economic welfare, but rather as yet another difficult constraint in the negotiation environment.

But what could the government do in the light of the Labour Court's report? The award had been made, the money paid, and consequently the desultory discussions that followed were of little effect. But there was an expectation at least that when it came to negotiating the second phase increase at the end of 1972, it would be within the terms of the national agreement. In January 1973, it appeared that, during the course of these negotiations, proposals had emerged for the shortening of scales and other improvements, and an alarmed Minister for Labour referred the matter once again to the Labour Court, who reported on 16 April 1973 that "the Court would not have found grounds within the terms of the National Agreement for recommending the shortening of any of the scales in question,"[8] nor would they have recommended certain adjustments which had been proposed for managers and assistant managers. While they agreed that some of the other proposals were within the national agreement, the substance of their decision was that for the second time, while protesting their compliance, the banks and the IBOA were concluding an arrangement quite at variance with the national agreement. It was in these circumstances that the government envisaged introducing legislation, the object of which would be to impose penalties on both the banks and the officials if they persisted in contravening the national agreement. However, before the bill was introduced, the Fianna Fáil government went out of office.

The new government inherited the difficulty, which in June became critical, as the banks and the IBOA, in their negotiations for a new agreement, seemed uncommonly like tossing the national agreement aside once again. Meetings with the government had apparently no effect, and early in July the Minister for Labour introduced the Regulation of Banks (Remuneration and Conditions of Employment) (Temporary Provisions) Bill 1973 which was rapidly enacted, and which had the same object as the proposed Fianna Fáil legislation, the major difference being that the penalties were confined to the banks. The Minister announced his intention to introduce the legislation while the annual conference of Congress was meeting in Killarney; the exemption of the union from penalty was designed to counteract the trade union dread of penal legislation while, at the same time, his hope was that the legislation itself would stiffen confidence in the concept of national agreements. The proposed legislation was welcomed by the Congress leadership and received calmly by the other unions, with little rumbling even from the radical fringe. No one in fact was prepared to espouse the bankers' cause, or even appear to do so.

It is difficult to say what the result will be of this confrontation. It is, in any event, being worked out at a time when a new national agreement is coming up for review, and when trade unions are once again questioning the very concept underlying this form of national bargaining; the banks' dispute has served to sharpen up its profile. This is particularly so in the matter of sanctions. Let us consider how these apply at present.

The moral and social pressures on unions to observe (or be seen to observe) national agreements is really very considerable, much greater than one imagines at first sight. In addition, as we have already recognised, there is in practice a prices and incomes policy of some sophistication

---

[8] *Report to the Minister for Labour under section 24 of the Industrial Relations Act 1946, concerning a proposed agreement covering employees of the Commercial Banks.* Report 1–73, Section 24, 16 April 1973.

operating in this country, although the NIEC perished on the way; and in the case of manufacturers, for example, one clear penalty is that applied by the National Prices Commission which will refuse to permit a price increase where it is attributable to a wage settlement in excess of the national agreement. However, the banks and the IBOA, in their isolation, tended to be insensitive to social pressures on the one hand, and on the other, bank charges are exempt from review by the National Prices Commission. True, the Central Bank has some role in this regard, but there are murmurs that this is not enough. It seems astonishing that the commercial banks, which normally would be regarded as the soul of economic good sense, should be distrusted in this way. Of course, they dread the idea of another protracted strike; it could result in a flood of business to the small but developing American and other non-associated banks, or could even lead to nationalisation; but it was shocking, nonetheless, that they should have persisted in dismissing the Labour Court recommendations. Some might claim that they were not the most judicious of recommendations, and perhaps other employers had given increases which were at the very least somewhat questionable (the cement industry and the fertiliser industry spring to mind), but nobody except the banks has deliberately set aside the basic structures on which good order rests.

What then could be done about it? It is important to remember that neither the banks nor the IBOA are direct parties to the national agreement, and the banks make some play in private of this fact, although it has less significance in their official position. But here we meet the real character of the national agreements of recent times; they have become much more than mere bargains, however extensive; they have indeed something of the character of public law; and it is a matter of irrelevance whether one has given personal consent to an agreement or not. Up to now, the agreement was supported by moral, not legal sanctions. In the special case of the banks, legal sanctions are also now applicable, but the essentially public character of the agreements had already been established and the recent legislation flowed from this.

There is a final, quite tantalising point. Despite the panic it created in the hearts of the government and the Employer-Labour Conference, the bank settlement in 1972, and again in the spring of 1973, did not appear to have sparked off any comparability drive among other salaried people, leading one to believe that the old exclusivity campaign was still bearing fruit. Of course a ten per cent. status claim had been moving through the public service, and this, likely enough, dulled the edge. Furthermore, the crisis in June seemed to take everybody by surprise; it was not preceded by unrest among other unions at the prospect of a special settlement for the banks. The fact is that the bank officials might still have been conceded, in practice by the other clerical workers, a special maverick position outside the comparability structure. The legislation, by clarifying and intensifying the issue, has now excluded such a possibility, and perhaps it is just as well. Nonetheless, the point in principle must not be overlooked. And so we come, once again, to the mystery of the consensus, where people may sense that the larger structure is more important than following the maverick. Even in our highly structured system of wages, there are quite a number of instances where settlements are exempted or indifferently followed. There can also be a rough equity at work here, when people sense that some special problems are being worked out. This is a necessary part of any prices and incomes system: it is the factor that humanises it. Yet it would be greatly helped by an adequate understanding of the problems involved. In Britain there was provision for special investigation in depth to identify such equities. No such general provision is made here; there is of course the Labour Court; and the National Prices Commission can call for a consultant's report if they wish, but these things are far from adequate. The fact is that, while we operate a quite highly-developed prices and incomes system, it is not possible for the Irish Congress of Trade Unions in particular to recognise that this is so, and consequently these supplementary, and very necessary, services of inquiry are difficult to establish.

II

Before going on to deal with the teachers' dispute, let us recognise how very significant, in national terms, some of these disputes have been, not only demonstrating the general climate of industry (as the ESB disputes did) but also affecting in a radical way the economic welfare of the whole state, and promoting, as a consequence, incomes and prices systems of growing sophistication. The 1966 maintenance agreement gave the headline for term agreements; the 1969 maintenance dispute led almost directly to tighter trade union control of picketing and also to the great national agreement of 1970. Here we see not only complex and detailed terms, but a judicial function exercised jointly by the employers and the trade unions; and inevitably a related commission on prices was also created. And finally, the bank dispute and its aftermath are now demonstrating that the national agreements themselves are taking on the character of public law. But the next dispute that we consider, the teachers' dispute, widens our horizons still further, reaching out into the whole cultural life of the country.

I must also make a personal point before we begin. During the whole period which we shall review, I was involved myself in a highly partisan way as general secretary of the Vocational Teachers Association. Nevertheless, the account here is as balanced as I can make it.

Nowhere were the great changes of the sixties, both in the Catholic Church and in society generally, more evident than in education, because, quite apart from the problems of growing affluence and changing religious perceptions, the education system was restructured in such an extensive way that its whole character was altered. The dispute on teachers' salaries, therefore, which ran right throughout the sixties, became tangled in the stresses and emotions arising from the great educational reforms of the period.

From the late thirties onwards, as Ireland became more and more inward-looking, forgetting its pluralist past and concentrating on its own parochial Gaelic culture, the Roman Catholic Church grew in importance, finding its rather triumphant Indian summer in the fifties, before the whole impressive system was jolted into an entirely new way of life. R. Dudley Edwards,[9] writing of 1951, makes the point that the position accorded to the Church in the Constitution was no mere fiction. And he also saw the growing strength of Catholicism in the remarkable increase in the number of persons following a religious vocation.

> In the case of the members of the Orders, there was more than double the number in 1951 as compared to 1921. The increase was not so great, however, in the case of secular clergy, though a twenty-five per cent increase is quite considerable. The number of houses of religious, including nuns, also increased by at least twenty-five per cent. Paralleling this development, of course, must be noted the general increase in prosperity in the country, and the substantial decrease of poverty. In conclusion, it may be said that there was an atmosphere of quietness which reflected the strength as well as the security, tinged sometimes with complacency, which the Church enjoyed in modern Ireland.

Furthermore, the Church, for reasons we discussed in the first chapter, had a heavily rural character, having its roots more often than not in a community which up to quite recent times was characterised by

> ... a closed, highly locality-bound intimate set of relationships rooted in family, kinship and neighbourhood ties; a very limited involvement in the market economy and a very low level of living, unaccompanied however by any feelings of deprivation since the standards expected were also low, and locally autonomous; and a distinctive but very rigid set of traditional beliefs and values.[10]

[9]'Church and State in Modern Ireland' in K. B. Nowlan and T. D. Williams (eds.) *Ireland in the War Years and After* 1939–51. (Gill and Macmillan, Dublin, 1969), p. 119.
[10]Damien Hannan, op. cit., p. 163.

There are great advantages in such a society. It is warm, supportive and surprisingly tolerant, once one sinks oneself right down into it, offering it no challenge. But equally it is highly resistant to change. It profoundly resents individual endeavour, particularly when this challenges the old ways and the old assumptions; and since it is itself highly autonomous, it also views with great anxiety and foreboding any efforts by a distant government to promote changes in its local institutions.

Let us come now to consider the education system in this context, but in doing so we must not see the Church standing, as it were, apart from society and providing a school system of some separatist character; rather must we see a whole people caught up in this way of life, feeding and enlivening a highly conservative parochial Church on the one hand, and an equally conservative parochial education system on the other, which because of its nature accepted the voice of the Church as of much greater significance than the voice of the state, despite the fact that the state provided most of the money. And this was a role which the state itself accepted right up to the sixties, to such effect that one Minister for Education described himself as an oil-can.

The Irish system of education has a marvellously complex and colourful background, shot through as it was with religious and political passions, and apparently always seen as a means of doing something or other in a social context: of filching children from the dissenter or the Romish priest, or of providing a ladder from destitution to jobs in government, or, in latter times, of restructuring the whole life of the nation so that the Irish people would speak a different language, socialise differently and, if the truth be told, think differently as well. It is pejorative to say that it was not child-centred; after all, it was designed for different times; but the child had to conform in a very strict way to what the institutions, whether state or church, required. However, during the post-war years, church and state in Ireland seemed to develop a happy identity in the matter of education, some would claim because of the supine posture of the state in the matter.[11] The schools were small, independent, and tightly under church control. The national examinations and the curricula were administered by the Department of Education in such a clear and rigid way that each school had a feeling of considerable autonomy, since there could be no interference except in accordance with rule. In such a steady state, the education system in the nineteen fifties saw its own reflection and was well-pleased.

Scattered throughout the country were the state primary schools, which were called national schools, often very small neighbourhood

[11] J. H. Whyte, *Church and State in Modern Ireland* (Gill and Macmillan, Dublin, 1971).

schools serving a sparse rural population, the accommodation usually being both aged and primitive; while the parish priest was the manager, they were run in fact by the lay teachers whose salaries were paid directly by the state. In the cities and large towns, the national schools were larger but here they were more often run by religious orders, whose type of organisation did not suit the rural crossroads. The vast majority of secondary schools were owned and run by religious orders; we have already seen how their numbers increased in the years since independence. They received a grant from the state for each student that attended, and they charged modest fees. They employed lay teachers to assist them, and salaries were paid partly by the state and partly by the school, the former paying the lion's share. The schools themselves were surprisingly small, often with a population of less than two hundred students. Single sex education greatly contributed to this: the girls went to nuns' schools and the boys to the religious orders of brothers or to the junior seminaries which the bishops had established. They all pursued an independent, wholly uncooperative way of life, secure in the strict gamesmanship of curriculum and examination. Indeed, if anything, the system was marked by a foolish competitiveness, greatly reinforced by the student grant system. The Protestant schools, serving perhaps five per cent. of the population, fitted readily into this highly individualistic system. There was, however, also a local authority system of vocational and technical education, which at first sight might appear to be independent. Whyte,[12] however, points out that whatever the letter of the law might say, clerical leadership was in practice accepted here as in other educational fields.

> The Committees of local authorities which administered technical education habitually co-opted clergy as members, and frequently elected a priest to be their chairman. This custom has continued and it is still common to find a priest as chairman of a vocational education committee. There was another safeguard also. This was not published at the time, but I have it on the authority of a subsequent Minister for Education that the then Minister for Education, Professor John Marcus O'Sullivan, gave the bishops a written assurance that the vocational system would stick strictly to its authorised field, and would not be allowed to develop so as to impinge upon the field covered by the denominationally run secondary schools.

Second level education was therefore deliberately stunted in vocational schools; usually it could not go beyond a two-year course and the student left school at fifteen or sixteen. Neither could he readily transfer to

[12]Op.cit., p. 37.

secondary school; once he had made his choice at thirteen years of age, he was committed. However, the vocational education committees had also a programme of adult education, and in the cities, they ran technical institutes and colleges.

But this is looking at it all with hindsight. In the fifties, there was complacent acceptance of the view that the Irish education system conferred a very special moral and intellectual character on the student. Somehow it seemed irrelevant that we had the highest non-agricultural unemployment rate in western Europe, and that the vast horde of emigrants from the agricultural areas was primarily unskilled. One gets a picture[13] of male rural workers jostling for heavy manual unskilled employment and emigrating to Britain when they could not get it here; so that by 1961 approximately thirty per cent. of all Irish males working in England and Wales were construction workers and labourers. And the young girls left as well. They had little alternative. The trains from the west and the south were packed with them on their way to the boat, with their bulging, shabby suitcases; and during the holiday periods, young men and women washed like a tide from England and back.

But in the enterprising climate of the sixties, this could not last; and in October 1962, the Minister for Education, Dr P. J. Hillery, established in cooperation with OECD a survey team headed up by Professor Patrick Lynch of University College Dublin to review investment in education in Ireland. The survey team did not expect to report for two or three years; but the break had come, the great defects of the system were becoming only too obvious, and the Minister found that he could not wait. In May 1963, he announced in a press interview some of the most radical changes in post-primary education that had taken place since 1930. He decided that the vocational schools would also do the secondary school type examinations, and in one stroke established a state system of education parallel to that of the religious. He also tried to break up the rather rigid academic education so profoundly a part of the religious schools and even established a number of state comprehensive schools to point the way. These proposals could not have been more radical, and all the changes which took place during the sixties stemmed from them. The monopoly of the religious schools was shattered, and yet there was almost no response at the time from them. The system was not geared to respond to such a challenge; but apart from that, the religious authorities, and indeed the people at large, found it difficult to take seriously a lay view on fundamental educational policy, although laymen might validly seek more mechanics for the factories.

[13]R. C. Geary and J. G. Hughes, 'Certain aspects of non-agricultural unemployment in Ireland' (Economic and Social Research Institute, Dublin, 1970).

The OECD survey team published its report in December 1965; it was quite devastating, and reinforced the good sense of the changes that had been made already.

> A considerable number of Irish pupils receive no post-primary education of any kind, and of pupils who begin post-primary courses a high proportion do not finish . . . There are, in addition, inequalities in the participation in post-primary education of children at all levels, based on social group and geographical location. There is, clearly, a need for public policy to concern itself with these anomalies.[14]

Moreover, the provision for technical studies was very inadequate. One sentence gave the key to the problems of the future and in particular to the role of the state:

> An unplanned expansion of the educational system, which would merely multiply the existing structure, would rapidly exhaust available resources and be accompanied by a declining return in terms of student output.[15]

Pumping more money in was of little account; the whole system would have to be restructured, and only the state could do so, using its vast capital resources for this purpose. The highly conservative school system, while appearing to accept that these inadequacies existed, considered that the problems could indeed be answered by the expansion of existing facilities, and they considered state restructuring to be dangerous and unnecessary meddling.

But when the Minister for Education of the time, Mr George Colley, came to consider these matters early in 1966, he found the teaching profession itself in much disarray, being locked in a wrangle that had persisted for ten years or more. The Irish National Teachers Organisation, which represented lay primary teachers, had conducted a bitter, protracted strike in 1946 and had a reputation for direct uncomplicated militancy. They were by far the largest union of the three, representing perhaps 14,000 teachers in all (incidentally in the North as well as the South) and in their early years expressed much of the anguished blundering-about which a highly centralised bureaucracy seems to invite. They had been stung to the quick in 1952 when the vocational teachers were given the same scales as secondary teachers (leaving the primary teachers trailing) and they had campaigned vehemently for parity ever since. Twice in the

[14]*Investment in Education* (Stationery Office, Dublin, 1965) Pr. 8311, p. 389.
[15]Op. cit., p. 392.

sixties they had tried to resolve the problem, by a government committee of inquiry in 1961[16] and by an arbitration hearing in 1963, both with disastrous results. But the union, by a display of militancy and by skilful political influence, managed to discount most of the damage, and their campaign for parity was still powerfully to the fore.

The Association of Secondary Teachers, Ireland, represented only the lay secondary teachers, perhaps 2,000, but the religious were deeply involved in their success, since the salaries paid by the state to their teacher members formed a substantial part of their income. The ASTI had always claimed a special position among teachers and a degree of exclusivity, principally because the vast majority were university graduates; their policy was therefore a little like that of the bank officials, on whom they modelled their actions to some extent. This policy of exclusivity was helped by the fact that the three groups of teachers—primary, secondary and vocational—had three separate schemes of conciliation and arbitration; and although there was great pressure to form one scheme, where the whole business could be discussed with everyone present, the ASTI would have none of it. All they would accept ultimately, and that with much reservation, was the appointment of the same arbitrator to chair the three separate arbitration boards, in the event of an issue going that far. The Departments of Education and Finance naturally sent the same representatives to each of the councils, where they approached their task with a complex and bureaucratic form of gamesmanship, which prolonged discussions inordinately and which convinced the teachers that the Department of Education in particular was immensely devious and wholly unreliable, making even sharper the stresses of centralised administration. Large institutions reflect in their policies the approach of their principal officers, all of whom do not see things the same way. It is not surprising, therefore, that we should find enlightened policies of educational reform being pursued hand in hand with a pettifogging and frustrating form of salary negotiation.

In February 1964, the ASTI had also been much disappointed in their salary negotiations, and that summer ASTI members refused to superintend the national examination or to act as examiners; the mood of the teachers was tense and ugly, and probably in an attempt to ameliorate this, the school managers, in May, had entered into a secret agreement with the secondary teachers by which they augmented their salaries by $12\frac{1}{2}$ per cent. Although this radically altered the official salary (which was of great significance to others), the managers considered that not only were they perfectly entitled to do this, but also to do it secretly,

---

[16]*Teachers Salaries Committee Reports etc.* (Stationery Office, Dublin) Pr. 5694.

since they were essentially private employers. Indeed, some additional sum had always been paid to some teachers, and they saw this as regularising as well as augmenting an existing practice. Although the managers showed in this great support for the lay teachers, nonetheless it is necessary to remark on the essentially inferior and supplementary role which lay secondary teachers had in religious schools, where they were infrequently consulted, given no institutional responsibility and never involved in matters of policy. Many would claim that some of the stormy events that followed owed something to the externalising of the frustrations of this arrangement.

The Vocational Teachers Association[17] had perhaps 1,200 members, many of whom were teachers of woodwork, metalwork and domestic science, much in contrast with the secondary schools. They had been infuriated by the secret salary deal for secondary teachers which they did not discover until the autumn of 1964. Throughout the years since 1952, they had drifted back from parity a little, but this increase meant the destruction of their salary policy, and an arbitration hearing in the summer of 1965 ended unsuccessfully and with much recrimination. In the aftermath of the ninth round increases, it was difficult to engage in new salary negotiations and they had to content themselves with some general assurance from the Minister that the position was not final. In the meantime, there was hope as well as anxiety in the plans which Dr Hillery had announced two years before.

These then were the three organisations whose representatives the Minister for Education, Mr Colley, met in January 1966 in the afterglow of the publication of the OECD report. His suggestion was direct and radical. He asked for views on the idea of a common scale for all teachers, with differing allowances. In this way, he hoped to respond to the considerable political pressure of the primary teachers, while at the same time opening up the idea of a coordinated system of post-primary education which would remedy the defects which were now only too obvious. He hoped that ". . . secondary and vocational schools, by the exchange of facilities and other forms of collaboration should make available a curriculum broad enough to serve the individual needs of all their students, and thereby to provide the basis of a comprehensive system in each locality." A common salary scale seemed a necessary part of such an arrangement. The three teaching groups, however, looked only to themselves on the issue, the secondary teachers in particular being extremely anxious about its implications.

But at this juncture in 1966 there was no prospect of a general salary

---

[17]In 1973 it changed its name to the Teachers Union of Ireland.

movement to dull the edge of the dilemma; and the vocational teachers, in particular, were now in a state of great anxiety because of the flat-footed way in which the proposed changes in post-primary education were introduced. There was no white paper, no comprehensive statement of policy; instead, a week before their Easter annual conference in Roscommon, the VTA were confronted with a bundle of syllabuses of an entirely new programme of education, which would come into operation the following September, bringing the full crunch of reorganisation far earlier than the teachers had expected. This, combined with their resentment on the salary issue, resulted in a stormy conference.

But events seemed to catapult forward. In the summer of 1966, Donogh O'Malley was appointed Minister for Education—a charismatic, innovative person who caught the imagination of the whole country, precipitating changes not only in post-primary education but in higher education as well that are still clamouring in our ears. In September 1966, he announced that post-primary education would be free to all; the secondary schools used to charge modest fees, but the minister offered them augmented grants if they consented to give free education; and most of them found that in practice they could not do otherwise. He also provided free transport which was of the greatest importance to the rural population. Soon civil servants from the Department of Education, changing their character completely, began to travel throughout the country urging reorganisation and cooperation between all post-primary schools at a county level. At first, the meetings were only among those directly concerned, but at O'Malley's insistence, they soon began to be held in public and whole communities were invited to debate the proposals for change. Much of it they viewed with suspicion and alarm; if a tiger changing its spots is never very credible, neither is a central bureaucracy coming down from heaven and asking advice. But the parents responded to O'Malley's imaginative character, and soon students were flooding into the schools, yellow school buses were pushing their way up lanes and by-roads, and in the years that followed, teachers were in considerable demand, the number in post-primary schools more than doubling in a very short time and inevitably giving an entirely new, very youthful look to the teaching profession.

However, all this was only beginning in the uncertain spring of 1967 when the VTA was trying to secure a salary increase which would recover the $12\frac{1}{2}$ per cent. which the secondary teachers had privately negotiated. The vocational teachers were passing through a great crisis of self-regard. The old vocational school system leaned heavily on practical subjects taught in a friendly way, not very demanding but close to community needs. Now, however, the changed programme meant new criteria,

criteria which emphasised examination performance in the student and university degrees in the teachers. There were many pleas for preserving the old traditions; but in practice the best that anyone could offer was that if the vocational schools had to become more academic, then the secondary schools had to become more practical—which probably missed the point of the whole thing, and did not help to allay very much the anxieties of the teachers, who feared that in a new coordinated system they would be regarded as second-rate. Of course, there were many vocational teachers too who welcomed the changes, seeing in them a great breakthrough for their students and their schools, but whether they feared or welcomed what was taking place, they were united in their anger that secondary teachers should have higher salaries than they. Comparability in pay was of obsessive importance to teachers, even more keenly felt, it would seem, than in the community at large which itself was highly sensitive on the same issue.

In the ordinary course of events, if agreement cannot be reached on a teachers' claim, it is referred to arbitration. But as we have seen, an arbitrator, even for the vocational teachers alone, must be appointed by agreement between all three groups of teachers as well as the minister; there was no alternative procedure; and it had been found impossible to get agreement. The ASTI were prepared to agree, but the INTO, the primary teachers, saw a separate arbitration for the vocational schools as a dangerous move, since the vocational teachers might be advanced once again, leaving primary teachers behind. They therefore blocked the appointment of an arbitrator, holding out instead for the imposition by the government of a common scale for all teachers. Frustration and anger mounted among the vocational teachers, their 1967 Easter conference was highly emotional, and by October they had decided on strike action.

O'Malley, however, resolved the problem by announcing that the government had decided to introduce a common salary scale, and he established a tribunal to recommend how it should be done. Because of the difficulty in reaching agreement on the members of the tribunal, it did not get under way until January 1968. Its chairman was Professor W. J. L. Ryan of Trinity College, who, in his capacity as chairman of the general purposes committee of the NIEC, had been the dynamic for much of the joint planning initiatives which had so greatly influenced the sixties. The tribunal reported[18] very quickly in May 1968, but tragically, some months before, Donogh O'Malley, who had given such colour and drive to education in the country, died suddenly. He seemed at the very height of his powers, glamourous and indestructible, and his funeral

[18] *Tribunal on Teachers Salaries* (Stationery Office, Dublin, 1968) Prl. 87.

in Limerick was thronged with the vast numbers of people who came to mourn him.

The tribunal had an immensely difficult task. The secondary teachers' agreement with their managers had given them approximately £200 a year, but the cost of bringing all primary and vocational teachers to this level was unthinkable; therefore the common scale had to be much less. It was fixed at approximately the current level of the vocational teacher scale. The secondary teachers had therefore to gain some compensation, even though the present incumbents would not be diminished. The tribunal recommended allowances for university degrees, from which the vast majority of secondary teachers would benefit, and also a system of posts of responsibility, the number of posts and their value being based on the age of the student; this too was intended to benefit secondary schools.

The primary teachers, although diplomatically mute, had achieved their objective. The vocational teachers recognised that there was now at least a common scale, and they were pleased with the posts of responsibility. They were greatly alarmed, however, at the provision for degree allowances which, although it permitted equivalence, had introduced a money difference in the vocational schools between the teachers of practical subjects and the growing number of university graduates; in this, it internalised, in a personal way within the community of the school, some of the stress that had existed in an external, and therefore more bearable, way between secondary schools and vocational schools. The issue was particularly distressing for a group of teachers, the validity of whose teaching was in any event under challenge; they shrank from the threat of a changed relationship with their colleagues in the school which would be made crudely explicit in this way. Understandably then, the graduate allowance dominated vocational teachers' policies from then on.

But the secondary teachers were in much greater difficulties. Their special salary advantage was gone; instead, they were offered posts of responsibility which also invited a major shift in personal relations within the school. This seemed a most forbidding idea. The tribunal had been quite blunt:

> In schools in which there are both clerical and lay teachers, either the principal or the vice-principal should be a lay teacher, and posts of special responsibility should be apportioned between clerical and lay teachers in accordance with the proportions which they constitute of the total teaching staff of the school.[19]

[19] Op. cit., p. 14.

But each secondary school saw itself as a private employer—and a small one at that—jealous of its right to hire and fire and its right to determine its own policy. The schools at that stage showed little enthusiasm for handing over to their employees something of their own unique, autocephalous authority. On the other hand, it would be difficult for the ASTI to campaign effectively for lay responsibility unless there was vigorous grass-roots support, which in turn would mean that small groups of lay teachers would have to suffer a confrontation with their own employers on an issue of great delicacy and complexity. Furthermore, many of the teachers had so adjusted to their supplementary role in the schools that they had no welcome for the proposal, seeing in it merely more trouble for an income to which they were entitled in any event. At best, therefore, the proposal was a pipe-dream, and at worst it was a cheat; and it seemed to the ASTI that they had blundered badly in having anything to do with the tribunal and in departing from their practice of bargaining separately and in an exclusive way.

In all this, we must recognise how little the demands of the teachers had to do with increased wealth and how much with status and self-regard. The graduate allowance in the case of vocational teachers was quite trivial in money terms, and as far as the secondary teachers were concerned, they were, at worst, losing only in prospect. These things of themselves could not account for the passions that were aroused. The public generally seemed to put it down to the fact that teachers as a body were quarrelsome and envious, and certainly, on the face of it, the whole episode, which got considerable publicity, was hardly edifying. But in fact teachers are no different in these matters from other people. The changes were too radical and too rapid for them to absorb without considerable stress.

But despite this, in the immediate aftermath of the tribunal report, it now appears that some small adjustments might well have carried the day. The tribunal's report was not a negotiated document but a recommendation for which only the tribunal was responsible. It is accepted generally that the act of reaching agreement by negotiation may push the price somewhat higher than a tribunal on its own might be able to justify. Therefore, in subsequent negotiations, some higher adjustments would not be unexpected, but, since the margins were narrow, such adjustments would have to be negotiated with great skill and sensitivity. As it was, the matter was left to the initiative of the Department of Education, where the civil servants concerned with such matters had in the past displayed an approach that was very unhelpful. Far from aiming at a consensus, they seemed to be caught up in a highly complex, devious business of balancing one group against another for the purpose of following their own view of what should be done. The fact was that the recommendation of the tribunal was merely the first stage, and it seems now that if, for example, Professor Ryan (who had already shown a remarkable talent for finding his way to a consensus) had been asked to chair the negotiations by which the recommendations might be implemented, much of the subsequent distress and disruption might have been avoided.

As things were, the proposals were rejected both by the vocational teachers and by the secondary teachers; but now the summer holidays were nearly at hand and, in the manner of ancient wars, the season overtook hostilities. In the autumn, the general eleventh round negotiations provided more money and therefore a greater possibility of settling; and this the vocational teachers did, recognising that they had more to gain than to lose. The problem of the non-graduate allowance was met by deciding to consider subsequently the question of equating the qualifications of teachers of practical subjects with those of graduates—which the non-graduates regarded with great suspicion. But the secondary teachers were adamant in their rejection, and sought to resolve matters by submitting claims to their own separate scheme of conciliation and arbitration. This now became the key issue. The tribunal, in recommending a common scale, had naturally recommended as well a common system of negotiation; but the separate schemes were subject to six months notice of termination, and the Minister for Education had not taken any steps to terminate them. The secondary teachers were therefore insisting on their right to exclusive negotiations, while the other teachers were noisy in their determination that all should henceforth be negotiated in common. Gradually the crisis began to take shape.

It is necessary before continuing to consider the position of the religious orders in this matter as well, since they owned and managed a substantial number of the secondary schools. These were men and women who had chosen to live a rigorous, celibate and often comfortless life because they believed that it gave a special quality to their vocation of teaching, a quality that justified their special position as owners and managers of schools and therefore, in a special way, as policy-makers. The opening up of the vocational schools, and, in particular, the proposed involvement of lay-folk in policy-making and in management (because this is what posts of responsibility implied) put in question all their personal sacrifice, their celibacy and the burden of their rule. Now, in that very September of 1968, when the secondary teachers' dispute was coming to the boil, a further development took place that seemed to confirm the worst fears of the religious orders. An academic journal,[20] edited by a Jesuit,

[20] *Studies* (Dublin, Autumn 1968).

carried an article by Mr Seán O'Connor of the Department of Education who was the assistant secretary in charge of development.[21] O'Connor was a career civil servant in a department that had been for years a backwater, but he had great perception and high courage, and breaking all the mute rules of the civil service, he set out in his article, on a personal basis, some of the challenging problems of Irish education, particularly in regard to the relations between church and state. His problem was how to cope not only with increased participation in post-primary education but how to provide a balanced curriculum at the same time, and faced with ". . . a hodge-podge of very small units," he considered that it would be sheer extravagance to provide each one with adequate facilities for language, science and technical studies. Since little headway had been made in cooperation between schools, he now considered that single community schools were the rational requirement. But of course one of the major obstacles here was the attitude of the church authorities to co-education:

> In some dioceses it is not tolerated at all; in many of the others it is a thing of last resort. Religious orders, by and large, oppose co-education. It is not uncommon to find two girls' secondary schools and a boys' school in a centre where the pupil potential is such as to warrant only one school. The difficulty here is apparent at once: a single school would make the presence of all but one of the Orders unnecessary . . . Nowhere yet has joint management of a single school been attempted by two religious orders . . . It seems clear that education is being adversely affected by institutional considerations not related to education.[22]

In questioning single-sex education, it is difficult to avoid questioning single-sex institutions such as religious orders. Furthermore, O'Connor made explicit what many had begun to recognise: the numbers joining religious orders were falling, in the crisis of identity that followed the second Vatican council, and this in turn put in question the claim of the religious to a virtual monopoly of post-primary education:

> There would seem to be a shrinkage in vocations for the priesthood and for the teaching Brothers. With an increasing enrolment in all post-primary schools the spread of religious over total teaching staff will be thinner than before. Yet, though they are unable to staff the schools they already own, they propose to establish more and better schools wherever the pupil potential shows an increase.[23]

[21]In the summer of 1973 he was appointed Secretary of the Department.
[22]Op. cit., p. 23.
[23]Op. cit., p. 25.

He followed this up with a crisp comment on the position of the secondary teacher and the role of the religious in the future:

> The lay secondary teacher remains always the hired man. His responsibility ends at the classroom door. He is consulted with, of course, because he may have something to offer, but he is never part of the decision-making... I lay stress on these things because I believe a change must be made; otherwise there will be an explosion, maybe sooner than later. No one wants to push the religious out of education; that would be disastrous, in my opinion. But I want them in it as partners, not always as masters.[24]

It was very shocking to the religious orders and to the clergy generally that this should have been said at all; the religious in Ireland had always lived in a warm wash of deference, and frank speaking in such circumstances was seen as an act of considerable hostility. Moreover, in their dealings with the Department up to then, they had often found it bureaucratic, devious and insensitive, and in those circumstances they found O'Connor's article most alarming. The Christian Brothers were convinced that O'Connor spoke for more than himself in this; that it was a sinister attempt by the state to push the religious out of education, and as a first step, they were now driving a wedge between "clerical, religious and lay teachers." Furthermore ". . . the approach to management reflected in Mr O'Connor's views corresponds to nationalization by stealth, whereby property is not taken over, but management is. Outright nationalization, through property purchase, at least has the attribute of being open and straightforward."[25] By no means all religious orders took this extreme view; some were quite willing to open up their schools to lay participation, but their voice as yet was hardly heard.

The ASTI, therefore, had the full support of the religious in their rejection of the idea of posts of responsibility and their claim for increased salaries instead, and in the early part of 1969, as emotions began to rise, it became generally known that if the ASTI went on strike, the religious would close their schools in support. And this in fact was what happened, when on 1 February 1969 the ASTI withdrew their services. This was more than a strike of teachers; it was a revolt of the schools.

This was very unsettling. At the height of the school year, children were aimlessly at home, the secondary schools were dark, and no one was clear how or when it would all end. It was damaging to the whole edifice of the establishment, since it seemed to set authority against authority. The bishops in particular became alarmed (they do not appear to have

---

[24]Op. cit., p. 25.
[25]Op. cit., pp. 58, 59.

been very involved up to then) and they approached the Minister for Education to try to find a solution. Quite apart from that, the religious orders were not only embarrassed in their new role but also without income, and it became clear after a little while that they proposed to reopen the schools in any event. After a fortnight, therefore, the minister came up with proposals which were accepted by the ASTI, and the strike ended.

The other teachers, and particularly the VTA, were highly indignant. Despite all the talk of joint negotiation, a separate settlement had been reached with the secondary teachers; and the terms of the settlement looked quite disastrous. Posts of responsibility, as Ryan proposed them, were abandoned, and the minister now proposed to give every secondary teacher after ten years service £100 a year, rising to £300 on the maximum for nominal responsibility. This in fact was a salary increase, although the Department claimed otherwise, and much discountenanced the VTA. But that was not the end of it. In contrast to this clear arrangement, no posts of responsibility had yet been created in vocational schools; instead, the VTA were locked in tedious, endless discussions with Department officials on how they might be introduced. Now, as well, teachers began to flow from the vocational schools into the secondary schools, attracted by the higher salaries, and the vocational schools seemed destined to be second-rate schools for second-rate students, with all the rather frightening implications which this would have for society later.

But the VTA were on the warpath. The national teachers rather gingerly followed their lead; they had little alternative, but in fact they thought that the VTA reaction was excessive. A claim was submitted for a £300 increase on the maximum (and other appropriate increases) and, when it failed to make headway, the VTA began a campaign of strikes, beginning with a two-day stoppage on 26 May and 27 May, and a mass rally in Limerick. The INTO followed with a one-day strike on 28 May. Within six months, therefore, all three organisations had been on strike. The Department capitulated and Professor Ryan was invited back to determine whether the tribunal recommendation had been breached by the secondary teachers' settlement. He found that it had.

This was now a pretty kettle of fish. The Department in fact could not keep faith with one group of teachers without a breach of agreement with another. Ryan's solution was to make the secondary teachers mark time in future general pay increases and use the money to give real posts of responsibility. But the secondary teachers were not parties to the Ryan discussions; they rejected the idea of joint negotiations, and stood firmly on an agreement which guaranteed them full increases in the future. Nevertheless, the Department tentatively attempted some breach, and in the autumn of 1969 they withheld a very small general increase from the secondary teachers who promptly charged them with violating their agreement. The Department, however, made no attempt to cut off the benefit of the £300 from incoming teachers, and the flow of teachers from vocational schools to secondary schools increased. The VTA saw in this further evidence of the Department's bad faith, and they saw in it as well the possible destruction of their system. In addition to that, an appalling wrangle had by this time developed between the VTA and the Department on the application of the graduate allowance to non-graduates, and also on the introduction of posts of responsibility. Ryan had made further recommendations on these matters, but there was a lot of muddle, particularly on the graduate allowance, and enormously high feeling. All this then launched the VTA once again on a campaign of strikes during the month of February 1970. Now they demanded an inquiry into the Department's whole personnel system, and, in the event, Seán O'Connor took over the personnel division and, soon after, Dermot McDermott of the Labour Court was invited to chair a conciliation conference. Strike action was suspended.

McDermott approached his task in a very flexible manner and, although the ASTI would not take part in joint discussions, he met them separately and tried in this way to reach agreement. But the special allowance of £300 was also having a bad effect on the staffing of rural secondary schools no less than vocational schools, and in May the Department at length announced that it would not apply to any future entrants. There was a stormy reaction from the ASTI who, in retaliation, refused to correct that year's examination papers. In the meantime, the discussions under McDermott failed, but they had done a great deal to clear the ground; the solution appeared to lie in winning a departure from the 1969 secondary teacher agreement by offering them compensation in the form of increments on the scale; and while O'Connor knew he could not get agreement from everyone on this, he thought the teachers might at least acquiesce to it—albeit with bad grace. When the talks broke down, the minister announced that he would himself implement what he considered to be an equitable solution; but he prudently waited until July, when the teachers were on holidays, before announcing the details.

But in the autumn of 1970, when this whole complicated wrangle was creating further bad temper in the schools, another major shift took place in educational policy. On 20 October, *The Irish Times* published a memorandum which had been sent by the Department of Education to the head of the Catholic Church in Ireland, Cardinal Conway, setting out their proposals for a new kind of post-primary school, which they called a community school. The hodge-podge of small school units had shown no capacity whatever to cooperate, and now many of them were seeking money for extensions and rebuilding in view of the school population explosion. The Department of Education were not prepared to agree extravagantly to rebuilding three small schools in a country town when one would do; the difficulty lay in devising some common management system in a totally non-cooperative climate. They proposed that the Roman Catholic bishop of the diocese should nominate four out of the six members of the management board, the vocational school authorities nominating the other two. The importance of the community school proposal lay in the fact that it could well become the typical post-primary school of the future; and therefore, some religious orders reacted vehemently, claiming that they were being pushed out of education. But when they came to think about it, they began to realise that the bishops no longer proposed to rely on religious orders with diminishing numbers for the greater part of Catholic schooling, and from this on, a less militant and more cooperative attitude seemed to develop.

But there was a powerful reaction to the proposals for other reasons, a reaction that was by no means confined to those in education. The proposals, in fact, would create a denominational system of public education in Ireland, essentially under the control of the Catholic bishops. It is likely in this matter that the Cardinal was influenced by his Northern Ireland background; but in the light of the developing tragedy of the North, many people in the South felt a great distaste for something so explicitly denominational in intent. In the year or so that followed, the proposal has in fact been amended to give it a non-denominational character.

But the ASTI, during January and February 1971 as they prepared to do battle once again with the Department of Education, could no longer rely on the secondary schools to close their doors in support as they had in 1969. The religious orders were now uncertain and had to look to themselves. Nevertheless, among secondary teachers, who had brushed aside the minister's July proposals, feeling was running very, very high. They had been deeply influenced by the bank officials, and they were determined not only to go on strike but to stay out until all was won. 15 February 1971 was the date decided on for the beginning of the strike, and quite a number of teachers had arranged to go to jobs in England immediately, confident that it would be a siege and not a battle. The plan was much influenced by the very large number of young teachers who were now in the profession. There were great perils, however, in this course of action. In practice, the issue might be left unresolved. Unlike the case of the banks, this was a feasible alternative. The secondary schools would remain open in any event, offering a limited service; the vocational schools were now doing full post-primary courses, and other post-primary schools could be created by the state. In a word, far from winning a strike, there was a danger of grievously damaging—and in a permanent way—the whole religious school system.

On the eve of the strike, Maurice Cosgrave, president of the Irish Congress of Trade Unions, intervened and asked the ASTI to defer their action. All three unions were affiliated to Congress and he asked them to join his executive in an effort to find a solution. The ASTI standing committee agreed to defer, much to the outrage of some of their members, who picketed Congress House during the discussions that followed and who, on one occasion, invaded the building itself. Congress had adopted a very difficult and ambivalent role, since it was hardly true that the row lay only among the teachers' unions. Furthermore, the margin within which a solution could be found was very narrow. However, a joint claim was hammered out, which contemplated further compensation for secondary teachers by way of a lump sum. The Department had been kept in the picture, and a week later an agreement along these lines was concluded among all the parties. Of course, waves of unrest continued to trouble the teachers, particularly because of the graduate allowance which almost ripped the VTA apart, but the basis for peace had been found.

What can we say of all this? Firstly, the circumstances were extremely difficult; so many changes had come so rapidly, and they had put in question not only the environs of a job but a whole ethos, a way of life. They had a cruel effect on a society little equipped to deal with such phenomena. No doubt they were inevitable; little enough could be done even to slow them down; but it is difficult to believe that the path could not have been eased somewhat. Instead, some of the approaches of the Department seemed to bring mayhem more than peace. On the other hand, the Department shone out like a beacon among institutions that at times displayed a most disedifying self-interest. It was motivated by the requirements of the students and of society more surely and more constantly than almost anyone else.

But let us step back a little from the tangle of events and recognise in this rather sophisticated area of Irish society the perilous inability of people to compromise. This really lay at the basis of the dispute. Ireland has experience in particular of command-type institutions, and even our government operates a command-type democracy. We have little experience of hammering out a solution by difficult and vigorous debate. There are two essentials to the business of agreement by compromise: the ability to confront and the ability to concede. We have little practice in confronting one another with a difficulty, and, without this, the process of compromise cannot begin; we often find it easier to destroy a man a from distance than disagree with him to his face. Secondly, we tend to regard a concession as a defeat and we expect the other fellow to take much the same view. Consequently, if we conflict with someone, our practice is not to persuade but to exercise some power which will compel him to our point of view. All sides in the teachers' dispute tended to move quickly to this position, but it is no less noticeable in some of the other disputes that we have examined. The problem of industrial unrest in the sixties lies deep in the nature of Irish society.

CHAPTER SEVEN

Conclusions and Temptations

I

INEVITABLY, in a concluding chapter such as this, we must attempt some general conclusions and recommendations, but the important part of the study, I suggest, lies in its attempt to convey the reality of the Irish situation. I offer three principal reasons for this. In the first place, so little has been written on Irish industrial relations. The Webbs, in their great pioneering work on trade unionism,[1] disposed of Ireland in a footnote on page 472 (which in fairness is lengthy enough to be carried over to page 473) and in an amused appendix on the Dublin gilds; and there the matter rests. There are a number of scholarly works on the early years in particular,[2] but little has been done in more recent times. True, we have had some useful studies of particular disputes, but it is difficult to judge their general significance for the want of a comprehensive picture. Secondly, we tend to see ourselves, as it were, reflected in a mirror of British endeavour, so powerful is the influence of Britain on our lives and so readily do British concepts and British models fall to hand. But social and economic patterns in Britain are really very different from ours, and the mirror can be a distorting one. There is the vast difference of scale (which requires a quantum shift in our understanding) but, apart from that, there are marked differences in social experience. We are here dealing with something much wider than industrial relations alone, but our study demonstrates the point as well as another. For example, it is too easy, as we noted in the first chapter, to see Irish trade union organisa-

[1]Sidney and Beatrice Webb, *The History of Trade Unionism* (London, 1920 edition).
[2]In particular, J. Dunsmore Clarkson, *Labour and Nationalism in Ireland* (New York, 1925).

tion as an interesting variation of the British system, just as it is too easy to see Irish trade union law as a British variation as well; but the reality of the troubled North and the British-based unions on the one hand, and the traditions cut deep into the Irish Constitution on the other, are far more than mere peculiarities in an essentially British environment. They are the substance of the Irish position, and this, therefore, must be our starting-point, not the British system. But the Irish material is so slender, and the British material so luxuriant, that inevitably we become a little bewildered and misled. The third reason for trying to catch at the reality of the Irish scene is indeed a related one. In our management schools in Ireland, we give considerable prominence to the behavioural scientists, and since our knowledge of our own situation is both fragmented and defective, this can be often irrelevant and occasionally alarming. In Irish management circles, Taylor and Mayo, McGregor and Leavitt, Katz and Maslow are household words, and attempts have been made, for example, to apply to the Irish bargaining scene the general theory of Walton and McKersie. They are popular because of their high level of generalisation, but however able the generalisations may be, these theories are woven out of the data of a particular society which is not our own, and they are valuable in so far as we can enrich them and validate them in our own experience. The paucity of Irish studies makes this very difficult. And the same defect means that we are not impelled by our own experience beyond the boundaries of the behaviourists. And yet we must reach beyond, if we are not to be bound by a frame which, while helping by its rigour to clarify our experience, may also constrict our understanding of it and banish something of its magic.

II

Of course, we should not exaggerate the incidence of industrial unrest in Ireland; nonetheless, during the sixties it was a major social and economic phenomenon, not perhaps because of the number of man-days lost (although these at times were great) but because of the impact it had on the life of the country generally. The maintenance dispute and the bank dispute spring immediately to mind, but some of the others were also important, if only for their potential for disaster.

In trying to evaluate them, we cannot escape from the general upheaval of the sixties which gave the disputes some of their intensity and intractability. We have seen how Ireland at the end of the fifties was still a very structured society; the relationships between people were clearly marked, their roles were set and explicit and, as a result, there was a powerful sense of *gemeinschaft*, which, while warm and supportive, had a great deal in it as well that was conservative and second-rate, making it vulnerable to the impatience that was to come. The dominant Gaelic subculture, complacent and inward-looking, gradually forgetting the larger pluralist Ireland of the past, sank into the warmth of a vast kinship, powerfully supported by the great unshakeable moral edifice of the Catholic Church. The minority religions in such circumstances only too readily formed their own kinship groups and the larger pluralism disappeared in their case as well. And then in the sixties, the growing affluence, the new technologies, the great shift in personal relations which television produced, and above all the revolution in the Catholic Church which made provisional much that appeared timeless and changeless—all this produced something of a state of *anomie*: that lonely anxious state where men no longer look to the warmth of fellowship, but seek all the time to acquire goods, to compete for success, to appear dominant since they have no other means of winning the regard of others and consequently of achieving self-regard; and because they must ruthlessly seek these things, they seem to be caught up by a greed that is never satisfied, and an envy that is so naked as to be disreputable.

But where the larger society becomes threatening or meaningless, men will also seek purpose and support in small interpersonal groups, a phenomenon which is related to what Van Beinum called the privatisation of the worker. People now look very much more to the firm they are employed in and to their own work situation. It is there that relativities really bite. They see themselves essentially as employees of their firm, and less and less do they identify with some national grouping such as electrician or typist or driver. Indeed, the broad general idea of a worker and of a working class tend to be more and more a notion of the trade union leadership.

Whether all this takes the form of a well-motivated and legitimate group interest, or a desire for some ruthless industrial buccaneering, its effect is a powerfully fissiparous one; large pluralist trade unions suffer great pressures, and even small unions, representing a single economic interest or a single occupation, are not free from stress. And the old excitement of a united campaign is now rarely experienced except perhaps among certain middle class trade unions intent on pursuing their own special interest in a manner which has little enough to do with the ideals of the past.

But the very same unions that suffer such fissiparous pressures are called upon more and more to engage in national affairs, to which many of their members are indifferent or perhaps even hostile. In this, as Van Beinum has remarked, resides the great dilemma of the trade union movement, a dilemma identified by Jimmy Dunne in his image of the two tiers, and which is imposing considerable personal stress on the trade union leadership. Let us, before considering the trade unions, their problems and disputes, consider first the men who were deemed to have led them.

In the kind of highly structured society of the fifties, there existed what could be best described as situational leadership. A man responded to the situation in which he found himself, adopting the appropriate posture, often to considerable effect. But there was little thought of wider principles; if he had to question himself, it would be the question which Julien Sorel is said to have asked silently after his first night with Mme. de Rênal: "Ai-je bien joué mon rôle?" A trade union leader during those years appeared to be brusque, impatient, down to earth, very much a man of affairs, both intimidating and reliable. There was little thrust, and almost no sense of strategy or planning for the future. Such men will tend to insist on conformism as a matter of course, and this in fact is characteristic of most trade union officials. Sometimes, as in France in 1968, the opposition of the trade union movement to any spontaneity is explained away in terms of Marxist policy, but it seems to me that such conformism is common to all large organisations and particularly to trade unions, whose members, being ordinary folk, tend to oppose change, to foster custom and practice, and to rely on those leaders who manifest the kind of solid conservative role-playing to which they are accustomed. The rapid sweep of events in the sixties found the trade union officials inadequate and at times resentful. They remained generally constant to the developments that were taking place, because it had in fact been their policy to seek them, but they were bewildered by forces among their own people which they did not fully understand. They were troubled by the rise of the egoist and the buccaneer, and the rules of the union, instead of conveying, as they were intended to do, a spirit of mutual help, now seemed to form an arena within which strident individuals fought out their special interests, using small groups of self-interest as both their clients and their cohorts. And even when a form of privatisation developed which was quite benign, it was difficult to distinguish. The official therefore saw in these private group movements something inimical to the union and perhaps to society generally. He found of course that an appeal to loyalty and community care was of little value; the really strong motives were limited and selfish. At times, in order to give himself authority in his leadership, he was tempted to greater militancy, trying to recover in this way some of the feeling of community which had evaporated; and this was a dangerous road to tread. Sometimes he tried to contain them, or just failed to exercise any leadership at all, and if an explosion came, as it sometimes did, there was an impression of great confusion, and blundering about and the rise of the second-string leadership.

We have seen, in the maintenance dispute and in some of the ESB disputes, how ugly this second-string leadership can be when it breaks through to grasp command, defiant of its own officials and indeed of everyone else. But even where such movements are led by normally decent and responsible people, one finds a strident self-interest. It seems that their very commitment to local and sectional loyalties causes them to have an uncertain appreciation of those large national issues which are so immediate to the top union officials; and the strong conforming nature of the small group can foster a sort of national lawlessness.

And it is here that the inadequacy of many trade union officials is revealed. So much has turned on the absence of a reasonable competence at a strategic point in a dispute. And if there are powerful voices, voices which are capable of changing the whole course of national affairs, they are heard against a background of general inadequacy. This is the reason for the quite extraordinary contrasts in industrial affairs; the débâcle of the maintenance dispute was followed by a national agreement of considerable sophistication; the negative response of the ESB unions to the Fogarty Report stands in contrast to the Workers Union of Ireland campaigning for Common Market entry and for an orderly policy on prices and incomes; and in the more domestic field, there was the ability of a man like Seán O Murchú who guided the building unions peacefully through the cataracts of the later sixties, much in contrast with the turmoil of 1964. These voices are so few, therefore, that where a competent person resigns his job, the likelihood is that he will be followed by one of inadequate ability. This is a major reason for the fragility of industrial peace. It is one of the reasons why negotiating groups have been unsuccessful on the whole, and why amalgamations have run into the sand. The events very often are too great for the men. There are inadequacies, too, among the employers, an imperception of reality at times great enough to pull the house down about their ears; and, as we shall see, the public conciliation service has its inadequacies as well. But here we are focusing on the trade union officials and how the position might be improved.

One would wish in no way to decry the education programme of Congress, which is directed to very practical ends; but the results from any education programme are a long time maturing. And the Irish Transport and General Workers Union have a programme of considerable significance in research and education, and because of their size, a sophisticated recruitment policy. But, for the rest, there are many difficulties, and education is not enough. One must, I believe, open up a large number of additional posts throughout the trade union movement, and recruit such able people as one can. The problem, of course, lies in the inadequacy of trade union finances, which even the Irish Transport must find constricting at the present time. Contributions are often far too low; but we must recognise how reluctant members are to agree to pay more (and where a number of unions are fishing in the same pool, they are reluctant to ask); and while one might in the long term get some improvement, it would be visionary to expect any dramatic increase. In such a dilemma, the answer may lie in the offering of generous public grants to unions, with no strings attached, for a variety of purposes other than their business of bargaining and disputes – grants for research, for education, for consultative conferences of all kinds and in this way to open up their financial ability to employ more officials. I myself share many of the fears which people have about such a proposal, fears of state dependence and so forth. But Congress itself receives substantial grants from the state for its educational and advisory services, and, although I opposed the idea originally when it was suggested, I must now recognise that it has in no way diminished the complete independence of Congress in all its activities, even those supported by grant. Nor should a union be reluctant to accept offers by employers of free office accommodation and the deduction of union contributions at source. There is, I suppose, a danger that the official might be seen as a company man, but this he himself can readily overcome, and, in any event, in practice the danger appears to be small. And, finally, the state itself will have to see in a young man with professional trade union experience a favourable candidate for public service appointment. If an official's salary cannot be very high, the job at least should provide a unique challenge for an able man, with many prospects arising from it. But where in all this, one may ask, can one look for dedication, that impalpable thing which distinguishes the trade union movement and makes it so attractive—even demanding—despite all the blunders? This kind of dedication is something of the spirit; it may be found – perhaps just as frequently – among able young recruits as among officials whose lives have been spent in continuous service.In any event, what is suggested here is not an alternative leadership but some badly needed help, not merely at the top but throughout the trade union movement.

It has been suggested that the answer lies primarily not so much in recruitment but in restructuring, whether it be merely better organised negotiating groups or full-scale amalgamations. But it takes considerable skill to effect restructuring, which neither judicious legislation nor hortatory conferences can replace; and in all, it merely serves to emphasise once again the significance of recruitment. There may be one exception to this however. During the earlier part of the sixties, John Conroy and Jim Larkin made together a considerable effort to reunite the Irish Transport and the Workers Union of Ireland; and both men seemed to have set the prospect of such an amalgamation as the crown of their work, bringing, as it would, a Larkin once again into the Transport Union and restoring a lost and valued unity. Discussions, for which there were high hopes, got bogged down, and when both men died, the hope gradually faded, although there is still a rumble of interest. If it were to occur, some other unions could be expected to pitch in as well, making a very large union in Irish terms well able to provide all the services and the expertise. Whether in the wider context this would be a good thing for the Irish trade union movement, whether it would obscure Congress and disturb the delicacy of the balance north and south, British and Irish, is quite another question.

One way or the other, we are on the brink of a major shake-up and a major opportunity. The accession of Ireland to the European Community means the involvement of Irish trade union officials in many international committees, both official and voluntary, and the demand on their time is becoming so considerable that additional recruitment must take place. Even more fascinating is the need for trade unions here to take part in international groupings, which respond to the European emphasis on industry-based structures. As things stand at present, a general union may have to serve a forbiddingly large number of different industrial interests, while small unions in the same industry may speak with divided voices. The way ahead is unclear, but there is a strong feeling that this marks a very radical departure, that we may be witnessing the end of an epoch.

III

Let us for a moment, then, open our discussion on trade union organisation to the wider European horizon. During a cold, wet and stormy June in Geneva in 1971, one of the trade union committees of the annual International Labour Conference found itself confronted in a somewhat painful way with two quite different perceptions of the trade union movement. Of course, the problem was resolved, in the way of international meetings, by a form of words which permitted the instrument to be agreed but which left the two points of view unbreached and unsullied. The point of dispute, however, touched on the central crisis of the trade union movement, particularly in these islands.

In the ILO, the practice is to discuss a major proposal twice, with the interval of a year between, and in 1971, the second discussion was under way on protection and facilities for " workers' representatives in the undertaking"; it was aimed at securing not only a recommendation but the much more solemn convention. The crux for the trade union side was what was meant by worker representative. The West Germans led the way in insisting that the instrument should apply to works council representatives, while the British (and the Irish) were highly alarmed at the recognition which this implied for representatives of house (or company dominated) unions. This is the heartland of trade unionism where one gets the surge of feeling and the tensions of inequity. Of course, in Geneva, matters were not helped by widespread misperceptions of each other's systems; but despite this, one could detect a marked difference of emphasis in the manner in which the problem was approached, West Germany with its industry-based, highly unitary trade unions, being concerned more with equitable management, while the British and the Irish were concerned primarily with the preservation of independent trade unions, operating in a free and open system of collective bargaining. Nor were the Irish the only ones to support the British point of view, if not at the first discussion in 1970, certainly at the second discussion in 1971. Support came from Canada and India, from Australia and New Zealand and from some of the African states, among whom the British tradition was so marked that some of the other delegates described their position, rather inelegantly and inaccurately, as the Anglo-Saxon point of view.

While we have taken pains at the outset of this chapter to emphasise the special character of Irish trade unionism, an essential part of it is nonetheless a shared tradition with the British trade union movement, as these discussions in Geneva show very clearly; but all the events which we have recounted in this study would seem to put in question much of the traditional approach, the approach which culminated in the vehement resistance of many unions to even a voluntary prices and incomes policy, and also in the reluctance to participate in a national wage agreement. It is a dilemma which was rather well-caught by Eric Jacobs in *The Sunday Times*[3] when he was reflecting in the spring of 1973 on the splurge of strikes in Britain:

> There is no doubt that the unions do face a difficult problem of identity. They are invited by events to make a shift – away from thinking of themselves as fighters against injustice, towards becoming administrators of justice. It is not an easy change, and union leaders have understandably shied away from it. But they must ask themselves what would happen if, one day, a political leader were to put the problem to their members in this way: Do you want the free

[3] 11 March 1973.

collective bargaining which your unions have always stood for, or do you prefer stable prices, full employment, steady economic growth and an end to industrial disruption – for the two do not any longer seem to be compatible?

British trade unionism came to flower in the liberal tradition of the nineteenth century with its assumption that sectional interests pursued in a balanced and enlightened way led necessarily to justice. But it was an optimism which rested on an evangelical religious tradition and a vast economic hegemony, and even if the environment has changed in modern Britain, there is still a creative tradition of dissent, creative in that the wider consensus is still reasonably firm and clear. Ireland, on the other hand, was never economically secure, and the consensus in these matters is more troubled. Jacobs's critical question may therefore come earlier and more acutely here, tempted as we always are, to heavy-handed centralised solutions; and this may well be the case also in developing countries in the British tradition of administration, where corporate and unitary solutions may be more appropriate than the optimistic pluralism of the British system.

The West German model is usually spoken of with approval in Ireland, and before it ever came into being, in the late thirties and early forties as we have seen, we were within a hair's breadth of a vast restructuring on a corporate basis of the whole trade union movement in the South. That experiment was impelled by a chauvinism which has been dissipated in the wider and richer diversity of tradition which is now recognised in the essential unity of north and south. Nonetheless, in the Republic at least, some kind of corporate solution, although anathema to many trade union leaders, is never very far from the minds of rank and file members. It may not arise in the direct challenge of trade unions but in a side-stepping of them, in a manner not too unlike the solution offered by the Fogarty commission in the case of the ESB.

There seems so much sense in recognising the essential unity and interdependence of any society, and if Britain can in practice afford to ignore it at times, it is probably because it is so manifestly there. More than that, there is an understandable impatience with those horizontally organised trade unions, usually craft, strung uneasily across a number of industries and rasping at any unifying initiative within an industry. And yet one cannot but feel troubled at the growth of powerful unitary institutions; one must consciously work for and preserve certain things: the candidness of debate, for example, the conscious tolerance of dissent, which characterised the traditional trade unionism of Sam Kyle of the Amalgamated Transport for example. There is a deeper fear, the fear of gargantuanism in our institutions, suffocating the interests of the individual or the small group. This is the fear that traditional trade unions plead when confronted by the corporate solution, although they themselves are frequently seen by their own members as gargantuanly insensitive. The answer lies not in the size of the institution but in its quality, in the manner in which there can be freedom, initiative and dissent for the individual and the group. This is what men seek; it is seen in Tavistock's concept of privatisation, no less than in the West German emphasis in Geneva on the representative of the works council. The future seems to lie then with the large organistic view of society, essentially unchallenged, but rich in initiative and tolerant of dissent; but while one readily recognises this powerful tendency to some form of corporatism, one suspects that the other qualities may get short shrift. The developing interdependence within society, therefore, which we must recognise, is likely to be distorted and made inequitable by our strong, heavy tendency to centrality in all our institutions. This is really the centre of the dilemma.

We are not alone in the dilemma of course; it is an endemic problem in modern society. But we seem to be far less conscious of our alarming centrality than we should be, far less conscious of the need to foster local autonomy and initiative.

IV

When we take account then of the great changes in our society, the tensions, the difficulties and the inadequacies, we can gain an understanding of why some strikes should have been so intractable, and why picketing on occasion should have had such a devastating effect. Such a condition of affairs will exaggerate our difficulties; but having said that, it is important that we should treat with great caution some of the other generalisations about the causes of disputes. It has been suggested from time to time that the industrial unrest had been greatly increased if not generated by Marxists, or, in latter years, by extreme republicans. It is true that, during the sixties, Sinn Féin, which was then socialist in character, vigorously involved itself with all forms of social protest; and this could give rise to a belief that industrial disputes were a part of some anti-social conspiracy. There are however no grounds for this. The disputes were straightforward disputes concerning immediate grievances and, while radical elements were sometimes an embarrassment and sometimes a help, they were essentially peripheral. It is fashionable too to discount the obvious reasons for a dispute in favour of some more acceptable underlying cause. The CIE bus dispute is a good instance of this. Although it was never explicitly stated, there was an assumption that the company was reasonable and the trade unions were reasonable; and this left the men themselves as the troublemakers. But most of them appeared to be decent and hardworking, and, consequently, as we have seen, it was decided to examine their morale, almost as one might examine the problems of a good-natured alcoholic. The fact, however, appears to be that the men had real and deep-seated grievances which were being exacerbated by company policy, and morale had little enough to do with it.

There are three statements, therefore, that we can make. The first is that the reasons given for the strikes are usually the real reasons (and there is great wisdom in holding firmly to this fact); the second is that once we look at strikes in depth, it is by no means surprising that they should have occurred; and the third is that each strike is quite unique, springing from the circumstances of a particular industry, and demanding a specific, not a general solution. If then our solutions must be particular to each case and not rather windy and general, we must above all look to our procedures and our institutions.

In this area, the outstanding development has been the Employer-Labour Conference, which fostered centralised bargaining, judicial procedures and the observance of good industrial practice. Since its development, we have experienced a period of substantial industrial peace, very much in contrast with the period that went before. This is the outstanding fact in Irish industrial relations, a fact that many attribute in very large part to the institution of the Employer-Labour Conference and the two national agreements which it has produced. But there are two major questions now facing us: firstly, whether the whole system of centralised bargaining may overheat and blow apart, pushing us back once again into widespread disputes; and secondly, whether, if it survives, the price, in inflationary terms, will be far, far too high. The first bears on the problem of wage comparabilities and equities, the second on the problem of a consensus on prices and incomes. Both problems, therefore, must be taken up in our discussion. We shall begin with the problem of a prices and incomes policy, since it was from an NIEC debate on this matter in 1969 that the reconstituted Employer-Labour Conference sprang. The discussion, as well, will serve to evaluate the various institutions in the field and will give some indication of the way ahead.

v

In an earlier chapter (p. 179) we traced, after the 1969 maintenance dispute, the pressure for some institutions to deal with prices and incomes, its failure, and the eventual success of the national agreement. It is necessary now to consider these matters in greater depth.

As early as 1965, the National Industrial Economic Council (in which the Irish Congress of Trade Unions had a powerful voice) raised in its report no. 11 the desirability of having an incomes policy,[4] and while "we have not found it possible in the time available to us to consider all the practical arrangements which would be required, we regard this as a matter of the utmost importance because it directly affects the form and character of our society. It is essential that an examination of these objectives should be initiated as soon as possible."[5]

This report of the NIEC, which was issued in November 1965, was greatly influenced by developments in Britain where, the April before, the National Board for Prices and Incomes was established, acting at that time as a royal commission before becoming a statutory body the following year. Associated with it, there was a goodly number of satellite documents, some of which had a great ring of excitement about them. In December of 1964, there had been the Joint Statement of Intent on Productivity, Prices and Incomes; in February there was the white paper, *Machinery of Prices and Incomes Policy*, and in the same month in which the board was established by royal warrant – April 1965—there was a further white paper, *Prices and Incomes Policy* setting out the criteria by which the public interest would be safeguarded. However, the NIEC did not get around to considering the matter again until the early summer of 1969, by which time the exciting voluntary character of the British system had long evaporated, and clouds had gathered over the whole experiment.

On the other hand, Britain now, in early 1969, appeared to be abandoning its current reliance on the Prices and Incomes Acts; it had been announced in the budget of April 1969 that the powers of the government would not be renewed at the end of 1969 to delay wage and price increases, that the country would return to a voluntary prices and incomes system, except for the power to delay for three months an increase that had been referred to the National Board.

Apart from this, a momentum of interest had gathered in Ireland itself; the Institute of Public Administration had held a seminar on the topic of incomes policies in May, and in July the Irish Congress of Trade Unions had, surprisingly, adopted a positive approach to some such arrangement, more confident now that it could avoid the peril of a legislated system.

In the manner of the NIEC, the matter was referred to its general purposes committee for examination, and Charles Mulvey, whom we

[4]National Industrial Economic Council, *Report on Economic Situation*, report no. 11, 1965.
[5]ibid., p. 38.

have already met in the Bord na Mona dispute, was commissioned to prepare a comprehensive paper on the British experience. Discussions initially were quite leisurely, but, in the autumn, alarm began to grow with regard to the bahaviour of the economy. 1968 had been the best year up to then in the economic history of the country; but the future looked threatening; the trade gap had widened, bank credit had expanded, and consumer expenditure was quickening dangerously. The government's fear, which was shared by T. K. Whitaker and other influential people, was that there would be exceptionally high pay settlements, following the lead of the maintenance craftsmen, once new agreements came to be negotiated. In March, the government had warned about the consequences of following the maintenance craftsmen's settlement, and Congress had discounted the need for any immediate measures, pointing out that the agreements in other employments had to run their course. The problem, however, in the autumn of 1969, could no longer be postponed, and as we have seen, the government hoped to get agreement on some voluntary restraint. In the event, the maintenance craftsmen's award worked its way fully throughout industry, constituting the twelfth round, but at this time, in the autumn of 1969, there were some prominent members of the NIEC who hoped that an incomes policy worked out between all the parties would contribute to a solution; and even if it could not be introduced quickly enough to affect current or prospective negotiations, at least the initial discussions would help to moderate expectations. In this way, a sudden urgency swept into the discussions.

The general purposes committee of the National Industrial Economic Council was by then its power-house and when it presented its reports to the Council itself, these were, usually, apart from some drafting changes, virtually in final form. This was not the case however with the draft report on an incomes policy which the general purposes committee presented to the Council in September 1969; there was much redrafting of an extensive and continuous kind, and a report did not issue until February of the following year. This in particular reflected the intense concern with the institutional arrangements which were suggested. The concern was intensified in two ways. Some council members saw the institutional proposals, *inter alia*, as a means by which the dangers of the current economic situation could be red-flagged publicly, and, therefore, the more rigorous they were the better; this rather alarmed the trade union side. Secondly, some of the more ambitious proposals were looked on with considerable disfavour by members of the Labour Court and to an extent by the prices section of the Department of Industry and Commerce, the two major institutions already in the field. Indeed, it was this second, rather than the first, which caused the more difficult and extensive redrafting.

Let us consider the elements of a prices and incomes policy which is voluntary, since the NIEC did not discuss a legislated system at any time in any serious way. In the case of incomes, the object was to avoid increases that were inflationary. This meant three things: an appreciation of what increases were possible nationally, a means by which these increases could be fairly given to all, and finally (and this was really the point) an acceptable means by which exceptions could be met and further increases permitted to special groups without blowing the whole system skyhigh. This last problem was greatly complicated by our devotion to the principle of comparabilities; and yet, as we have seen on more than one occasion, it was the suppression of these exceptional cases in the general interest which led to very bitter disputes. In the matter of prices, the object was to avoid unjustified increases by means of price surveillance, rather than by price control, principally in order that competition could operate fairly. This required, of course, that the government would have adequate reserve powers, but, further, it also required that there should be a means by which certain cases could be investigated in depth and reported on publicly. But the key to the whole thing was to recognise that incomes and prices were highly interrelated and interdependent, and therefore the institutions to deal with them should reflect this.

Let us then take all these elements separately, rooting our discussion in the NIEC report no. 27[6] which was published in February 1970. The report began by considering the phenomenon of inflation, its consequences and the role of a prices and incomes policy as an important means of meeting the problem. Certainly, on the face of it, it seemed grave indeed that our capacity to produce wealth should have to be damped back because we were unable to handle its equitable and sensible distribution; but the consequences were seen as more perilous than that, and early drafts frankly contemplated the possibility of devaluation of the Irish pound. Indeed a certain urbanity (necessary no doubt in the circumstances) is noticeable in the final report which subdues somewhat the anxiety of the earlier discussion.

The report then repeated once again the substance of that part of the earlier report no. 11 which dealt with a prices and incomes policy, the object of which was the equitable distribution of increasing wealth. Equity was the corner-stone, equity publicly and widely understood. All increases of all kinds, incomes and prices alike, must be seen as being legitimate within a general consensus, and differentials in income

[6]National Industrial Economic Council, *Report on Incomes and Prices Policy*, report no. 27, 1970 (Prl. 1102).

must also be legitimated in the same way. Pressures exerted by the same widely-held consensus would also constitute the sanctions against the maverick and the predator. All this was intended not only to introduce the discussion on institutions but to inform and alert opinion in regard to the current critical position, in a word to 'influence attitudes.' The report therefore urged two things: understanding of the economic and social climate, and commitment to a remedy. The latter was of the greatest significance and the report was caustic about the current trade union deficiencies which seriously limited their effectiveness. (The employers organisations also got critical mention, one suspects for reasons of balance).

The new institutional arrangements were conceived as follows. Broad guidelines of what increases in money incomes were possible would be enunciated by the NIEC itself. These, however, would be very general and uncontentious. They would be translated into terms which were 'operationally useful' by a new national employer/employee body. It is interesting to note that the functions contemplated for this body were both more modest and more shadowy than in the event it itself developed; while it might produce occasional national agreements, it was seen essentially as being also in the business of offering guidelines – more specific, however, and directed in particular to negotiators at firm and industry level, with the added responsibility of riding herd on them to ensure compliance. This latter seemed to be a doubtful starter, and certainly the body was thought to be quite incapable of handling examinations, critically and in depth, of powerful sectional groups, and it was this that led to the idea of an independent prices and incomes board.

And so we come to the centre of the debate. The council set out the functions of a new "independent Incomes and Prices Board, similar to the National Board for Prices and Incomes in Britain," deciding what would justify divergences from guidelines in the particular cases referred to it, exploring the industry, the pay structures, the links between incomes and prices, and acting as the guardian of the community's interest, its concern being as much with growth as with current income distribution. However, the council decided not to recommend such a Board, and the reasons are worth quoting in full.

> [There] is no agreement within the council in favour of setting it up at this stage, because of certain practical difficulties that would be associated with its establishment and operation and the danger that the failure of an ambitious institutional step of this kind could have a disproportionately damaging effect on incomes and prices policy in its early stages. Some members have doubts about such a

Board succeeding within the context of a voluntary incomes policy. In our discussions, we have not found it possible to reach agreement on how to tackle many of the problems that an Incomes and Prices Board would pose or precipitate. The most important of these practical problems is how to avoid conflict or overlap between the new Board and the Labour Court. Furthermore, we feel that there would be considerable difficulty in attracting suitable personnel in adequate numbers to a new and untried body.[7]

The relations with the Labour Court was really the conundrum that could not be resolved. The difficulty ran deep. The council was conscious of the fact that, while the Board it contemplated would be a guardian of the public interest, the Labour Court

> was originally, but is now no longer, required by statute to have regard, in making its recommendations, to the national interest. The Court's main function is to provide a basis for reaching agreement between the opposing parties so as to settle or avoid industrial disputes. It has never operated in a situation in which the national interest was spelled out in terms of guide-lines....[8]

We must remember in evaluating this that members of the Labour Court were consulted during the council's discussions. It is not surprising, then, that the council feared that there would be conflicting recommendations from the proposed Board and the Labour Court; or worse, that the Court would be seen as an appeals body from the Board, in circumstances where a case decided by the Board in the public interest could be upset on grounds in which the public interest had little part.

Nor was the prices section of the Department of Industry and Commerce very happy about an Incomes and Prices Board with investigatory powers; if there were inadequacies, they felt that they would be met on the extension of the function of the Fair Trade Commission to the services sector of the economy. Faced with all this, the council came up with an ingenious, if rather tortured, solution.

The idea was to establish a body, to be known as the Incomes and Prices Committee, which would advise the appropriate minister on the cases which should be referred for investigation; but in doing so, it would spell out the scope and the issues in each case, and these it could publish. The point was, however, that the Incomes and Prices Committee would not itself investigate, or issue reports, or take part in their drafting. Instead, in the matter of incomes, the investigation would be carried

[7]Op. cit., p. 32.
[8]*idem*, p. 33.

out by the Labour Court, suitably refurbished, and in the case of prices by the Department of Industry and Commerce, or by the Fair Trade Commission, or – and this was of great importance – it could be recommended that a case be investigated by a joint working party, and in this way the interdependence of prices and incomes could be held in focus. The Incomes and Prices Committee, however, would review the performance of the investigatory bodies, and since it would have this function and also the function of explicit and public recommendation on what should be investigated, it would on the one hand have status, and on the other it would avoid the tangle of conflict. The Labour Court, now fulfilling the role of investigation as well, would be unlikely to conflict with itself, although it was recognised – and accepted – that its conciliation service might still take a somewhat divergent line.

There is one remark about the Labour Court which must be made in passing. To cast it in the role of a body which would settle disputes at all costs would be very wrong; it would be fairer to say that its perception of the public interest sprang from a somewhat special experience, and the proposed system, it was hoped, would tend to broaden this view.

There is no doubt that this was seen as a beginning, and the Incomes and Prices body, although a rather shadowy device, could, if judiciously manned, grow greatly in power and prestige. It was recommended that it would consist of an independent and agreed chairman, five other non-official members (selected after consultation with the employer-employee body) and five official members (the chairman of the Labour Court, the chairman of the Fair Trade Commission, a representative from the prices section of the Department of Industry and Commerce, from the Department of Finance and from the Department of Labour). But this was all subject to early review.

> If it seemed to be having little effect, then, in our view, more radical institutional changes would have to be considered. It might then be necessary to set up a single institution within which the prices and incomes functions of the existing bodies would be integrated.[9]

It was a very fair assumption indeed that something quite significant would have been made of the Incomes and Prices body. We have since seen the National Prices Commission, which was established towards the end of 1971 under the vigorous chairmanship of Professor Louden Ryan, become an important instrument of public policy formation. Its monthly reports have dealt not only with individual price application and more general price surveillance, but also with topics such as local prices committees, consumer advisory councils, and even with a brief analysis

[9] ibid., p. 40.

of the phenomenon of inflation. It would have been fascinating to see the same vigour applied to an Incomes and Prices Committee.

We have already seen (p. 180) how the annual conference of Congress in July 1970 shattered all hopes of such a system; instead, Congress turned to the reconstituted Employer-Labour Conference. This body is bipartite: that is, it consists of representatives of trade unions and employers merely, and has neither independent members nor government representatives. This statement must be modified in two ways; we have already seen how Basil Chubb, the independent chairman, felt obliged in 1970 to declare a personal view, and secondly, the government as an employer is represented on the conference; but in substance, there is no doubt that it is a bipartite body. No tripartite body, such as an incomes and prices committee, was created, and more than that, the NIEC was allowed to wither and die in the discussion on what should succeed it. In these circumstances, the Employer-Labour Conference developed, through the two national agreements, an institutional character of a magnitude and influence much in contrast with the subsidiary and rather ambiguous role which the NIEC report contemplated.

We have also seen earlier (p. 182) how the national agreements had the effect of centralising bargaining and limiting the area of industrial action.[10] We must now turn to the issue which was the particular concern of the NIEC report, the manner in which exceptions were identified and legitimated. We shall for this purpose concern ourselves in particular with the second national agreement that concluded in July 1972. First there was the universal provision which would apply as current agreements concluded; once again it consisted of two phases: the first provided for percentage increases on wages and salaries from 9 per cent. ranging down to 4 per cent., and the second phase, arising after twelve months, provided for 4 per cent. with a cost-of-living escalator clause in the form of a threshold clause, as the British now like to call it. There were a number of other important developments, particularly the acceptance of the principle of equal pay for men and women, which need not delay this outline discussion.

This then was the maximum position, with three broad exceptions. There was, as before, provision for dealing with anomalies (somewhat more flexibly now), provision for dealing with incentive payments; and now, in addition, the whole thorny field of conditions of employment was gingerly opened up. When one looked for a decision on how these ex-

---

[10]For a comprehensive report on the workings of the national agreements up to the summer of 1973, see *Report to the Employer-Labour Conference on the National Agreements of* 1970 *and* 1972, published by the Employer-Labour Conference, 31 August 1973.

ceptions would operate, and when one looked for guidance on a difficult point of interpretation, where could one turn? In answering these questions, we come to the root of the difference between the Labour Court on the one hand and the Employer-Labour Conference on the other, and we see the profiles of each institution much more clearly. It has been said that the difference between the two institutions lies in this: that while questions of interpretation are dealt with by the Employer-Labour Conference, questions of fact and questions of implementation are dealt with by the Labour Court. I have found this distinction to be of limited value; the Labour Court, as we shall see, does fulfil an interpretative role, and the Employer-Labour Conference does concern itself with implementation. The real distinction, it seems to me, lies in this: the Labour Court has a stabilising role, following trends when they have emerged but not as a rule initiating trends itself, while the Employer-Labour Conference is essentially innovatory, certainly in the last two national agreements where its task was to create radically new frames within which increases took place. This helps, incidentally, to explain a great deal about the Labour Court. From a trade union point of view, it is useful in bringing an employer into line, but is less likely to be sympathetic to a new initiative even where it had a good deal to recommend it. (This was certainly in the minds of the maintenance craftsmen when in 1969 they refused to appear before the Court.) From the point of view of the NIEC economist, it will tend to discount economic arguments in favour of stabilising a movement which appears to be inevitable. It is from this, I think, comes the confusion regarding the significance of the public interest. While this role of the Labour Court is of considerable importance, there is a danger that the most difficult disputes of all, those setting major national trends, must be settled in the jungle. And this in fact is what happened in the past. On the other hand, these are precisely the matters which the Employer-Labour Conference attempted to resolve by means of the great national agreements.

Let us glance first at the functions of the Labour Court for the purposes of the National Agreement of July 1972. It is the final arbiter in certain matters concerning equal pay for women; it determines whether an employer should be exempted from the agreement because of inability to pay, and above all, where agreement cannot be reached between the parties on a question of anomaly, or on a question of conditions of employment, the question must be referred, without industrial action, to the Court. This last, the major point really, has resulted in a great deal of Court activity in recent times.

All this is straightforward enough; and so also is the normal interpretative function of the Employer-Labour Conference. Many cases can be dealt with in accordance with precedent, but, if a case is particularly difficult, the steering committee refers it to a subcommittee of the Employer-Labour Conference which is known as the interpretation committee and which meets as a rule without a chairman. Here we come to the first point of departure. I must confess that I had assumed that in its interpretative role, which after all is largely a judicial matter, the interpretation committee, since it consisted of the two sides in equal strength, would tend to depend more and more on precedent, finding this the only practical course to adopt and becoming more and more hidebound as a result. In fact, this does not appear to have occurred to any great extent; on the contrary, interpretation appears in some instances to extend the agreement. The explanation offered is that the parties are in fact putting in written form what was actually intended at the time, although not recorded. It is recognised that national agreements are written at a tempo which requires later review and refinement; and this function is fulfilled by the interpretation committee. Clearly, the débâcle after the ninth round agreement has had its effect. But it is a development of the greatest fascination, because it raises the possibility of a continuously evolving agreement, rather than one solid frame substituting for another.

The second point of departure is the adjudication committee which was established by the Employer-Labour Conference in June 1973. It is concerned not with interpretation, not even with settlements; it is concerned with actions by trade unions or employers which are in breach of the national agreements, that is industrial action on the part of the trade unions, and—on the part of the employers—such matters as refusal to pay on the foot of the agreement, or the unilateral changing of conditions of employment. It is best seen not as a judicial or as a conciliatory function, but as one of policing the agreement. It apparently arose from the exigencies of one or two cases. The steering committee normally advises the parties on such matters as these, but its voice is not necessarily compelling. We have already noted one instance where a plenary session of the Employer-Labour Conference was necessary to reinforce the steering committee decision—the case of AGEMOU and AUEW in the CIE garages (p. 176); but this is a heavy-handed manoeuvre. An adjudication committee, which was given the prestige of the conference as a whole, could examine issues more closely and adjudicate more fairly; and furthermore, it would not be embarrassed by the possibility of having among its members one of the partisans in the dispute. (This was quite possible, certainly on the trade union side, if a plenary session were called, since all the members of the executive council of Congress are *ex officio* members of the Employer-Labour Conference.)

The third point of departure is the question of the reference of settlements for evaluation in the public interest. Here we are not concerned with disputes; we are concerned with the possibility of an arrangement (even perhaps a conspiracy) between an employer and a trade union to reach an agreement contrary to the national agreement and contrary to the public interest. We have met this already in the case of the banks where settlements had been referred to the Labour Court by the Minister for Labour on just such grounds; and in 1972, before a settlement was confirmed between the government and the teachers, a similar reference was made to the Labour Court. On the other hand, when the Devlin Review Body[11] recommended increased pay in the upper reaches of the public sector, Congress referred the matter, not to the Labour Court, but to the Employer-Labour Conference. This looks confusing on the face of it, but it has a certain logic. The Minister for Labour is in a special legislative relationship with the Labour Court; he is empowered to refer such questions to them for report under Section 24 of the Industrial Relations Act, 1946. He has no such relationship with the Employer-Labour Conference, but in practice he is aware that the Labour Court, in preparing its report, would consult with the Employer-Labour Conference in any event. On the other hand, Congress has a special relationship with the Employer-Labour Conference, being one of its pillars, and quite apart from that, in the case of the Devlin recommendation, the chairman of the Labour Court, and perhaps others close to it, were possible beneficiaries.[12]

But there is need for yet a further service which could be provided by the Employer-Labour Conference. The final ESB report urged the continuous testing of the industrial relations temperature, and responding to problems in good time. The fact is, however, that most strikes, particularly the difficult ones, send their stormclouds well before them; the difficulty really lies in making an adequate response. Again and again, we have seen how a simple demand required a complex answer, in the case of the building workers, the maintenance workers, the banks, the teachers, the many disputes in the ESB. Demands for more pay or reduced hours concealed behind them a formidable tangle of relationships and implications for the future, quite apart from the magnitude of the claims themselves and the difficulty of meeting them within the margins available, but being often only partially identified, they invited sometimes wrong-

---

[11]*Review Body on Higher Remuneration in the Public Sector,* July 1972 (Stationery Office, Dublin) Prl. 2674.

[12]Subsequently, an anomaly claim on behalf of higher civil servants was referred to the Labour Court (despite the possible involvement of the chairman personally) which reinforces the thrust of the argument.

headed and perilous solutions, or perhaps resulted in a paralysis of uncertainty as the tension mounted. It is here that the reports commissioned by the Minister for Labour have been of great value, but what we now badly require is the carrying out in full of the NIEC proposals, the establishing of a panel of people to undertake the studies and to provide an integrated service so that one report would enrich another, giving rise, one would hope, to general reports from time to time indicating major problems and major strategies. Professor Fogarty, after his experience of two commissions of inquiry, would bring the idea further, and he suggested in 1971[13] a permanent commission on industrial relations such as was set up by the Labour government in Britain following the Donovan Report. He distinguished such an idea from the *ad hoc* inquiries established after the event and with limited terms of reference, and he also distinguished it from the Labour Court which he claimed is a court not for inquiring into disputes but for settling them. Such a commission, he suggested, would not act as any kind of a court, nor as a conciliation agency, but would "look into the practice and procedure of industrial relations in any part of the economy which seemed to need this and to persuade the parties towards reform." Nor would he exclude certain powers to compel the introduction of proper procedures. Such a joint body, he hoped, would promote the continuing and consistent reform of industrial relations. There is a great deal to recommend all this, although on balance I believe the advantage would lie in establishing instead the permanent panel of experts, as suggested by the NIEC, under the aegis however of the Employer-Labour Conference. Making it all responsible to the Employer-Labour Conference would give the service itself more acceptability and the Conference more certainty in undertaking national initiatives.

Some of the difficulty here may lie with the Department of Labour in what appears (to an outsider, in any event) to be a reluctance to see established permanent systems as alternatives to the civil service. We see it as well perhaps in the case of the two rights commissioners (these are not civil servants) who receive little administrative support, not perhaps for any wrong reason but because the Irish civil service finds difficulty in dealing with these kinds of arrangements, preferring to lodge matters within a traditional frame of responsibility. Even the conciliation service of the Labour Court, which has a considerable and well-deserved reputation, could benefit from recruits from outside the civil service proper. It seems wise then to recognise the limited role of the Labour Court, to confirm it in that role and to foster, particularly under the Employer-

[13]Michael P. Fogarty, 'Voluntary Association, Industrial Relations and the Common Good', *Administration,* vol. 19, Autumn 1971.

Labour Conference, such additional procedures and institutions as are necessary.

Before leaving the functions of the Employer-Labour Conference, it is as well to remember that, although it has been engrossed in recent years in national agreements, its terms of reference are broader than that, and in fact it has engaged in a number of studies, the check-off system of collecting union contributions being one, and another being worker-participation in industry. It has also prepared a report on fair employment and dismissal procedures. These are valued, apart from their intrinsic worth, as keeping firm the broader structure of the conference in the event of national agreements going out of fashion.

vi

Here then, built on a shaky and strike-torn foundation, a system of considerable sophistication has developed, where comprehensive and detailed agreements are concluded for the whole nation, their terms vigorously upheld and special problems dealt with by an effective judicial arrangement. More than that, the system appears to have brought with it the blessings of industrial peace. What can we say of the way ahead?

At the outset we asked ourselves two questions: firstly, whether the whole system of centralised bargaining may overheat and blow apart, pushing us back once again into widespread disputes; and secondly, whether, if it survives, the price, in inflationary terms, will be far, far too high.

Let us deal first with the stresses on the system. I believe that in recent times we have experienced industrial peace not merely because pay increases have been substantial (this, as we have seen, is often as much a hazard as a help to good relations) but because they have been considered fair—because they maintained the appearance of equity; and this highly political, rather than economic, concept lies at the very heart of the problem. Where, as Aubrey Jones[14] has pointed out, the appearance of equity is lost, the pressure for higher incomes is intensified. Of course, the Employer-Labour Conference is deeply concerned with these matters. With regard to terminal dates—that is, the different dates on which the agreement is implemented for different groups of workers—they have made some headway. And in particular they have tried to make the agreement, although centrally conceived and instituted, more sensitive to sectoral difficulties, with the consequence that many groups have gained substantial increases in addition to the basic sum agreed, particularly where they were skilful in interpretation and presentation. This has of

[14]Aubrey Jones, *The New Inflation* (Penguin, Harmondsworth, 1973), p. 47.

course greatly eased the tension. But on the one hand, such increases tend to put in question the legitimacy of the whole arrangement; on the other hand, there are inevitably a large number of disgruntled and unsatisfied workers, who find themselves unable to rise beyond the minimum of the agreement, either because their leadership is not skilled enough, or more likely, because the system is hostile to their particular claim. A highly centralised system must insist that all questions be asked in its terms—not in the terms in which they might arise in the real world. A system such as this must above everything else be consistent; indeed its legitimacy depends on this consistency, and therefore, despite this sensitivity and skill, many claims must be pushed back into the system causing tension to build up, and inviting the danger that, when a movement comes, it will come for all and it will come explosively. If tension is not too high at present in the summer of 1973, when negotiations must soon begin on a new national agreement, it is a tribute to the Employer-Labour Conference and the manner in which they have managed the delicate boundary between legitimacy on the one hand and flexibility on the other.

But at the back of it all there is the black dog of comparabilities pushing expectations higher, and making the whole system even more unstable and inflationary. Let us review this phenomenon in Irish industrial relations, recognising how much more difficult it makes the achieving of equity. Throughout most of the disputes, the principle of comparability was dominant in a very special and intense way, more dominant apparently than it was in any other country that we are aware of. It seemed to spring from some deep need in our society, whether by reason of our size or of our social disposition; even where we had spontaneous wage-rounds, or free-for-alls, one finds a tendency to uniformity, although, as Mulvey and Trevithick[15] remark, one might intuitively expect such rounds to incorporate a variety of settlements, in an attempt to correct imbalances from previous national agreements. The principle of comparability was so axiomatic that when solutions were attempted, they remained within its terms: there was the Quinn tribunal which recommended precisely the same salary scale for all the clerical recruitment grades throughout the civil service, the local authority service and the semi-state service; there was the proposal of the government to give the Labour Court the function of coordinating the lot by placing its members on virtually every arbitration board in the state; and only last year, 1972, we had the heady and rather alarming experience of seeing the salaries of judges, senior civil servants, politicians and heads of state-sponsored bodies, all dealt with together in one report,[16] with a powerful implication of some relationship

[15]Op. cit., p. 205.
[16]*Review Body on Higher Remuneration in the Public Sector,* op. cit.

between them. Indeed the national agreements themselves, when one reflects on them, are powerfully influenced by the same idea. And when, in the past, the principle of comparability was challenged, it was either sheer buccaneering, and recognised as such, or one union breaking loose in order to lead a general movement.

Until the Fogarty reports on the ESB, nobody seems to have questioned the good sense of the whole idea; nobody seems to have recognised that, pressed to its logical conclusion, it would lead to a vast and rather lunatic edifice of interlocking rates of wages, salaries and allowances, with negotiators on both sides intent on shoring it up in order to avoid disaster, and hostile therefore to claims which fell outside its scope, the pressure of the shop floor for example, or an intractable conflict of skills.

We must recognise then that the problem lies not primarily in the control of the operation of the comparability principle, but in its displacement. Blum suggested emphasis on other criteria, and Mulvey and Trevithick looked also to an improvement in the labour market; but the answer lies primarily, I think, in the emerging trend towards privatisation, as Van Beinum described it. If there has been a privatisation of the work and the worker, so also must there be a privatisation of bargaining, not in the sense of excluding a union but rather in relating the bargain to the private and individual situation of the firm, not to a national category. We can see something of this in the present programme of the ESB. A firm, for example, would no longer employ an electrician or a fitter on the basis of a national wage, with certain plus rates; rather would they appoint to a post unique to the firm for which such a skill was required but which itself was larger in scope and responsibility. Thus we are confronted with a complex and difficult task of job reorganisation.

The primary purpose of job reorganisation, however, must be to benefit the firm itself, not to obscure national comparabilities. And there are indeed strong reasons which compel us to embark on this. There is a growing desire among workers for a democratisation of the job, for more personal discretion and more job control; there is an anxiety on the part of many firms to make sense of the jungle of special plus payments which they must meet and which they would wish to resolve in a single scale (Chubb, for example, found a dizzying complexity in the maintenance rates); and there is need to relate all workers together within the firm in an integrated salary policy (and wage earners are particularly impatient with the discrimination of the past); otherwise, one's firm is hostage to all sorts of national influences which in the domestic context can be conflicting and disruptive. But apart from the apathy and imperception of managers, there is much to impede what appears to be a reasonable and natural growth. Some unions will oppose it, for good reasons as well as bad; the argument from comparabilities is a powerful argument and a considerable defence against inequity; but there is also the dread of the union itself—particularly the small craft union—of becoming irrelevant in such a situation. Furthermore, much of the business of reorganisation would bear on job redesign which is difficult to accommodate in an industrial world which seems to reinforce current job design by a vast panoply of training techniques aimed at quick learning. Finally, there is the influence of the national agreements, despite their immense contribution to industrial peace. And here at least some headway is possible.

There are two things one might do. There should be some means, as there was in Britain, by which claims for an increase in income could lead, in an exceptional case, to a comprehensive report on the whole industry, the quality of the report validating any departure from the norm. This in fact could be a function of the panel which the NIEC recommended for the purpose of investigating disputes, and, in the absence of a prices and incomes body (or even if such a body were set up), could be established under the general responsibility of the Employer-Labour Conference.

The second point is a much more difficult one, particularly in view of all that has been achieved. I fear that we must rethink our national agreements, contenting ourselves with far less at national level. I do not suggest any cut-back in the sophisticated structures that we have created; but the bargaining itself must move closer to what the Swedes have termed the solidaristic wage system, where only the parameters are agreed nationally, and where real bargaining continues all the way down to plant level. But to achieve this is a formidable task. If there are to be significant increases throughout employments in addition to the nationally agreed amounts, then the nationally agreed amounts must be more modest; but, in fact, our expectations have been cast very high by the last two agreements, and it is difficult to see how they can be moderated. The answer in such a transitional period may lie in a more modest agreement for perhaps a year, or an evolving agreement which builds out some general understanding. These things are now possible since the Employer-Labour Conference has developed strongly as an institution. The problem really is whether we can afford the cost, which one way or the other is bound to be high. And this brings us to our second major question.

Aubrey Jones, in his rather remarkable book, *The New Inflation*,[17] from which we have already quoted, summarises the position very well:

> Now, in a society which is content to abide by a traditional standard of living and which is not consumed by a passion for equal increases or equal absolute levels of pay, pressures need not arise to push up

[17] Op. cit., p. 25.

earnings faster than the rate of growth in the gross national product. But in a society which is accustomed to constantly rising living standards and which seeks to imitate the largest increase in earnings that it sees around it, the tendency, as we have shown, will be for earnings to exceed the rate of increase in the gross national product and for labour costs per unit of output to rise. Such a society, for social and political rather than for economic reasons, will have an inflationary bias.

In fact, not only have we experienced this inflation—the highest in western Europe, as the 1973 annual report of the Central Bank points out—but at the same time we have a major unemployment problem and profoundly serious difficulties of regional imbalance. Of course, there are many causes for this, of which the rise in money incomes is only one: there is also the rise in import prices, the rise in export prices, the growth of government expenditure and so forth. Nevertheless, the growth in money incomes was very substantial, much exceeding its value in real terms, and it is in this area of large settlements which bring little gain that current anxiety arises. The National Prices Commission, in a recent report,[18] looked back on the NIEC warnings regarding inflation and affirmed their continuing validity:

> There was universal acceptance that dire consequences would follow if Irish inflation proceeded for long at a rate faster than inflation in neighbouring countries. At the same time, no body or agency was prepared to accept that it or its members had made, or were making, a major contribution to inflation. Unless those who contributed to inflation were prepared to recognise and accept responsibility for their contribution, there was very little hope of keeping inflation in Ireland within the bounds of what was occurring in other countries. It was the unanimous view of the NIEC that, if the then current rate of domestic inflation was not curbed, even the existing level of employment could not be maintained and that it would be utterly unrealistic for Ireland to aspire towards full employment. In addition, the country would be faced with social tension and unrest, because inflation frequently brought unmerited gains to some individuals while bearing particularly heavily on those on fixed or low incomes.

There are some who would claim that the Employer-Labour Conference in its national agreements takes account adequately of these things as far as wages and salaries are concerned, and indeed the preamble to the 1972 agreement subscribes to ". . . the following social and economic

[18]National Prices Commission, *Monthly Report No.* 16, March 1973, p. 16.

undertaking CIE (the transport authority) which employs nearly 21,000, and the Electricity Supply Board, employing nearly 12,000. It also counts each local authority as a separate undertaking, with the exception of Dublin City.

Undertakings employing		Count
more than 10,000		2
more than 5,000 but less than 10,000		2
" " " " 4,000 " " " 5,000		2
" " " " 3,000 " " " 4,000		9
" " " " 2,000 " " " 3,000		2
" " " " 1,500 " " " 2,000		12
" " " " 1,000 " " " 1,500		30
" " " " 900 " " " 1,000		7
" " " " 800 " " " 900		15
" " " " 700 " " " 800		20
" " " " 600 " " " 700		17
" " " " 500 " " " 600		22
" " " " 400 " " " 500		40
" " " " 300 " " " 400		68
" " " " 200 " " " 300		150
" " " " 100 " " " 200		375
" " " " 50 " " " 100		707
" " " " 25 " " " 50		1254
" " " " 10 " " " 25		1400
Undertakings employing less than 10		1027

	1969	1971
Total employment in non-agricultural economic activity	770,000	789,000
Total employed in the public sector	184,000	

Employment in the public sector: 1969 (figures are approximate)*

State-sponsored bodies	55,000
Civil service	
General service and departmental grades	28,000
Industrial	10,000
Others	3,000
Total civil service	41,000
Local authorities	28,000
Health authorities	18,000
Harbour authorities	1,500
Vocational educational committees	1,500
Total local authorities etc.	49,000
Teachers	24,000
Defence forces	8,500
Garda Síochána (police)	6,500
Total public sector	184,000

**Trade Union Information*, June-July 1969

APPENDIX 2

Industrial Relations in the Republic

Industrial relations in Ireland are characterised essentially by free collective bargaining and by custom and practice. As a general rule, wages are not regulated by law, the principal exception being agricultural employees. Legislation provides a legal framework within which, broadly speaking, employers and employees make such bargains as they please. The following are some of the institutions in the field:

The Labour Court
It was established under the Industrial Relations Act 1946. It is not a court of law. It investigates industrial disputes and issues recommendations. It consists of employee representatives, employer representatives and independent chairmen, all full-time and appointed by the Minister for Labour. The Court appoints a conciliation service consisting of industrial relations officers, all civil servants. The Court also fosters joint industrial councils with clear procedures and independent chairman; seventeen exist at present, including the construction industry, flour milling and the banks.

The Labour Court may register agreements under Part III of the Industrial Relations Act 1946, the effect being to make the agreement legally enforceable. There are very few industry-wide agreements of significance, the two major ones being in the footwear industry and (of outstanding importance) the construction industry. There are twenty-one statutory joint labour committees, and employment regulation orders made by the Labour Court on the basis of proposals submitted to it by these committees are legally enforceable. The Court may provide an arbitrator in a dispute, if both parties wish, or arbitrate itself, but only if both parties agree beforehand to accept its findings.

Agricultural wages The Agricultural Wages Board, established under the Agricultural Wages Acts 1936–1969 is empowered to prescribe the statutory minimum rate of wages for farm workers.

Conciliation and arbitration This system of bargaining was introduced in the civil service in the early nineteen fifties. It consists of two levels: a conciliation council, equally representative of the staff and the state sides, but chaired by the permanent head of the appropriate department of state or his deputy) and secondly an arbitration board, also equally representative but chaired by an agreed independent chairman appointed by the government. The system was extended in separate schemes to national teachers, secondary teachers and vocational teachers. In an adapted form, it was introduced as well for local government officials and also for some other public servants.

Employer-Labour Conference It was established first in 1963 but was reconstituted in its present form in 1970 with Professor Basil Chubb as independent chairman and with joint secretaries, D. J. McAuley, Director-General of the Federated Union of Employers and Ruaidhri Roberts, General-Secretary of the Irish Congress of Trade Unions. It was established for the purpose of providing a national forum for the discussion and review of all major industrial relations problems. The national pay agreements of 1970 and 1972 were negotiated within the conference.

The employer side consists of the Federated Union of Employers, the state service (in its capacity as an employer), the local authority managers, the semi-state bodies, the Construction Industry Federation, Irish Printing Federation, Electrical Contractors Association, Society of the Irish Motor Industry, and Dublin Master Victuallers' Association.

The trade union side consists of all the executive council members of the Irish Congress of Trade Unions.

APPENDIX 3

Trade Union Membership in Ireland

	Republic	Northern Ireland	All Ireland
Number of trade unions	95	77	147
Membership of:			
general unions	216,600	103,400	320,000
white-collar unions	89,600	71,600	161,200
other unions	80,600	88,000	168,600
Total membership	386,800	263,000	649,800
men	286,800*	193,500	480,000
as percentage of total	74%	74%	74%
women	100,000*	69,500	169,500
as percentage of total	26%	26%	26%
White-collar members	130,000*	83,000*	213,000
as percentage of total	34%	31%	33%
Percentage of employees in trade unions			
men	57%	66%	61%
women	40%	36%	38%
total	52%	54%	53%
Ten biggest unions:	265,000	168,000	
as percentage of total	69%	72%	
Main unions			
ITGWU	150,400	6,400	156,800
ATGWU	18,100	83,200	101,300
AUEW (ES)	5,400	27,300	32,700
WUI	31,000	—	31,000
EETU/PTU	1,700	17,000	18,700
IUDWC	15,900	—	15,900
Unions affiliated to ICTU	371,500	231,200	602,700
as percentage of total	96%	88%	93%
Unions with head offices			
in Republic	322,000	27,900	359,900
as percentage of total	86%	9%	55%
Northern Ireland	—	15,400	15,400
as percentage of total	—	6%	2%
Britain	54,800	219,700	274,500
as percentage of total	14%	84%	42%

*Rough estimate.

Abbreviations: ICTU – Irish Congress of Trade Unions; ITGWU – Irish Transport and General Workers' Union; ATGWU – Amalgamated Transport and General Workers' Union; AUEW (ES) – Amalgamated Union of Engineering Workers (Engineering Section); WUI – Workers Union of Ireland; EETU/PTU – Electrical, Electronics and Telecommunications Union/Plumbing Trades Union; IUDWC – Irish Union of Distributive Workers and Clerks.

Source: Irish Congress of Trade Unions, *Trade Union Information* June 1971, January 1972, February 1972. The figures relate to the year 1970.

APPENDIX 4

The National Wage Rounds

1946–47 (first round) Increases varied but, on average, wage rates rose by about one-fourth.

1948 (second round) Average increase on the basis of a national agreement resulted in £0.40 to £0.50 per week for men and about half these amounts for women.

1951 (third round) A general movement resulting in various increases ranging for men from £0.50 to £0.90, women getting about two-thirds of the men's increase.

1952 (fourth round) A national agreement, partially negotiated on the trade union side but generally implemented, resulted in an increase of £0.625 per week, women getting about two-thirds of this.

1955 (fifth round) A general increase, with some workers, during the round coming back for more; there was great diversity in the increases, ranging from £0.55 to £0.85 per week.

1957 (sixth round) A national agreement for £0.50 per week, women getting from £0.25 to £0.375 per week.

1959 (seventh round) A general movement took place resulting in increases for men of from £0.50 to £0.75 per week and for women £0.325 to £0.50. It was followed in 1960 by a movement for a reduction in working hours and for the five-day week.

1961 (eighth round) By the summer of 1961, increases of up to £0.70 per week had been negotiated, but settlements for electricians and building workers pushed up the rates; and by the end of the year, they ranged from £1.00 to £1.25 a week for men and from £0.50 to £0.75 for women.

1964 (ninth round) A nationally negotiated increase gave increases to everyone of 12 per cent. subject to a minimum increase of £1.00 for men.

1966 (tenth round) In the absence of a national agreement, the ICTU recommended a maximum of £1.00 a week, which was later supported by the Labour Court and generally applied.

1968 (eleventh round) During 1967, the practice of negotiating two-year comprehensive agreements began, and this became the feature of the eleventh round, the increases being £1.75 to £2.00 per week for men, in two or three phases; women got about 75 per cent. of this.

1969–70 (twelfth round) Electricians in November 1968 and, in particular, maintenance craftsmen in April 1969 led the way for settlements which were of the order of £4.00 a week in two or three phases over an eighteen-month period. Women's increases averaged about 80 per cent. of men's. There was a very wide spread of termination dates by this time.

1971 (thirteenth round) This was a national agreement concluded on 21 December 1970, providing for a phased agreement over eighteen months, the first phase being £2.00 per week (women a minimum of £1.70) and the second phase 4 per cent. with an automatic adjustment for increases in the consumer price index figure.

1972 (fourteenth round) This was a national agreement concluded on 31 July 1972, providing for a phased agreement of (in general) seventeen months, the first phase giving 9 per cent. on basic pay up to £30 a week, $7\frac{1}{2}$ per cent. on next £10 and 4 per cent. on the remainder (with some additional provisions), and the second phase, which arises after twelve months, giving 4 per cent. on basic pay with an automatic adjustment for increases in the consumer price index figure.

Index

AEF (*see* Amalgamated Union of Engineering Workers)
Aer Lingus, 157
AEU (*see* Amalgamated Union of Engineering Workers)
AGEMOU (*see* Automobile, General Engineering and Mechanical Operatives Union)
Alexander, Paul, 53
Amalgamated Society of Woodworkers (*now renamed* Union of Construction, Allied Trades and Technicians), 51-2, 79-80, 156, 161, 165
Amalgamated Transport and General Workers Union, 41, 43, 44, 46, 49, 50, 51, 64, 101, 103, 107, 113, 114, 126, 128, 136, 165, 226
Amalgamated Union of Engineering Workers, 86, 87, 107, 112, 155n., 156, 162-6, 172, 176, 180, 237
Ancient Guild of Brick and Stonelayers, 79
Andrews, C. S., 59, 65, 69, 136
Ascendancy, the, 4
Association of Secondary Teachers, Ireland, 152, 204, 207, 209, 212-16
Assurance Representative Organisation, 87
ASTI (*see* Association of Secondary Teachers, Ireland)
ASW (*see* Amalgamated Society of Woodworkers)
ATGWU (*see* Amalgamated Transport and General Workers Union)
AUEFW (*see* Amalgamated Union of Engineering Workers)
AUEW (*see* Amalgamated Union of Engineering Workers)
Automobile, General Engineering and Mechanical Operatives Union, 161-2, 176, 237

Baker, T. J., 25n.
Bakers Union (Irish Bakers', Confectioners' and Allied Workers' Union), 165
Banks,
  bill 1973, Regulation of Banks (Remuneration and Conditions of Appointment) (Temporary Provisions) Bill 1973, 193-4
  dispute, 15-16, 184-198
  joint industrial council, 187-9
  staff relations committee, 187
Barr, Andrew, 52-3
Belfast and District Trades Union Council, 52-3
Bell, William, 52
Bennett, Louie, 41n.
Binks, Harold, 52, 53
Blaney, Neil, 22
Blease, William, 58
Blum, Albert A., 122, 167, 168, 242
Bord na Mona, 16, 58, 90, 93, 98, 177, 190, 230
  dispute, 136-9
  trade union group, 137-8, 141-9
Bridlington Agreement, the, 56

Britain, 3, 173, 218, 219, 225, 226, 229, 230, 235, 239, 243, 245
TUC, 43
Civil Service Pay Research Unit, 111
Building dispute, 16, 77-84
Building Workers Trade Union, 79, 80
Busmen's dispute (*see under* Córas Iompair Éireann)
Byzantine schism, 11

Callaghan, Frank, 161
Campbell, Seán, 41n.
Candon, Jim, 52
Cassidy, Jack, 52, 161, 162
Catholic (*see* Roman Catholic)
Catholic Standard, 43
Cement Ltd., 163n., 165
Central Bank, the, 184, 197, 244
Centrality,
  of bargaining, 154-5
  of institutions, 12-15, 227, 246-7
Christian Brothers, 212
Christle, Joe, 106, 118
Chubb, Basil, 5n., 89, 179, 181, 235, 242
Chubb, F. B. (*see* Chubb, Basil)
CIE (*see* Córas Iompair Éireann)
CIU (*see* Congress of Irish Unions)
Civil service,
  cultural background, 5
Civil Service Alliance, 152
Civil Service Executive and Higher Officers Association, 152
Clarkson, J. Dunsmore, 218
Clerical and Administrative Workers Union, 53
Colley, George, 203, 205
Commission on Vocational Organisation 1939-43, 39n., 41
Common Market (*see* European Economic Community)
Comparability principle in wage and salary increases, 73, 110-111, 121-4, 138, 140, 168, 183, 186, 197, 198, 207, 231, 241-6
Congress (*see* Irish Congress of Trade Unions)
Congress of Irish Unions, 23, 44
Connolly, James, 8, 41, 47, 48, 51, 55
Conroy, John, 44, 46, 47, 49, 51, 53, 54, 65, 80, 84, 92, 94, 95, 107, 224
Constitution of Ireland, 33, 34
Conway, William Cardinal, 214, 215
Córas Iompair Éireann, 15, 57, 136, 152, 176, 227, 237
  Dispute of Dublin Busmen, 16, 58-71, 148, 149, 190
  Clontarf Garage, 64
Cork Examiner, 88
Cork Trades Council, 153
Cosgrave, Maurice, 126, 131, 152, 174, 216
Cox, Jim, 161, 162, 163
Crawford, Leo, 23, 53-4, 63, 79, 80, 84, 94, 105, 106, 108
Crowley, Patrick, 87
Cuffe, Charles, 78
Cusack, C. A., 167

Dáil Debates, 74n., 81n.
DATA (*see* Draughtsmen's and Allied Technicians' Association)

INDEX 257

Department of Education (*see* Education, Department of)
Department of Finance (*see* Finance, Department of)
Department of Industry and Commerce (*see* Industry and Commerce, Department of)
Department of Labour, (*see* Labour, Department of)
Desmond, Barry, 56, 84
Devlin Review Body (*Review Body of Higher Remuneration in the Public Sector* 1972), 238
Dobbin, Maurice, 81
Donovan Report (*Royal Commission on Trade Unions and Employers' Associations* 1965-68), 35, 239
Dooley, Paddy, 61
Downtown rate in wage bargaining, 104, 108, 124, 139, 154
Doyle, Gerry, 79
Draughtsmen's and Allied Technicians' Association, 130, 133
Dublin Busmen's dispute, (*see under* Córas Iompair Éireann)
Dublin City Busmen's Union, 64
Dublin Trade Union Council, 43, 44
Dublin Typographical Provident Society (*see also* Irish Graphical Society), 51
Dunne, Jimmy, 52, 87, 88, 151, 161, 163, 170, 220
Durkan, J., 25n.
DTPS (*see* Dublin Typographical Provident Society)

Economic and Social Research Institute, The, 17, 25, 116, 184
Education, Department of, 200-216
    Minister for, 200-216
Educational Company case, 34
Edwards, R. Dudley, 199
EEC (*see* European Economic Community)
EI, Shannon, 98
Electrical Trades' Union (Ireand), 18, 104, 106-8, 112, 113
Electricians' Association, 112
Electricity (Special Provisions) Act 1966, 90, 113, 115, 118
Electricity Supply Act 1927, 100
Electricity Supply Board, 15, 16, 24, 31, 56, 136, 139, 145, 157, 169, 176, 190, 193, 198, 222, 226, 238, 242
    Day Workers Association, 113, 126, 130, 131, 134
    Disputes, 99-135
    Fogarty inquiry (final report) (*Final Report of the Committee of Industrial Relations in the Electricity Supply Board* 1969), 97, 99-135, 222, 226, 238, 242
    Fogarty inquiry (interim report) (*Interim Report of the Committee of Industrial Relations in the Electricity Supply Board* 1968), 99-135, 146
    Gleeson Report (*Electricity Supply Board Commission of Inquiry* 1961), 100, 108n., 117, 122
    Industrial council, 118, 131
    Linesmen's Association, 113, 126
    Local union representation, 127, 128
    National Joint Industrial Committee, 100, 104, 108
    National Strike Committee 1968, 116
    Officers Association, 103
    Salaried Staff Conference, 101
    Shift Workers Association, 130-134
    Trade union group, 109, 126, 130
    Tribunals, 100, 109, 112, 117, 118, 122, 123
Electricity (Temporary Provisions) Bill, 105
Employer-Labour Conference, 32, 50, 55, 58, 73, 74, 76, 175-182, 194, 197, 228, 235-247
Equity in distributing incomes, 240-7

ESB (*see* Electricity Supply Board)
ETU(I) (*see* Electrical Trades' Union, Ireland)
European Economic Community, 24, 50, 55, 155, 222, 224

Fair Trade Commission (*now* Restrictive Practices Commission), 233, 234
Federated Union of Employers, 14, 23, 75, 78, 82, 83, 86, 88-91, 98, 123, 124, 138, 139, 154-169, 182, 192
Federation of Builders, Contractors and Allied Employers of Ireland (*now* the Construction Industry Federation), 78, 81
Federation of Irish Industries (*now* Confederation of Irish Industry), 74
Federation of Rural Workers, 137
Fianna Fáil, 22, 95n., 196
Finance, Department of, 234
FitzGerald, Garret, 26
Fitzpatrick, William J., 51, 52, 53, 87, 88
Fixed term agreements, 177-9
Fogarty, Michael P., 98, 116, 117, 120, 184-193, 239
Fogarty Report (*see under* Electricity Supply Board)
FUE (*see* Federated Union of Employers)

Gaelic subculture, 2-7, 40, 51
Geary, R. C., 202n.
Geneva, 224-7
Germany
  unification of, 3
  West Germany,
    labour relations, 30
    worker representation, 119-120, 225-7
Gleeson Report (*see under* Electricity Supply Board)
Gogarty, John, 194
Grace, E. A., 187
Gray, Edward, 187, 192-5
Groethuysen, Bernard, 6
Guinness salaried employees, 101

Hannan, Damien, 10n., 18, 101, 199
Haughey, Charles J., 22
Heuston, R. F. V., 33n., 34
Hillery, P. J., 113, 202, 205
Hughes, J. G., 202n.
Hull, Charlie, 176
Hutchinson, Bertram, 7n.

IBOA (*see* Irish Bank Officials' Association)
ICPSA (*see* Irish Conference of Professional and Service Associations)
ICTU (*see* Irish Congress of Trade Unions)
IEI & ETU (*see* Irish Engineering, Industrial and Electrical Trade Union)
IETA (*see* Irish Electrical Technicians Association)
IGS (*see* Irish Graphical Society)
ILGOU (*see* Irish Local Government Officials Union)
ILO (*see* International Labour Office)
Industrial Relations Act 1946, 29
Industrial Relations Act 1969, 31
Industrial Relations Act 1971 (UK), 35
Industrial Relations Act 1972, 153
Industrial Relations Bill 1966, 90

INDEX

Industry and Commerce,
  Department of (prices section), 230-4
  Minister for, 91 (*see also* Department of Labour)
INPC (*see* Irish National Productivity Committee)
Institute of Public Administration, 14n., 229
International Labour Office, 171, 172, 224
INTO (*see* Irish National Teachers Organisation)
Investment in Education (see OECD)
IRA, 3, 9, 22
Irish Bank Officials' Association, 185-197
Irish Conference of Professional and Service Associations, 55, 101, 102, 171, 186
Irish Congress of Trade Unions, 1, 18n., 26, 27n., 36, 38n., 44-8, 51, 74-92, 98, 105-8, 114, 115, 126, 127, 130, 132, 133, 144, 151-182, 186, 188, 192, 196, 198, 216, 222-4, 229, 230, 237, 238, 246
  Annual conference 1963, 55
  Annual conference 1964, 72-4
  Annual conference 1965, 86-90
  Annual conference 1966, 91
  Annual conference 1967, 92
  Annual conference 1968, 93
  Annual conference 1969, 153, 170
  Annual conference 1970, 170, 171, 174, 175, 180
  Annual conference 1973, 183
  Appeals board 56-7, 132, 152
  Construction Industrial Committee, 171
  Disputes committee, 56, 57
  groups of unions, 57, 58, 170-1
  industrial committees, 171
  Industrial Relations Committee, 176
  Northern Ireland Committee, 58, 72
  Northern Ireland Officer, 58
  picketing policy, 172-5 (*see also* picketing)
  Public Services Committee, 152, 171
  reorganisation, 56, 152, 169-172, 223
  wages conference 1966, 89
Irish Electrical Technicians Association, 130
Irish Engineering, Industrial and Electrical Trade Union (now incorporated by amalgamation into NEETU) 56, 104, 130
Irish Exporters Association, 74
Irish Federation of Musicians, 87
Irish Graphical Society, 51 (see also DTPS)
Irish Jurist, 33n., 34
Irish Local Government Officials Union (*now* Local Government and Public Services Union), 152
Irish National Painters and Decorators, 79, 80, 82
Irish National Productivity Committee (*now* Irish Productivity Centre), 50, 54, 56
  Human Sciences Committee of, 65, 153
Irish National Teachers Organisation, 45, 52, 203, 207, 213
Irish National Union of Vintners, Grocers and Allied Trades Assistants, 52
Irish Press, The, 88
Irish Times, The, 27, 85, 86, 100, 214
Irish Trade Union Congress, 23, 39, 43, 44, 45, 51
Irish Transport and General Workers Union, 40-4, 47, 49-54, 59-66, 70, 80, 87, 93, 107, 136, 137, 164, 165, 180, 222, 223, 224, 246
Irish Union of Distributive Workers and Clerks, 51, 101, 103
Italy, unification of, 3

IT&GWU (*see* Irish Transport and General Workers Union)
ITUC (*see* Irish Trade Union Congress)

Jackson, Archie, 80
Jacobs, 163
Jacobs, Eric, 225, 226
Jenkins, William, 72
Job evaluation, 111
Johnson, Tom, 8
Joint Statement of Intent on Productivity, Prices and Incomes 1964, 229
Jones, Aubrey, 240, 243, 245

Keane, Tim, 87, 161
Kennedy, Fintan, 49, 51, 61, 88, 91
Kennedy, Norman, 44, 46, 47, 48, 50, 51, 53, 72, 87
Kennedy, Tom, 50
Kyle, Sam, 43, 44, 226

Labour
   Department of, 92, 119, 172, 234, 239
   Minister for, 98, 113, 116, 117, 132, 157, 159, 184, 189, 194, 195, 196, 238
Labour Court, 23-34, 62, 76, 78, 82, 84, 90, 92, 110, 112, 114, 117, 118, 123, 132, 137, 138, 140-4, 152, 154, 158, 161-7, 178, 179, 183, 187-9, 192-8, 230, 233, 234, 236-241
Labour Party, 43, 45, 52
Larkin, Denis, 50, 53, 173
Larkin, Jim, 44-50, 55, 57, 65, 84, 86, 102, 106-108, 224
Larkin, Jim (Big Jim), 39-44
Law and trade disputes, 32-5
Lemass, Seán, 22, 26, 41, 42, 45, 55-7, 74, 75, 81, 86-92, 96, 105, 150
Leonard, Brian, 161-3
Limerick Operative Housepainters Society, 79
Local government,
   Dublin, 13, 14
   Minister for, 13n.
Lynch, Jack, 22, 150, 167
Lynch, Patrick, 202
Lutheran Reformation, 11

Macgougan, Jack, 36, 48, 87, 152
McAllister, Dan, 49
McCarthy, P. D., 117, 119, 125
McCartney, J. B., 33n.
McCullough, Billy, 53
McDermott, Dermot, 82, 161, 162, 166, 187, 214
McGonagle, Stephen, 87
McGrath, Nicholas, 51
McInerney, Michael, 62
Maintenance craftsmen's dispute, 16, 130, 150-169, 188, 198, 222
Malone, P. J., 87
Management theorists, 219
Marine, Port and General Workers Union, 52, 82, 151, 164, 165, 167
Marxism, 46, 47, 53, 227
Meenan, James, 97, 98n.
Merrigan, Matt, 50-1, 114
Morrow, James, 87, 161, 171, 173

INDEX

Mortished, R. J. P., 23
Mulvey, Charles, 98, 110n., 136-149, 229, 241, 242
Murphy, Con, 98, 151, 155, 157-170
Murphy, Dominick, 52, 83, 87, 88, 152
Murphy, Patrick, 137

NATE (*see* National Association of Transport Employees)
National Association of Transport Employees, 59, 62
National Board for Prices and Incomes, 229, 232
National Boot and Shoe Operatives, 53
National Busmen's Union, 18, 64-6, 71, 86, 176
National Economic Council, 180, 246
National Engineering and Electrical Trade Union (*see also* IEI&ETU and NEU), 155-166
National Engineering Union (now incorporated by amalgamation into NEETU), 52, 56, 130
National Federation of Building Trade Operatives, 80
National group of maintenance craft unions, 155-162
National identity, 2-7
National Industrial Economic Council, 25, 26, 28, 50, 54, 55, 72, 85, 88, 92-8, 136, 153, 179, 180, 182, 196, 207, 228-245
National Labour Party, 43
National pay agreement,
 1964, 73-7, 88-90, 190
 1970, 174-7, 181, 182, 193-8
 1972, 182, 235-240
 penalties for non-performance, 196-7
National Prices Commission, 96, 182, 196-8, 234, 244, 245
National teachers, 5
National Union of General and Municipal Workers, 87
National Union of Sheet Metal Workers and Coppersmiths (*now after amalgamation*: National Union of Sheet Metal Workers, Coppersmiths, Heating and Domestic Engineers), 52
National Union of Tailors and Garment Workers, 48, 152
National Union of Vehicle Builders, 165
Nationalism, 10
NBU (*see* National Busmen's Union)
NEETU (*see* National Engineering and Electrical Trade Union)
NEU (*see* National Engineering Union)
Nevin, Donal, 41, 42n., 53, 54
NIEC (*see* National Industrial Economic Council)
Northern Ireland, 1, 14, 17, 22, 38, 48, 51, 173, 174, 186, 195, 203, 215, 224
 Communist Party, 52
 Committee of Congress, (*see under* Irish Congress of Trade Unions)
 National Economic Council, 58
Norton, William, 45, 52
NUVB (*see* National Union of Vehicle Builders)

O'Brien, William, 40-4, 47
O'Connor, Seán, 211-12, 214
O'Donoghue, Martin, 187, 188, 193
OECD education survey team 1962-65, 202-05
 Investment in Education, 203n.
O'Leary, Michael, 30
O'Mahony, David, 19, 20, 23n., 29, 37, 38n., 58n., 70
O'Malley, Donogh, 206, 207-08

O Murchú, Seán, 80, 222
O'Neill, Matt, 51, 52
O'Neill, Terence, 87
Operative Plasterers' and Allied Trades' Society of Ireland, 54, 79
O'Reilly, Donal, 79
O'Sullivan, Derek, 81, 104
O'Sullivan, Harold, 152n.
O'Sullivan, John Marcus, 201
Owen, Robert, 41

Paine, Tom, 7, 51
Peace pledges, 125, 175-7
Pelagius, 10-11
Picketing (*see also under* Irish Congress of Trade Unions) 17-18
Political representatives,
  cultural background, 5
  local government (*see also* Local government), 13
Port and Docks Board, 85
Post Office Workers Union, 45
Potez, Galway, 56, 58
Prices and Incomes Policy, 153, 179-181, 196, 198, 222, 228-247
  Bill 1970, 181
  White Paper 1965, 229
Privatisation of the worker, 67, 68, 127, 128, 220, 221, 227, 242
Provisional United Trade Union Organisation, 44

Quinn v. Leathem, 33
Quinn Tribunal (on pay in recruitment of clerical grades in the public service) 85, 103, 110-12, 122, 193, 241

Radio Telefís Éireann, 58
Republicanism, 7, 8
Rice, Arthur, 163
Rights Commissioners, 31, 153, 239
Roberts, Ruaidhri, 37, 41n., 44, 45, 53, 54, 55, 77, 84, 85, 93, 174, 177
Roman Catholic Church, 198, 199, 214, 215, 220
  authoritarian image, 2
  authority and influence, 8-12
  spiritual influence, 9
  traditional rural, 5
  university education, 12
RTE (*see* Radio Telefís Éireann)
Ryan, Louden, (*see* Ryan, W. J. L.)
Ryan, W. J. L., 207, 210, 213, 234

Sams, K. I., 57n.
Schmemann, Alexander, 11
Shillman, Bernard, 33n.
Sinclair, Betty, 52, 174
Sinn Féin, 227
Skinnider, Mairead, 52
Stonecutters Union of Ireland, 79
Strikes,
  character, 15-18
  incidence, 18-21
Studies, 210n.

Sunday Times, The, 225
Swedish system of solidaristic bargaining, 243

Taff Vale case, 33
Tavistock Institute of Human Relations, 65-70, 116, 127
TCD (see Trinity College, Dublin)
Teachers,
  dispute, 198–217
  salaries committee, 204
  tribunal on salaries, 207-217
Theatrical and Kine Employees Union, 53
Thompson, Bob, 87
Thompson, E. P., 7
Titterington, John, 185, 187, 191, 192, 194, 195
Trade Union,
  Act 1871, 33
  Act 1941, 34, 42-3
  Act 1971, 172
  Bill 1966, 90, 152
  Commission of Inquiry 1939, 42
  history, 39-47
  organisation, 36-9
Trades Disputes Act 1906, 33
Transport Salaried Staffs Association, 52
Trevithick, J., 110, 241, 242
Trinity College, Dublin, 6, 12, 207

UCD (*see* University College, Dublin)
United House and Ship Painters, 79, 80
United Kingdom (*see* Britain)
University College, Dublin, 202

Van Beinum, Hans, 65, 220, 242
Vatican II, 2, 8-10, 211
Vocational Teachers Association (*now* Teachers Union of Ireland), 53, 198, 205-16

Wage rounds, 23-8
Walsh, Brian, Justice, 33n.
Webb, Sidney and Beatrice, 218
West Germany (*see* Germany)
Whitaker, T. K., 24, 180, 230
Whyte, J. H., 8n., 200n., 201
Workers Union of Ireland, 40, 44, 49, 50, 59, 62, 64, 65, 107, 137, 165, 174, 180, 222, 224
Working class, cultural background, 7
WUI (*see* Workers Union of Ireland)